Table of Contents

Introduction	6.
Chapter 1. The Macro Economic Instability of Madison's Ruling Class Plutocracy.	31.
Chapter 2. Madison's Myth of "We, the people."	40.
Chapter 3. Hamilton's Ruling Class Economic System.	62.
Chapter 4. George Mason's Anti-Federalist Arguments Against Ratification.	77.
Chapter 5. Madison's Constitutional Plutocracy and Lincoln's Civil War To Save the Plutocracy.	98.
Chapter 6. The National Plutocracy of Crony Corruption and the Culture of Plunder During the Gilded Age.	113.
Chapter 7. The Emergence of the Global Corporate American State.	176.
Chapter 8. The Creation of the Federal Reserve Bank.	191.
Chapter 9. Re-constructing A Fair Constitution Under Jefferson's American Dream of an Entrepreneurial Capitalist Society.	231.
Chapter 10. Re-constructing Jefferson's Entrepreneurial Capitalist Society.	243.
Chapter 11. The Constitutional Economics of Jefferson's Entrepreneurial Capitalist Society.	268.
Epilogue	280.
Bibliography	282.

Schedule of Exhibits and Diagrams

Exhibit 1. The History of American 18.
Economic Collapse and Financial Panics.

Exhibit 2. The Chronology of the Restoration 28.
Of Elite Rule.

Diagram 1. NBER Data on Recession 32.
Presented by the St. Louis Regional Federal
Reserve Bank.

Diagram 2. Pareto Optimality in Jefferson's 122.
American Dream.

Diagram 3. Social Welfare in the American 124.
Society, Between 1792 and 1860.

Diagram 4. Social Welfare in the American 125.
Society in the Gilded Age, Between 1877
and 1907.

Diagram 5. Monetary Manipulation, Investment 155.
Speculation, Corruption, Economic Collapse
and Labor Strikes During The Gilded Age.

Diagram 6. St. Louis Federal Reserve Bank 212.
GDP-Based Recession Indicator Index.
1967 – 2020.

Diagram 7. GAO Audit: Appendix IV: Ten 221.
Largest Domestic Bank Holding Companies
by Total Asset Size as of December 31, 2010.

Diagram 8. Data from GAO Audit on the Five 221.
Banks Who Obtained The Biggest Federal
Reserve Board Bailouts During the 2008
Economic Collapse.

Diagram 9. Data from GAO Audit of Five Foreign Banks Who Obtained The Biggest Federal Reserve Board Bailouts During the 2008 Economic Collapse.   222.

Diagram 10. U. S. National Debt to GDP.   227.

Diagram 11. Total Assets of Federal Debt Owned by Fed.   228

Diagram 12. Components of U. S. GDP.   229.

Diagram 13. Gross Private Domestic Investment.   229.

Introduction.

Our book presents a thesis of American history as a perpetual social class conflict caused by the conflict between Jefferson's promise of liberty for common citizens, and Madison's constitutional rules of civil procedure, which permanently elevated the financial interests of the natural aristocracy, over the economic interests of common citizens.

The conflict generally reveals itself in times of social or economic crisis when an observer comments that America is a great nation, but has never lived up to Jefferson's promise of equal liberty.

For example, Noah Feldman, in the conclusion of his recent book, The Broken Constitution, provides a version of the explanation that the nation never lived up to Jefferson's promise because the constitution is a living, evolving document. (The Broken Constitution: Lincoln, Slavery, and the Refounding of America. Noah Feldman. Farrar, Straus & Giroux, 2021.).

Feldman writes,

"The reality is that the moral Constitution, like all constitutions, is not an end state but a promise of ongoing effort. Through the Constitution, we define our national project. But we never fully achieve it. Lincoln's legacy, then, is not the accomplishment of a genuinely moral Constitution. It is the breaking of the compromise Constitution, and the hope and promise of a moral Constitution that will always be in the process of being redeemed."

Feldman argues that there are two versions of the constitution, a "moral" constitution, created after the Civil War, and an immoral, "compromise" constitution, created by Madison, which protected slavery.

The conflict between Jefferson's moral Declaration, and Madison's immoral rules of civil procedure, is a metaphor for two conceptions of the "American Dream."

Jefferson's ideology of liberty leads to the American Dream of upward occupational success through equal opportunity. Jefferson's American Dream, today, is entrepreneurial capitalism in a commonwealth of politically equal independent producers, who voluntarily agree to obey the rule of law.

Madison feared the majority power of , "We, the people," and his rules created a plutocracy for the benefit of the natural aristocracy, now known as the Ruling Class.

"We, the people," was just a very clever rhetorical ruse to hide the fact that "We, the people," was really just 39 self-selected elites, who met in secret to create the constitution.

Madison's rules perpetuated a political culture of ruling class shared plunder in government policies and speculation in the economy. Madison's version of the American Dream is "Get-Rich-Quick."

He used the British mixed government model of society, and recreated a version of the British social class society in America, where the American natural aristocracy had their own branch of government, and was insulated from the influence of common citizens.

Madison's more perfect union was not a union of states, nor a union between common citizens and the new government. Madison's more perfect union was a compact between the natural aristocracy and the agencies of government, held together by the cultural value of shared plunder.

Madison's rules created the legal framework for elite rule, and Hamilton then added the financial system that benefitted the plutocracy.

The origin of the conflict between two versions of the American Dream lies in how the story of American history is told by scholars and academics, like Feldman, who combine and conflate two distinct, and separate historical events at the beginning of the American nation.

The two distinct and separate events are combined by academic historians into a historical myth of one consolidated event, called "the founding."

The myth allows defenders of Madison's constitution to use the Declaration's principles of equality as evidence that Madison's constitution is not immoral, it is simply evolving to become a "more perfect union."

Feldman's argument relies on slavery as the exclusive, single, immoral feature of Madison's constitution.

We offer an alternative explanation of the immorality of Madison's constitution that features the disenfranchisement of the consent of the governed of common citizens, in a transfer of sovereignty from citizens to a consolidated tyrannical central government.

In violation of both Locke's and Jefferson's image of citizens agreeing to a voluntary transfer of their rights to more fully secure their natural rights, when the citizens leave the state of nature, the common citizens lost natural rights without gaining any benefits in the exchange with Madison.

The citizens were never given a chance to vote to ratify the transfer of sovereignty and never agreed upon the establishment of Madison's plutocracy.

In the only popular vote of citizens, for or against ratification, the 3,000 citizens in Rhode Island voted 99% to reject Madison's constitution. There is considerable historical evidence that the overwhelming majority of common citizens, in other states, shared the views of the voters in Rhode Island.

The rest of the so-called ratification conventions secured ratification through force and fraud, including the use of police agents in Pennsylvania to hold convention delegates, against their will, to obtain an illegitimate quorum for the ratification vote.

We agree with the analysis of Feldman in his review of the debates between Lincoln and Douglas, where Douglas argued that the solution to the slave issue in the territories was to let citizens in each state to vote on slavery.

Feldman writes,

"Douglas was correct about popular sovereignty [states voting on slavery] because the people of the states never voted to ratify the compromise constitution."

Our argument about the immoral constitution follows Feldman's logic. The citizens in each state never voted to ratify Madison's constitution, which would have been the correct moral founding of the U. S. Government.

To summarize, Madison's constitution was immoral because it perpetuated slavery, because it disenfranchised the sovereignty of the consent of the governed of common citizens, and was implemented in a fraudulent ratification process.

The only shred of legitimacy of consent of the governed in Madison's rules was the ability of the common citizens to vote, periodically, on the elites who would rule them.

And, that last shred of legitimacy was violated on November 3, 2020, when the Democrat Marxists overthrew the representative republic to install their version of a more perfect Marxist union.

The enactment of the 13th, 14th, and 15th Amendments changed nothing about the power of the Ruling Class to make economic and political decisions in the absence of the consent of the governed.

We argue that what Hamilton created, beginning in 1792, was an economy that ran on elite investment speculation, credit and debt, not on cash.

We explain that the cause of perpetual economic collapse, in Hamilton's economic system, is the unbalanced centralized power of the early national banks, and the subsequent unchecked power of the Federal Reserve Bank, to manipulate the monetary system, to the benefit of New York bankers, and the American Ruling Class.

Madison's rules finally devolved into a centralized Marxist political tyranny, which functions with the collaboration of a global corporate state.

We use the analysis of W. J. Cash, in The Mind of the South, to explain that the history of American class conflicts can be interpreted as a three-stage chronology of economic collapse, common citizen rebellion, and restoration of the ruling class power. (The Mind Of The South, W.J. Cash. Vintage Books, 1941.).

Our reliance on the thesis of W. J. Cash provides a direct contrast with Feldman that there are two constitutions, a moral one, which replaced an immoral one. Feldman argues that American history can be seen as a clean break between the two constitutions.

Rather, we argue that the Civil War did not change the power of the Ruling Class to subjugate the common class of citizens. We argue, as does Cash, that there is on-going continuity of the Ruling Class power.

In fact, the aftermath of the Civil War resulted in a more powerful ruling class, commonly called the Plutocrats, during the so-called "Gilded Age."

We agree with the analysis of Steven Hahn, that the Ruling Class became even more powerful after the Civil War.

Hahn writes,

"Especially important was the creation and dramatic empowerment of a new class of finance capitalists through the marketing of government securities and their close alliance with the national state mediated chiefly by the railroads…The alliance between new finance capital and the new nation-state proved of considerable developmental importance because it favored creditors over debtors…"

The elite rule, after the Civil War, created the economic instability that damaged the prospects of success for Black people, farmers, Indians, industrial workers, and West Coast Chinese immigrants, between 1865 and the election of McKinley, in 1896.

We argue that there is no logical or moral justification, for these people to have been mistreated by the Plutocrats. Under a different constitutional configuration, that promoted Jefferson's concept of the American Dream, they would not have suffered.

The historical class conflict dynamic of Cash is explained by the ability of the financially wealthy families to transfer unelected, economic power to illegitimate political authority, under the guise of Madison's constitution.

After the Civil War, the ruling class used their power to create an unstable economic and financial system that collapsed about every 10 years

We argue that there is no macro-economic marginal price theoretical reason for the economy to collapse every ten years. The economic instability is caused by Madison's constitutional rules, not by a failure in the price system of the competitive free market.

We revive William Graham Sumner's description of the American "Forgotten Man," as a description of how Madison's political rules, and Hamilton's economic system, worked in tandem to deny common citizens an equal opportunity for financial success.

Sumner stated, in an 1883 lecture in Brooklyn, that the Forgotten Man would be compelled to pay to support the Ruling Class advantages.

Sumner wrote,

"A government produces nothing at all, they leave out of sight the first fact to be remembered in all social discussion—that the State cannot get a cent for any man without taking it from some other man, and this latter must be a man who has produced and saved it. This latter is the Forgotten Man. Hence the real sufferer by that kind of benevolence which consists in an expenditure of capital to protect the good-for-nothing (Ruling Class) is the industrious laborer."

We revise Sumner's phrase "the forgotten man" to mean, today, that the financial and economic interests of working and middle class citizens are not represented in the centralized, deep-state, Marxist tyranny.

Sumner explained that common citizens bore the brunt of taxes imposed by the ruling class. The burden of taxation caused two outcomes.

First, the taxes crushed the incomes and resources of common citizens because Hamilton's system ran on credit and debt, not on currency, and common citizens never had the money to pay their taxes or debts.

When the common citizens failed to pay their taxes or debts in gold and silver, the legal rules allowed the elites to confiscate their farms and property.

Second, the government tax revenues were used by the elite to speculate on investment projects, and the speculation always ended in an economic collapse, generally leaving the elite financial interests unharmed.

The first event of economic collapse is caused by excessive money creation, which leads wealthy people to speculate. The speculation causes the economy to collapse, on a periodic basis, about every ten years. (see Exhibit 1. below).

The common citizens suffer job loss and lose their farms, during each economic collapse. The government agents then bail out the wealthy class to restore the status quo of elite rule. (see Exhibit 2. below).

The political model of Cash is easy to understand. In any small town, or larger political jurisdiction, a set of wealthy people control the political machinery to benefit themselves, to the disadvantage of common citizens.

In Aristotle's description, America's political system would be described as rule by the few. In the national government setting, Cash's model is applied to the few who control the levers of power through the "spoils" system, and control the national laws on the financial and banking system.

There is no force in Madison's framework to compel the elected representatives to represent the common good, or the public purpose. Once the elected representatives arrive in DC, they collaborate with the special financial interests to enrich themselves.

Cash applied his model to the historical era of reconstruction, when the ruling class in the South restored the image of the plantation in both society and industry, as a way of reasserting their political control over common citizens.

Cash wrote,

"The burning concern thus generated in the minds of the master class met with and married with that other concern which, as we have seen, was generated in them by their own economic difficulties...brought to a full conviction...that without ever abandoning cotton growing, the arm of the land must somehow be extended."

The solution to the elite's loss of political power, after the Civil War and Reconstruction, according to Cash, was pretty simple.

For them, the economic future of the South should look just like its past.

"Progress was being accomplished so completely within the framework of the past that the plantation remained the single great basic social and economic pattern of the South...that is exactly what the Southern factory almost invariably was: a plantation."

We argue that the Cash's metaphor of restoring the plantation fits as an explanation for every economic crisis in American history. After each economic collapse, the Ruling Class restores the image of the economic plantation.

In order to achieve their desired goal of restoring their power, the master class, after Reconstruction, needed to manipulate the White yeoman farmer's prime value of economic opportunity to serve the needs of the elite.

The pathway of attack was along the farmer's intersection of values of individualism and local allegiance to community and family.

In other words, the ruling class began substituting communal, or socialist values, for the former values of individualism and self-sufficiency of White yeoman farmers.

Bruce Palmer described how the Bourbon Democrats, beginning around 1895, began

"...an effort to reconcile individual material self interest with the welfare of the community, (which) led to the abandonment of the core of the (farmer's) former idea - that society was held together and progressed because of the action of each person's material self-interest - and moved toward a consideration of society as a group of people rather than a collection of individuals." (Man Over Money: The Southern Populist Critique of American Capitalism, Bruce Palmer. UNC Press CH, 1980.).

According to Gavin Wright.

"Virtually every industrial beginning may be traced to someone's attempt to make a capital gain on property in land, by selling the land for the industrial plant. (Old South, New South: Revolutions in the Southern Economy Since the Civil War. Gavin Wright. New York: Basic Books, 1986.).

Following Wright,

"there was a sense in which the beneficiaries really could be seen as 'the community' ...What was most misleading about the cotton mill rhetoric was the implication that non-property owning (white) laborers and concern for their welfare played a major role" in the booster's motivations. The master class was using the appeal of "more and better jobs" for the 'community' in a way that appealed to the farmer's need for upward mobility while at the same time, undermined the farmer's traditional values of individual freedom."

According to Cash,

"The southern textile industry stressed communal values. Its image for social relationships in mill villages was not the market but the paternalistic family."

Under the jurisdiction of the plantation elite, the mill building movement used the values of the Agrarians, individual initiative, ambition and economic independence, which led to social relationships in mill towns that featured, according to Newby, "a kind of social atomism, suspicion of strange people and new ideas, and resistance to social innovation of any sort," including the political innovations promoted by the Agrarians. (Plain Folk in the New South: Social Change and Cultural Persistence, 1880-1915. I. A. Newby. Louisiana State University Press, 1989.).

According to Cash,

"...the cotton mill worker of the South would be stripped of his ancient autonomy and placed in every department of his life under the control of his employer...by 1910, the barons and the stockholders of the mills were exhibiting a tendency to turn a smaller proportion of the total profits back to building of more mills or the expansion of industry and business in general, and to take more for their own personal purposes."

As noted by Cash, the Ruling Class economy ran on cheap labor.

"Whatever the intent of the original founders of progress, the plain truth is that everything here rested finally upon one fact alone: _cheap labor_...the wages were on average just about adequate to the support of a single individual - such wages as required that every member of a family moving from the land into Factory-town, who was not incapacitated by disease or age or infancy, should go into the mills in order that he too might eat."

What Cash said about the historical era after 1877, applies equally well to our historical thesis of explaining American history as a series of economic collapse, followed by common citizen economic despair, followed by a restoration of elite rule.

The class conflict originates in the dynamic incompatibility of Jefferson's promise of liberty and Madison's framework of permanently empowering the natural aristocracy.

The political ideology of race hatred is a constant tool of the ruling class to restore elite rule. Throughout American history, it did not matter to the elite if the race hatred was Whites hating Blacks, or in the most recent era, of Blacks hating Whites.

We disagree both with the historical analysis of Democrat Marxists that America was founded upon the sin of slavery, in 1619, and their solution of a collectivist communist tyranny.

America was founded in 1775, under Jefferson's promise of liberty.

In contrast, the United States Government was founded in 1787, under Madison's constitution that empowered the elite over the common citizens.

The Democrat Marxists are correct that Madison's constitution protected slavery, not because slavery was the essential value that held elites together, but because protecting slavery in the South was essential to maintaining elite rule in the North.

The 38 self-selected Federalist elites who walked out of Independence Hall, on the afternoon of September 17, 1787, knew that their rules would lead to a civil war, but their self interest in forming the plutocracy overrode their moral concern about slavery. (Note: Only 38 elites signed the document. One of the 39 elites signed the document twice, once for himself, and once for his buddy, who could not be there that day).

The two events, Jefferson's Declaration, in1776, and Madison's constitution, of 1787, do not constitute the "founding."

Rather than interpreting the two events as a consolidated single "founding," we agree with Michael Klarman, in his book. The Framers Coup, (Oxford University Press, NY. 2016.), that the 39 elites who met in secret, in Philadelphia, to hammer out Madison's rules, constituted a Ruling Class coup over the Articles of Confederation, not a founding.

Klarman wrote,

"Madison objected to the injustice of state legislation on creating paper money and debtor relief laws ... Madison viewed society as two classes: creditors or debtors, rich or poor... Madison declared that the Senate ought to come from and represent the wealth of the nation. The Senate should serve as a bastion of privilege. Dickinson wanted the Senate to bear the likeness of the British House of Lords. Pinckney argued that, "only the wealthy would be able to afford to serve."...As Butler put it, "the great object of government was to protect property...the Senate would block any populist economic measures that might emanate from the House."

Madison said that the Senate needed to be a "check on the democracy. It can not be made too strong."

That "check on democracy" is now in the hands of Marxist Democrats, who staged America's second coup, in November 2020, overthrowing Madison's representative republic.

Our book explains that patriots today, who are trying to resurrect, or reconstruct Madison's constitution, in order to defeat the Marxist Democrats are on a fool's errand.

Madison and Hamilton created a ruling class plutocracy, and going back to their "founding" would not resolve the conflict in the two visions of the American dream.

The economic system of credit and debt created by Hamilton would continue to collapse about every 10 years, due to money growth and speculation by the Ruling Class.

And, restoring Madison's centralized government would not eradicate the grip that the Democrat Marxists have on the deep state apparatus.

Our argument about the fallacy of going back to Madison's constitution to eradicate Marxism echoes Lincoln's argument about the Slaveocracy going back to Madison's constitution, instead of seceding.

As noted by Feldman, Lincoln stated,

"The only solution Lincoln offered to the crisis was to "go back to [the] old policy." He told the South , and his audience," If you would have the peace of the old times , readopt the precepts and policy of the old times."

That advice to the Southern states was as false then for dealing with the issue of slavery, as the strategy of resurrecting Madison's constitution today for dealing with the issue of Marxism.

It was the flaws in Madison's rules for creating the British social class system in America that allowed the Marxists to gain their illegitimate power. In their ascendancy to illegitimate power, they are simply replacing the Ruling Class, to gain unchecked control over Madison's Leviathan.

We offer a better strategy for common citizens to both eradicate the Marxist threat to liberty, and to eradicate the power of the global corporate state to undermine national sovereignty.

A better idea is to start over at the point of history of Jefferson's Declaration, and reconstruct Jefferson's American Dream of an entrepreneurial capitalist society.

Exhibit 1. The History of American Economic Collapse and Financial Panics. Data compiled from End the Fed, by Ron Paul and data sources in Wikipedia and other internet sources.

Panic of 1785.

The panic of 1785, which lasted until 1788, ended the business boom that followed the American Revolution. The causes of the crisis lay in the overexpansion and debts incurred after the victory at Yorktown, a postwar deflation, competition in the manufacturing sector from Britain, and lack of adequate credit and a sound currency. The panic among business and propertied groups led to the demand for a stronger federal government.

Copper Panic of 1789.

Loss of confidence in copper coins due to debasement and counterfeiting led to commercial freeze up that halted the economy of several northern States and was not alleviated until the introduction of new paper money to restore confidence.

Panic of 1796–97.

Just as a land speculation bubble was bursting, deflation from the Bank of England (which was facing insolvency because of the cost of Great Britain's involvement in the French Revolutionary Wars) crossed to North America and disrupted commercial and real estate markets in the United States and the Caribbean.

1802–1804 recession.

A boom of war-time activity led to a decline after the Peace of Amiens ended the war between the United Kingdom and France. Commodity prices fell dramatically. Trade was disrupted by pirates, leading to the First Barbary War.

Depression of 1807. The Embargo Act of 1807 was passed by the United States Congress under President Thomas Jefferson as tensions increased with the United Kingdom. Along with trade restrictions imposed by the British, shipping-related industries were hard hit. The Federalists fought the embargo and allowed smuggling to take place in New England.

1812 recession.

The United States entered a brief recession at the beginning of 1812. The decline was brief primarily because the United States soon increased production to fight the War of 1812, which began June 18, 1812.

1815–21 depression.

Shortly after the war ended on March 23, 1815, the United States entered a period of financial panic as bank notes rapidly depreciated because of inflation following the war. The 1815 panic was followed by several years of mild depression, and then a major financial crisis – the Panic of 1819, which featured widespread foreclosures, bank failures, unemployment, a collapse in real estate prices, and a slump in agriculture and manufacturing.

Panic of 1819.

The Panic of 1819 was the first major peacetime financial crisis in the United States. Public land debt ballooned from $3 million in 1815 to $17 million in 1818.

1822–1823 recession.

After only a mild recovery following the lengthy 1815–21 depression, commodity prices hit a peak in March 1822 and began to fall. Many businesses failed, unemployment rose and an increase in imports worsened the trade balance.

1825–1826 recession.

The Panic of 1825, started as a stock crash following a bubble of speculative investments in Latin America, which led to a decline in business activity in the United States and England.

1828–1829 recession.

In 1826, England forbade the United States to trade with English colonies, and in 1827, the United States adopted a counter-prohibition. Trade declined, just as credit became tight for manufacturers in New England.

1833–34 recession.

The United States' economy declined moderately in 1833–34. News accounts of the time confirm the slowdown. The subsequent expansion was driven by land speculation.

Panic of 1837.

The Panic of 1837 was a financial crisis in the United States that touched off a major recession ... The crisis followed a period of economic expansion from mid-1834 to mid-1836.

1836–1838 recession.

A sharp downturn in the American economy was caused by bank failures and lack of confidence in the paper currency. Speculation markets were greatly affected when American banks stopped payment in specie (gold and silver coinage). Over 600 banks failed in this period. In the South, the cotton market completely collapsed.

1839–late 1843 recession.

This was one of the longest and deepest depressions. It was a period of pronounced deflation and massive default on debt. The Cleveland Trust Company Index showed the economy spent 68 months below its trend and only 9 months above it. The Index declined 34.3% during this depression.

1845–late 1846.

This recession was mild enough that it may have only been a slowdown in the growth cycle. One theory holds that this would have been a recession, except the United States began to gear up for the Mexican–American War, which began April 25, 1846.

1847–48 recession.

The Cleveland Trust Company Index declined 19.7% during 1847 and 1848. It is associated with a financial crisis in Great Britain.

1853–54 recession.

Interest rates rose in this period, contributing to a decrease in railroad investment. Security prices fell during this period. Panic of 1857

June 1857–December 1858 recession.

Failure of the Ohio Life Insurance and Trust Company burst a European speculative bubble in United States' railroads and caused a loss of confidence in American banks. Over 5,000 businesses failed within the first year of the Panic, and unemployment was accompanied by protest meetings in urban areas. This is the earliest recession to which the NBER assigns specific months (rather than years) for the peak and trough

1860–61 recession.

There was a recession before the American Civil War, which began April 12, 1861. Zarnowitz says the data generally show a contraction occurred in this period, but it was quite mild. A financial panic was narrowly averted in 1860 by the first use of clearing house certificates between banks.

1865–67 recession.

The American Civil War ended in April 1865, and the country entered a lengthy period of general deflation that lasted until 1896.

1869–70 recession.

A few years after the Civil War, a short recession occurred. It was unusual since it came amid a period when railroad investment was greatly accelerating. Several months into the recession, there was a major financial panic.

Panic of 1873 and the Long Depression.

Economic problems in Europe prompted the failure of Jay Cooke & Company, the largest bank in the United States, which burst the post-Civil War speculative bubble. The Coinage Act of 1873 also contributed by immediately depressing the price of silver, which hurt North American mining interests. The deflation and wage cuts of the era led to labor turmoil, such as the Great Railroad Strike of 1877. In 1879, the United States returned to the gold standard with the Specie Payment Resumption Act. This is the longest period of economic contraction recognized by the NBER.

1882–85 recession.

Like the Long Depression that preceded it, the recession of 1882–85 was more of a price depression than a production depression. From 1879 to 1882, there had been a boom in railroad construction which came to an end, resulting in a decline in both railroad construction and in related industries, particularly iron and steel.

1887–88 recession.

Investments in railroads and buildings weakened during this period. This slowdown was so mild that it is not always considered a recession. Contemporary accounts apparently indicate it was considered a slight recession.

1890–91 recession.

Although shorter than the recession in 1887–88 and still modest, a slowdown in 1890–91 was somewhat more pronounced than the preceding recession. International monetary disturbances are blamed for this recession, such as the Panic of 1890 in the United Kingdom.

Panic of 1893.

Failure of the United States Reading Railroad and withdrawal of European investment led to a stock market and banking collapse. This Panic was also precipitated in part by a run on the gold supply. The Treasury had to issue bonds to purchase enough gold. Profits, investment and income all fell, leading to political instability, the height of the U.S. populist movement and the Free Silver movement.

Panic of 1896.

The period of 1893–97 is seen as a generally depressed cycle that had a short spurt of growth in the middle, following the Panic of 1893. Production shrank and deflation reigned.

1899–1900 recession.

Though not severe, this downturn lasted for nearly two years and saw a distinct decline in the national product. Industrial and commercial production both declined, albeit fairly modestly. The recession came about a year after a 1901 stock crash.

Panic of 1907.

A run on Knickerbocker Trust Company deposits on October 22, 1907, set events in motion that would lead to a severe monetary contraction. The fallout from the panic led to Congress creating the Federal Reserve System.

Panic of 1910–1911.

This was a mild but lengthy recession. The national product grew by less than 1%, and commercial activity and industrial activity declined. The period was also marked by deflation.

Recession of 1913–1914.

Production and real income declined during this period and were not offset until the start of World War I increased demand. Incidentally, the Federal Reserve Act was signed during this recession, creating the Federal Reserve System, the culmination of a sequence of events following the Panic of 1907.

1918–1919. Post-World War I recession.

Severe hyperinflation in Europe took place over production in North America. This was a brief but very sharp recession and was caused by the end of wartime production, along with an influx of labor from returning troops. This, in turn, caused high unemployment.

Depression of 1920–21.

The 1921 recession began a mere 10 months after the post-World War I recession, as the economy continued working through the shift to a peacetime economy. The recession was short, but extremely painful. The year 1920 was the single most deflationary year in American history; production, however, did not fall as much as might be expected from the deflation. GNP may have declined between 2.5 and 7 percent, even as wholesale prices declined by 36.8.

1923–24 recession.

From the depression of 1920–21 until the Great Depression, an era dubbed the Roaring Twenties, the economy was generally expanding. Industrial production declined in 1923–24, but on the whole this was a mild recession.

1926–27 recession.

This was an unusual and mild recession, thought to be caused largely because Henry Ford closed production in his factories for six months to switch from production of the Model T to the Model A.

1929–March 1933. Great Depression.

A banking panic and a collapse in the money supply took place in the United States that was exacerbated by international commitment to the gold standard. Extensive new tariffs and other factors contributed to an extremely deep depression. GDP, industrial production, employment, and prices fell substantially. A small economic expansion within the depression began in 1933, with gold inflow expanding the money supply and improving expectations; the expansion would end in 1937. The ultimate recovery, which would occur with the start of World War II in 1940, was credited to monetary policy and monetary expansion.

Recession of 1937–1938.

The Recession of 1937 is only considered minor when compared to the Great Depression, but is otherwise among the worst recessions of the 20th century. Three explanations are offered as causes for the recession: the tight fiscal policy resulting from an attempt to balance the budget after New Deal spending; the tight monetary policy of the Federal Reserve; and the declining profits of businesses leading to a reduction in business investment.

Recession of 1945.

The decline in government spending at the end of World War II led to an enormous drop in gross domestic product, making this technically a recession. This was the result of demobilization and the shift from a wartime to peacetime economy.

Recession of 1949.

The 1948 recession was a brief economic downturn; The recession also followed a period of monetary tightening.

Recession of 1953.

In 1951, the Federal Reserve reasserted its independence from the U.S. Treasury and in 1952, the Federal Reserve changed monetary policy to be more restrictive because of fears of further inflation or of a bubble forming.

Recession of 1958.

Monetary policy was tightened during the two years preceding 1957, followed by an easing of policy at the end of 1957.

Recession of 1960–61.

Another primarily monetary recession occurred after the Federal Reserve began raising interest rates in 1959.

Recession of 1969–70.

The relatively mild 1969 recession followed a lengthy expansion. At the end of the expansion, inflation was rising, possibly a result of increased deficits.

1973–75 recession.

A quadrupling of oil prices by OPEC coupled with high government spending because of the Vietnam War led to stagflation in the United States. The period was also marked by the 1973 oil crisis and the 1973–1974 stock market crash. The period is remarkable for rising unemployment coinciding with rising inflation.

1980 recession.

The NBER considers a very short recession to have occurred in 1980, followed by a short period of growth and then a deep recession. Unemployment remained relatively elevated in between recessions. The recession began as the Federal Reserve, under Paul Volcker, raised interest rates dramatically to fight the inflation of the 1970s.

Early 1980s recession.

The Iranian Revolution sharply increased the price of oil around the world in 1979, causing the 1979 energy crisis. Tight monetary policy in the United States to control inflation led to another recession.

Early 1990s recession.

After the lengthy peacetime expansion of the 1980s, inflation began to increase and the Federal Reserve responded by raising interest rates from 1986 to 1989. This weakened but did not stop growth, but some combination of the subsequent 1990 oil price shock, the debt accumulation of the 1980s, and growing consumer pessimism combined with the weakened economy to produce a brief recession.

Early 2000s recession.

The collapse of the speculative dot-com bubble, a fall in business outlays and investments, and the September 11th attacks brought the decade of growth to an end.

2007–2009. Great Recession

The subprime mortgage crisis led to the collapse of the United States housing bubble. Falling housing-related assets contributed to a global financial crisis, even as oil and food prices soared. The crisis led to the failure or collapse of many of the United States' largest financial institutions: Bear Stearns, Fannie Mae, Freddie Mac, Lehman Brothers, Citi Bank and AIG, as well as a crisis in the automobile industry. The government responded with an unprecedented $700 billion bank bailout and $787 billion fiscal stimulus package.

Exhibit 2. The Chronology of the Restoration of Elite Rule.

1775-1776. Jefferson's Original Promise Documents.

1781. State Sovereignty Promise of Articles of Confederation.

1783. King George surrenders and transfers the Crown's sovereignty to the sovereignty of 13 Independent States Britain acknowledges the United States (New Hampshire, Massachusetts Bay, Rhode Island and Providence Plantations, Connecticut, New York, New Jersey, Pennsylvania, Delaware, Maryland, Virginia, North Carolina, South Carolina, and Georgia) to be free, sovereign, and independent states, and that the British Crown and all heirs and successors relinquish claims to the Government, property, and territorial rights of the same, and every part thereof,

1787. Madison usurps the Articles of Confederation, First Restoration of elite rule. If you like your state, you can keep your state. 7 Grand compromises endorsing slavery.

1788-1789. Anti-Federalists betrayed by Federalists in sham ratification conventions.

1788. North Carolina holds out for Declaration of Rights and is oppressed by Congress for failure to ratify.

1791. Bill of Rights added.

1798. Federalists enact Alien and Sedition Acts to eliminate opposition.

1800. Jefferson's Failed Counter Revolution to restore liberty.

1829. Jackson elected. Beginning of Democrat Party. Forced removal of Indians. First state's rights nullification crisis.

1858. Extension of slavery into the territories. Lincoln quotes Jefferson as justification for the Civil War.

1866-1877. Failed Reconstruction. Natural aristocracy restores elite rule.

1880 – 1898. Failed Agrarian Revolt. Ruling Class restores elite rule.

1896. Beginning of American Apartheid and restoration of the rule by crony capitalism. McKinnley elected.

1929. Great Depression. First failed American experiment in socialism. Roosevelt tries out a version of Mussolini's corporate fascism.

1958. Eisenhower warns of military industrial elite related to combined corporate government power.

1992. Corporate elites pass first acts of corporate crony globalism.

1999. Corporate elites admit China into WTO under status of a "developing nation."

2008. Housing collapse and corporate bailouts. Fed restores elite rule.

2008. Obama elected

2016. Failed Trump presidency to avert a coup.

2020. Democrat Marxist coup. Coalition of Republican crony corporations and Democrat Marxists.

Chapter 1. The Macro Economic Instability of Madison's Ruling Class Plutocracy.

The National Bureau of Economic Research (NBER) was founded in 1920, largely in response to controversies between free market advocates and proponents of centralized government planning, over the "fair" distribution of income in the American economy.

As a result of an early agreement between the adversaries, both sides agreed that the mission of the NBER was to present data on when an economic recession began and ended.

In other words, the NBER was bound by a self-imposed restriction that their studies may present data and research findings, but may not make policy recommendations or make normative statements about the cause of economic recessions.

It could present the data, but it could not explain why the American economy was subject to multiple, periodic recessions, because explaining the theoretical cause of the economic recessions may lead to discussion about the "fair" income distribution, which would not be scientifically objective, or value free.

In the absence of an NBER explanation of the cause of the economic instability, conventional economic wisdom explained that periodic recessions were simply a normal, natural, "boom-bust" consequence of the American free market economy.

Diagram 1 describes the NBER chronology of economic recessions from 1860 to 2020.

Diagram 1. NBER Data on Recession Presented by the St. Louis Regional Federal Reserve Bank.

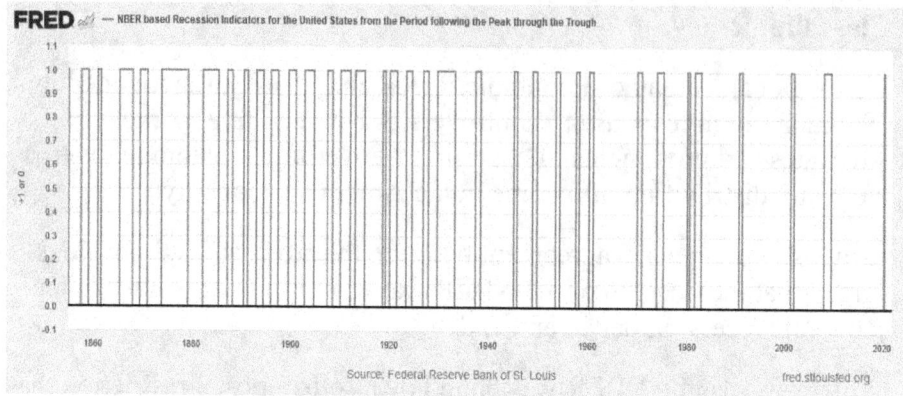

As noted above, in the Introduction, Exhibit 1, (The History of American Economic Collapse and Financial Panics,) American economic recessions occur with periodic regularity about every 10 years.

We argue that there is nothing normal or natural about the economic instability in the American economy.

Nor, is there anything in contemporary marginal general equilibrium theory to explain, or predict that these periodic recessions are a "normal" consequence of the marginal adjustments of price and quantity in macro economic theory.

The naturally observable phenomena of economic recession is observable over a long period of time, and can be explained by a combination of economic theory and political theory.

But, the economic theory is not found in conventional neo-classical marginal equilibrium theory.

Quantity and price adjustments in marginal equilibrium theory do not lead the society to any pre-determined optimal social welfare end point, or to any pre-determined rate of real economic growth.

Prices, in the market, are not independent variables that serve to guide society to some magical point of social welfare optimality.

Prices are dependent variables that are caused both by the interaction of the set of rules and legal entitlements enacted through a constitutional convention, and by investments made in previous periods, under supply and demand conditions that existed in those prior time periods.

Any point along the production possibility frontier will generate a non-unique set of prices, if the distribution of income between social classes is changed. The set of prices at that point of production possibilities reflects the existing distribution of income.

Marginal price adjustments are a reflection of changing rules and laws, not simply the result of changes in supply and demand forces for money. Price adjustments lead to a future equilibrium point, not to a social welfare maximum, or to optimal rates of economic growth.

That future equilibrium point could easily be what academic economists call a "Nash Equilibrium," resting at a low level of economic activity, visualized as an economy slowly rotating around a suboptimal point of production.

The Nash equilibrium conditions are reached over a long period of time, generally about 10 years, based upon allegiance of the ruling class to maintain the status quo income distribution, at that time period, at that unique point along the production possibilities frontier.

In other words, at that point of production, given the existing distribution of income, the Nash equilibrium becomes stable. The wealthy families are content at that lower level of production because the low level of economic activity does not disrupt their existing distribution of income.

As economic growth slows, income competition becomes more intense, with the more powerful agents able to extract greater income from less powerful agents, as a result of political manipulation of the rules of reward.

The speculative private capital investments, made by the ruling class in the prior time period did not generate real economic growth in the latter time period, causing real economic growth to stagnate at the Nash equilibrium point.

The response by the central bankers to the economic slowdown is to increase the supply of money, causing a mirage of economic activity, while at the same time, protecting the existing distribution of income and wealth.

During this period of time, as long as the declining marginal profits can cover the variable costs of production, slight product innovations will occur in the existing legacy production and manufacturing plants in the economy.

As marginal rates of profit decline, the economy traces out a trajectory to the next Nash equilibrium at a much lower level of economic activity.

Political and financial elites who benefit from the existing status quo distribution of existing products and markets can therefore be expected to engage in crony capitalist rent-seeking, using government revenues to maintain their income.

The equilibrium associated with the Nash attractor point, and the productivity improvements associated with mass produced standardized products, do not lead to economic growth in the next period, because future economic growth depends on prior capital investments in real production, not fake money creation.

The social conditions of low economic growth at the Nash equilibrium lead to greater levels of conflict between elites, who desire to maintain their incomes, and the social classes described by Sumner as the 'forgotten man.".

The political institutional structure, created by Madison, grants unelected political power to the elites who use the agencies of government to maintain their income through crony capitalist control over government taxes and spending.

The financial system, created by Hamilton, allows unelected central bankers to manipulate the money supply, in order to control the direction of the market, to suit their own social welfare.

The early casualties of the Nash equilibrium are the erosion of trust in exchanges in long-term investment decisions and the erosion of voluntary allegiance to obey the rule of law.

The later victims are non-elites (forgotten man), in the future time period, who suffer reduced levels of income and wealth as a result of the political power associated with Madison's Ruling Class inbreeding.

In an open, diverse political environment, the functioning and operations of the competitive free market, absent of elite political control over the distribution of income, the sovereign national economy could be expected to trace out a trajectory to a higher welfare point on the social welfare possibilities frontier.

Obtaining that hypothetical welfare point depends on productive private capital investment in equipment and machinery, in the prior economic time period, generally about 10 years before.

However, as mentioned above, that new social welfare point, along the production possibilities frontier, logically implies a new distribution of income, which results from consumers selecting new technological products that did not exist in the earlier time period.

In other words, prior private capital investments create new prices and new future markets, which threaten the status quo distribution of income. The ruling class cannot manipulate money creation or control revenue flows from government agencies, in the new markets because political control and money supply affect current markets, not uncertain future markets.

The best idea for maintaining control for the elites is to have the future markets look just like the past markets, or to borrow from W. J. Cash, a return to the plantation.

The theoretical explanation of the periodic economic recessions, seen above in the NBER chart, describe the return to the plantation, about every ten years, so that the existing status quo of income distribution and political control is maintained by the Ruling Class.

After each periodic recession, the NBER could also describe the factors that brought the economy out of recession.

The transition out of a low level of economic activity has traditionally been increased government spending on fighting a war. Because of Hamilton's initial dependence on credit and debt, not cash, the wars are financed by increasing government debt.

At the end of the war, the real economic growth, based upon real private capital investment, is not sufficient to pay the government debt, which is then financed by the increase in the mirage of money supply creation by the central bankers.

The owners and holders of the debt are wealthy families and banks who were lucky to buy the bonds, during and after the war, in the secondary market, at a discount.

For example, the bond buyer may pay $20 in the secondary market for a bond that was initially issued by the U. S. Treasury at $100.

The government and banks then agree that fairness, for the owners of the bonds, requires that the government redeem the bonds at full face value, resulting in a quick profit of $80 for the owner of the bonds, plus the repayment of interest on the bonds, generally over a bond maturity of 10 years.

This bond exchange technique of a quick profit for bond owners is how Hamilton secured the loyalty and allegiance of the wealthy natural aristocracy to support the new government.

The quick profit technique has been used by bankers and the U. S. Treasury, over and over again, throughout American economic history, after each war.

To review, the get-rich quick, speculative investments made by the natural aristocracy do not lead to real economic growth, and after about 10 years, the U. S. economy settles into a period of recession.

Generally, the recession ends when increased government spending on the military leads to a period of real economic growth. The war is financed by the issuance of government bonds, which are bought by banks and wealthy families.

Generally, the terms for bond interest and redemption are very favorable to the bond buyers, as was the case for J. P. Morgan, in 1894, when his bank financed the continued operations of the U. S. government in the depression of 1893.

Morgan's terms for buying the bonds constituted a guaranteed rate of profit, backed by the full faith and credit of the government, given that the government survived.

Given an initial distribution of income between the natural aristocracy and common citizens, in 1792, Madison's constitutional rules, in conjunction with Hamilton's financial system, could determine both price inflation and price deflation for an indefinite future period of time, as long as those interests controlled the rate of money creation.

The implication for neoclassical marginal theory is that the marginal equivalencies of profit maximization and utility maximization only, and exclusively, work in a capitalist market characterized by a stable institutional structure of money creation, based upon allegiance to the rule of law.

The longer the rule of law endures in a competitive capitalist economy, the more likely it is to lead to greater levels of future economic growth, because private capital investors are confident that they can obtain their future reward.

Oddly, the longer the Ruling Class maintains control over money supply, the greater the likelihood that economic growth will settle into a suboptimal Nash equilibrium as a result of political inbreeding.

Homans describes this part of social interaction "distributive injustice," as contrasted with distributive justice, which is where reward is based upon merit.

In the Nash equilibrium period, an injustice occurs when a person does not get the amount of reward he had expected to get, based both upon what he had seen rewarded in the earlier period, and also based upon what he gets in comparison to the reward another person gets in the same time period.

Injustice, in this case, is legitimate expectations of reward denied unfairly because the rule of law and the application of the rule of law is unequally tilted to the most powerful agents, who have captured control over the use of the police power of the state.

Capturing the police power of the state by special financial interests in order for them to preserve the status quo distribution of income is a manifestation of political inbreeding in the British social class society created by Madison's constitution.

For example, when Angelo Codevilla describes the American ruling class, he identifies the set of citizens in the Northeast who live in the same neighborhoods, go to the same universities, join the same social business networks and marry each other, in order to inbreed. (The Ruling Class: How They Corrupted America and What We Can Do About It. Angelo M. Codevilla, New York, Beaufort Books, 2010.)

As Homans points out, capital is not just money used for investment.

"Capital may take the form of a moral code, especially a code supporting trust and confidence between men; a well-founded belief that they will not always let you down in favor of their private short-term gain." (Social Behavior: Its Elementary Forms, George, C., Homans, New York, 1974).

Capital, seen as trust in Homan's case, means the ability to invest in one time period and expect to obtain reward in the later time period. The social institutional structure of capital investments must be stable long enough for the reward of the investment to be obtained in the later time period.

Contemporary economists call this type of capital "social capital."

Granovetter has called this social value of trust the "moral economy."

In his concept, the moral economy is the,

"...degree to which a group's operations presuppose a moral community in which trustworthy behavior can be expected, normative standards understood, and opportunism foregone." (Mark Granovetter, quoted in Dosi, Giovanni, et. als., eds., Technology, Organization, and Competitiveness: Perspectives on Industrial and Corporate Change, Oxford, 1998.)

If the rules on money supply keep changing, investors will not invest in the present time period because obtaining their future reward is uncertain.

We argue that Hamilton created a financial system that ran on the moral value of "shared plunder" where the banks, throughout American history, controlled the supply of money to suit the welfare function of the ruling class.

The financial goal for the elites in changing the money supply and the rate of interest, was aimed at preserving the status quo distribution of income that existed between social classes, since 1792.

Short-term reward and gaming the system in get-rich schemes replaced the moral value of trust in Jefferson's moral economy. In the shared plunder economy, there is no trust because everyone is engaged in plunder, and there is no long term investment horizon.

We argue that shared plunder and get-rich quick is the basis of the second version of the American Dream, which competes with Jefferson's version of the American entrepreneurial capitalist Dream.

Hamilton's economy of shared plunder was sustained and supported by Madison's constitutional rules that granted the police power of the state to manipulate the creation of money, exclusively to the natural aristocracy.

To the extent that the future reward becomes uncertain because obedience to the rule of law is uncertain, current period investment will not be made, and the economy will slip into decline from the point of the previous Nash equilibrium, to the next Nash equilibrium.

As William Baumol observes, "private capital entrepreneurs are economic animals…variations in reward structures determines the impact of new venture creation."

Baumol explains that,

"It is easy to imagine how the reward structure which benefits the governing elite might be perpetuated by that elite, with the simultaneous effect of discouraging [capital investment] disruptions which might threaten their power." (William Baumol, cited in Hall, Peter, Innovation, Economics and Evolution: Theoretical Perspectives on Changing Technology In Economic Systems, New York, 1994).

Our theoretical explanation for the regularly observable economic recessions in the NBER chart is that politically-inbred elites (also known as the Federalists) captured the police power of the state, in Madison's constitution, and they then used their unelected, illegitimate power to direct legacy incomes and rewards to themselves.

This explanation would be a truth that the NBER staff dare not speak, not because the explanation is unscientific, but because speaking the truth would get them fired from their cushy jobs.

Chapter 2. Madison's Myth of "We, the people."

Our main argument is that Jefferson's promise of liberty is founded on an American dream of individual success, whereas Madison's constitution is based upon rules that permanently elevated the financial interests of the natural aristocracy over the interests of common citizens.

The two conceptions of the American Dream are incompatible and irreconcilable.

Madison feared that, "We, the people," would combine majority power, in a national democratic republic, to deprive the minority of wealthy elites of their rights to property and social class privileges.

Madison cited the experience of the 13 state legislatures in depriving the natural aristocracy of their privileges as a mistake to be avoided in the new government.

His rules created a national plutocracy for the benefit of the natural aristocracy, now known as the Ruling Class.

The dilemma confronted by Madison, in 1787, was how to modify the concept of sovereignty of consent of the governed to fit his constitutional framework of a Ruling Class representative republic, which did not require on-going consent of the common citizens.

When King George transferred the sovereignty of the Crown to American citizens, the citizens, themselves, became the sovereign power.

The sovereign power of the people, at that point in history, was absolute and supreme, and the citizens obtained the natural right to alter or abolish the government, as explained by Jefferson, in the Declaration.

Prior to the patriot victory in 1781, the patriots were in Locke's imaginary state of nature, and Jefferson's Declaration was based upon the Lockean framework of natural rights, when citizens left the state of nature to form a new government.

Madison had to find a way to limit the majority voting power of the common citizens, so that the sovereign authority of the people was circumscribed.

Madison started out his constitution with the phrase "We the people," as if to suggest that the parties to the contract were the individual citizens and the nascent government.

After that initial reference to the people, it becomes apparent that the parties to Madison's contract are not the people, as individuals, but people as social classes.

"We, the people" was in fact, and reality, only 39 self-selected elites, who wrote the constitution, as if those 39 elites constituted the sovereignty of "We, the people."

Madison's notes for September 12, 1787, contain his acknowledgement of how he implemented the modification of sovereignty from the people to the social class of elites.

From Madison's notes: September 12.

"Committee of Style reported an amendment to Article 7, which was read by paragraph. This document (the Constitution), is preceded by a preamble, which begins, "We the People of the United States, in order to form a more perfect union..." rather than "We the people of the states of New Hampshire, etc..."

The other delegates had never seen this version of the Preamble before. The text that they had seen before referenced the people of each state, which would have been consistent with King George's transfer of sovereignty.

As explained by Merrill Jensen, in his book, Articles of Confederation, what the anti-federalist did not understand was the degree of ideological commitment of the elites to creating a government that protected their privileges of the natural aristocracy.

Jensen writes,

"...the nationalists adopted a theory of the sovereignty of the people, in the name of the people, and erected a nationalistic government whose purpose was to thwart the will of the people in whose name they acted..."

The issue of where sovereignty resides in America has continued to plague social class conflict in America. For example, based upon their understanding that the citizens of the states were sovereign, the Slaveocracy in Southern states assumed that they had a right to own slaves, and a right to secede.

Another example of the uncertain location of sovereignty arises after the Civil War, as described by C. Vann Woodward, in Origins of The New South,

"In their attack on the national banking system, the agrarian economists were on solid ground in contending that private privilege was exercising a sovereign power, a power of regulating national currency, for private gain, rather than for meeting the needs of the country."

In that era, a private special financial interest, created by Hamilton's banking system, was exercising an undelegated sovereign political power over farmers.

That undelegated special financial interest was protected by Madison's constitutional rules, which insulated the private financial interests from the majority will of the common citizens.

As Sean Wilentz wrote, in his book, The Rise of American Democracy: Jefferson to Lincoln,

"The people had no formal voice of their own in government. And, that was exactly how it was supposed to be – for once the electors had chosen their representatives, they ceded power, reserving none for themselves until the next election...[We]The people, as a political entity, existed only on election day."

Madison's "We, the people," created an artificial personality to which the name the "State" is given. This same artificial legal personality was extended to private corporations, during the 1870s, under Madison's constitutional rules.

The sovereignty created by Madison was transferred from "We, the people," to the "State" as an organic totality, or consolidated political unit.

Madison's sovereignty resides in the organs of government, under the powers granted to the government by the Constitution, as if the "State" has its own existence, independent of the people.

Madison did not create an artificial personality to correspond with "We, the people" because his intent was to modify the sovereignty of the people as a whole, viewed as a political unit.

Following the logic of Jefferson, all legitimate authority was derived from the consent of the governed.

Following Madison, all legitimate authority was derived from the "State," directed by the ruling social class, which managed and administered the agencies of government.

Madison created an American version of "virtual representation" drawn from the British model of the King's Privy Council. The chronology of events, prior to 1776, is that the King's Privy Council virtually represented the interests of the colonists, and therefore, the British colonists did not need actual representation in London, in the British mixed government social class model.

According to Michael Klarman in The Framers Coup, Madison thought that his centralized rules would operate like the authority of the British Privy Council's to block populist legislation in state legislatures related to state issuance of currency and debt relief.

In 1783, the King transferred sovereign power from the Crown to the unorganized 13 states, as 13 independent legal entities. The Treaty of Paris begins with King George acknowledging that he is surrendering to 13 independent sovereign states.

The King acknowledges, and names, the United States (New Hampshire, Massachusetts Bay, Rhode Island and Providence Plantations, Connecticut, New York, New Jersey, Pennsylvania, Delaware, Maryland, Virginia, North Carolina, South Carolina, and Georgia, to be free, sovereign, and independent states, and that the British Crown and all heirs and successors relinquish claims to the Government, property, and territorial rights of the same, and every part thereof.

In 1787, Madison created a new "State" that replicated the King's Privy Council, and transferred sovereignty from citizens to the State.

Both by principle and by legal authority, the doctrine of sovereignty in the United States defines sovereignty not as an independent, unlimited, indivisible power of "We, the people", but in the narrow sense of the power of the agencies of government to compel obedience, and the elite's freedom from liability from exercising political power over citizens,

In his book, The Moral Foundations of the American Republic, Robert Horwitz, quotes John Randolf to capture the essence of the location of sovereignty under Madison's constitution.

Randolf states:

"When I mention the public I mean to include only the rational part of it. The ignorant and vulgar are as unfit to judge the modes as they are unable to manage the reins of government."

In Federalist #39, Madison argued for a new sort of representative republic. It would rest on the,

"total exclusion of the people, in their collective capacity, from any share in government."

Hamilton wrote at the time that he considered the "people as a great beast, howling masses, not fit to govern."

In entering Madison's constitution contract, individuals, who were not part of Madison's definition of the natural aristocracy, gave up freedoms without extracting an equal measure of benefits to pursue their sovereign interests.

The common citizen's political and financial interests would be virtually represented by the natural aristocracy, who were deemed by Madison to have the moral virtue of placing the citizen's interests above their own private, selfish interests, in managing the affairs of the government.

Merrill Peterson, in The Jefferson Image in the American Mind, cited Madison's failure to establish liberty as the mission, or purpose of government, in his Preamble.

Peterson wrote:

"that Madison's division of powers,...became the chief means of checking the exaggeration of the democratic principle, and thus of securing an equilibrium of majority power and constitutional guarantees..."

In other words, Madison's rules became an effective instrument of control over common citizens precisely because the rules, once adopted in the Lockean framework of leaving nature, could never be reformed in the direction of more democracy, by the common citizens.

Following Hobbes, Madison created the Leviathan, whose awesome, terrible powers could never be revoked.

In The Natural Rights Republic, Michael Zuckert calls Madison's constitutional rules, "institutional instrumentalism."

This description means that Madison constitution created the institutional rules that are instrumental in effecting the distribution of power in the republic.

For Madison, the purpose of government was not to provide a mechanism of rights claims and reciprocation of trust among citizens who possessed equal rights, as rights would be in the Jeffersonian model.

Rather, Madison's rules were the instruments to balance and check financial and political power in order to insure that social elites, the natural leaders, who made important decisions on behalf of all society, were insulated from the tyranny that could be imposed by a political majority of "We, the people."

In The Creation of the American Republic, 1776 – 1787, Gordon S Wood quotes Richard Henry Lee on how remarkable Madison's modification of the concept of sovereignty had been.

Lee states:

"It will be considered, I believe, as a most extraordinary epoch in the history of mankind, that in a few years there should be so essential a change in the minds of men [regarding sovereignty]. Tis really astonishing that the same people who have just emerged from a long and cruel war in defence of liberty, should now agree to fix an elective despotism upon themselves and their posterity."

Madison's rules created a republic without defining the res publica of the republic.

As described by Robert Hoffert, in A Politics of Tensions: The Articles of Confederation and American Political Ideas,

"The purpose of republic is res publica, the public thing, or the public good."

During the Convention, the delegates were mostly set against the inclusion of a bill of rights in the new Constitution, defeating efforts by George Mason and Elbridge Gerry to consider one.

Madison played both sides of the issue, saying in a letter to Thomas Jefferson,

"I have always been in favor of a bill of rights... At the same time I have never thought the omission a material defect, nor been anxious to supply it even by subsequent amendment."

Five of the states that conditionally ratified the Constitution included a list of amendments that would be required in the new Constitution, if they were to extend unconditional approval.

After Madison first fought against the inclusion of a Bill of Rights, he switched sides. In his election campaign against James Monroe for the new U.S. House, vowed to fight for a bill of rights.

He informed the Congress on May 4, 1789, that he intended to introduce the topic formally on May 25; but on May 4, the Congress was embroiled in a lengthy debate on import duties, and when May 25 rolled around, the debate continued.

He rose again on June 8 to introduce the subject, but he was blocked, with other members noting that the Congress had more pressing matters to attend to.

In the ensuing debate in Congress, about the 10th Amendment, Madison modified the text to take out the word "expressly" because of the legal damage the word would do to the centralized power of the government.

Madison argued that the Articles of Confederation had been created by the 13 states, while this new constitution was created by "We the People."

Madison wrote,

"Should all the states adopt it, it will be then a government established by the thirteen states of America, not through the intervention of the legislatures, but by the people at large. In this particular respect the distinction between the existing and the proposed governments is very material. The existing system (The Articles), has been derived from the dependent derivative authority of the legislatures of the states; whereas, this is derived from the superior power of the people."

Madison cited North Carolina's opposition to the Constitution as his motive for including the Bill of Rights.

Madison wrote:

"I allude in a particular manner to those two States that have not thought fit to throw themselves into the bosom of the Confederacy. It is a desirable thing, on our part as well as theirs, that a re-union should take place as soon as possible. I have no doubt, if we proceed to take those steps which would be prudent and requisite at this juncture, that in a short time we should see that disposition prevailing in those States which have not come in, that we have seen prevailing in those States which have embraced the constitution."

Madison then invoked his deception that the Bill of Rights could be adopted without damaging the supreme sovereign power of the central government.

His deception hinged on excluding the word "expressly" in the 10th Amendment.

Madison wrote,

"I do conceive that the constitution may be amended; that is to say, if all power is subject to abuse, that then it is possible the abuse of the powers of the General Government may be guarded against in a more secure manner than is now done, while no one advantage arising from the exercise of that power shall be damaged or endangered by it…(the amendments can be adopted) without endangering any part of the constitution, which is considered as essential to the existence of the Government by those who promoted its adoption."

Madison's opening argument for the amendments cites the authority of "We the people," who granted the new government its powers. Madison placed the text for "We the people" in the Preamble.

Madison wrote,

"First, That there be prefixed to the constitution, (in the Preamble) a declaration, that all power is originally rested in, and consequently derived from, the people…The powers not delegated by this constitution, nor prohibited by it to the States, are reserved to the States respectively."

Madison then switches sides to argue that specific powers not delegated by either the states or "the people," are discretionary powers of the government.

The Bill of Rights could be added, argued Madison, because those rights did not interfere with the discretionary power of the government.

As noted by Thomas Paine, Madison's Preamble was "a nominal nothing without principles." The Preamble failed to state the public purpose of government.

Mason argued that a "more perfect union", or the res publica, had been left undefined in Madison's Preamble. It could mean anything.

In the hands of the natural aristocracy, a more perfect union meant elite rule, based upon the shared cultural value of shared plunder in the operation of the agencies of government, and in the operation of the private banking system.

In the hands of Democrat Marxists, today, a more perfect union means a more perfect Marxist tyranny. The centralized power of "the State" is equally applicable as a more perfect union to either the Ruling Class, or to Democrat Marxists.

Madison explained the logic of his instrumental rules in Federalist #51:

"In framing a government of men over men, one must first empower the government to control the people, and then oblige it (the government) to control itself."

Madison's civil rules of procedure created a Leviathan to control the people without creating any mechanism of citizen control over the Leviathan, once it had been created.

Madison's flaw allowed the central government to operate directly upon the citizens without providing the mechanism for citizens to operate directly on the government.

Madison's arrangement reserved no sovereign powers to the citizens, and the result, today, is a special interest tyranny, called the "Deep State."

As Elisha Douglass pointed out in Rebels and Democrats, Whig leaders like North Carolina's Sam Johnston understood that the problem for the new constitution was ,

"...how to establish a check on the representatives of the people."

Once established, just like the Leviathan, the check on common citizens was irrevocable.

Few, if any of Madison's cohorts worried about the basic contradiction unleashed by their flawed constitutional scheme.

As Douglass noted,

"Hence, a double paradox: to preserve their own liberty, the unprivileged masses must be prevented from infringing on the privileged few; to maintain a government based on consent, a large proportion of the people must be deprived of the ability to extend or withhold consent."

According to C. B. MacPherson, in The Political Theory of Possessive Individualism: From Hobbes to Locke (1962),

"It was not that the interests of the laboring class were subordinated to the national [Ruling Class] interest. The laboring class was not considered to have an [independent sovereign] interest; the only interest was the ruling-class view of the national interest."

Following a part of Locke's theory of political authority, Madison accepted the premise that civil society consisted primarily of an exchange of values in either the economic or the political market.

It did not seem to matter to Madison, or to Hamilton, that the values and instruments in economic exchange may be different than the values in political exchange.

From Madison's point of view, when the proprietors of labor (common citizens), left the state of nature to form the social contract, they agreed that the purpose of the contract was to establish rules governing the exchange relationships, and that the new government must have power to enforce the orderly mechanisms of exchange.

Madison set about to create the constitutional rules that would bring about the orderly exchange mechanism by emphasizing the separation of powers through his system of formal checks and balances.

His emphasis was on creating constitutional rules of exchange that could be enforced in a morally neutral environment, called the "State."

This flaw in Madison's Preamble helps to explain why, in the time of Jackson's Democratic Party, [1835], the Democrats could legitimately claim that the public purpose of government was the protection of the weak from the strong, while the Whigs could claim, with equal legitimacy, that the constitutional public purpose was served when government facilitated the development of private financial institutions.

Madison's separation of powers does not address the ends to which that power is directed. It devolves, in other words, to winning and keeping power between two social classes.

Allegiance to the rule of law, in Jefferson, is based upon a shared sense of civic obligation to follow the rules, which gives way, in Madison, to rule evasion, based upon the cultural value of shared plunder.

During the Convention in Philadelphia, the delegates debated the best strategy for securing ratification of their work. Madison had already determined that securing ratification through the state legislatures would not be a good idea because it was the state legislatures that had been causing the problems for the natural aristocracy.

A better idea for securing ratification of the proposed Constitution, according to Madison, was to avoid ratification by the legislatures, and to have self-selected delegates in state conventions endorse the proposed constitution.

Madison stated that "the state legislatures did not speak for the people, [the natural aristocracy] but only for particular people [the common citizens].

Madison's logic for keeping the deliberations secret and for evading the legitimate rules for ratification by the legislatures, then in place, under the Articles, was explained by Madison on August 30.

The rules for ratification by conventions, and not legislatures, would allow the elites, as Madison stated, to obtain ratification "over the whole body of the people."

The two parts of Madison's ratification strategy were to keep the common citizens in the dark, by not ever releasing the record of the convention, and to place the ratification process in the hands of the corrupt elites, at the state level, who used their corrupt power to secure the votes on the ratification.

The entire ratification process, debated on August 30 is about the minimal number of state conventions required to ratify.

Madison suggested that just 7 states would be required. The part about the number of states required had been left blank, and the debate that day revolved around that issue.

From Madison's notes, August 30.

Mr. MADISON remarked, that if the blank should be filled with "seven," "eight," or "nine," the Constitution as it stands, might be put in force over the whole body of the people, though less than a majority of them should ratify it.

As Mr. King noted, the rules for ratification would allow a minority to impose a government on the majority:

Mr. KING thought this amendment necessary; otherwise, as the Constitution now stands, it will operate on the whole, though ratified by a part only.

The next day, in a precursor to the 10th amendment debate, King attempted to limit the operation of the central government to only the states which ratified it.

In Convention. — Mr. KING moved to add to the end of Article 21, the words, "between the said States;" so as to confine the operation of the Government to the States ratifying it.

The hidden agenda of Madison's ratification strategy was exposed on August 31, in the debate between King and Gouverneur Morris.

From Madison's notes, August 31.

Mr. GOUVERNEUR MORRIS thought the blank ought to be filled in a two-fold way, so as to provide for the event of the ratifying States being contiguous, which would render a smaller number sufficient; and the event of their being dispersed, which would require a greater number for the introduction of the Government.

Mr. GOUVERNEUR MORRIS moved to strike out, "conventions of the," after "ratifications;" leaving the States to pursue their own modes of ratification.

Mr. KING thought that striking out "conventions," as the requisite mode, was equivalent to giving up the business altogether. Conventions alone, which will avoid all the obstacles from the complicated formation of the Legislatures, will succeed; and if not positively required by the plan, its enemies will oppose that mode.

Mr. GOUVERNEUR MORRIS said, he meant to facilitate the adoption of the plan, by leaving the modes approved by the several State Constitutions to be followed.

In other words, Morris disclosed that Madison's entire ratification process was designed to gain illegitimate approval in a procedure under the control of the elites in each state. Morris thought the elites in each state should do whatever they wanted to do.

King responded that the amendment not to seek state legislative approval was equivalent to giving up on a legitimate ratification process.

As explained by Martin, the ratification process would fail, unless common citizens were, "hurried into it by surprise."

Mr. L. MARTIN believed Mr. MORRIS to be right, that after a while the people would be against it; but for a different reason from that alleged. He believed they would not ratify it, unless hurried into it by surprise.

From Madison's notes, August 31.

Mr. MADISON considered it best to require Conventions; among other reasons for this, that the powers given to the General Government being taken from the State Governments, the Legislatures would be more disinclined than Conventions composed in part at least of other men; and if disinclined, they could devise modes apparently promoting, but really thwarting, the ratification. The difficulty in Maryland was no greater than in other States, where no mode of change was pointed out by the Constitution, and all officers were under oath to support it. The people were, in fact, the fountain of all power, and by resorting to them, all difficulties were got over. They could alter constitutions as they pleased. It was a principle in the Bills of Rights, that first principles might be resorted to.

Mr. L. MARTIN insisted on a reference to the State Legislatures. He urged the danger of commotions from a resort to the people and to first principles; in which the Government might be on one side, and the people on the other. He was apprehensive of no such consequences, however, in Maryland, whether the Legislature or the people should be appealed to. Both of them would be generally against the Constitution. He repeated also the peculiarity in the Maryland Constitution.

On August 31, the ratification process was amended twice.

From Madison's notes, August 31.

Article 21, as amended, was then agreed to by all the States, Maryland excepted, and Mr. JENIFER being aye.

Article 22 was then taken up, to wit: "This Constitution shall be laid before the United States in Congress assembled, for their approbation; and it is the opinion of this Convention that it should be afterwards submitted to a Convention chosen in each State, under the recommendation of its Legislature, in order to receive the ratification of such Convention."

Mr. GOUVERNEUR MORRIS and Mr. PINCKNEY moved to strike out the words, "for their approbation."

On this question, — New Hampshire, Connecticut, New Jersey,1 Pennsylvania, Delaware, Virginia, North Carolina, South Carolina, aye, — 8; Massachusetts, Maryland, Georgia, no, — 3.

Mr. GOUVERNEUR MORRIS and Mr. PINCKNEY then moved to amend the article so as to read:

"This Constitution shall be laid before the United States in Congress assembled; and it is the opinion of this Convention, that it should afterwards be submitted to a Convention chosen in each State, in order to receive the ratification of such Convention; to which end the several Legislatures ought to provide for the calling Conventions within their respective States as speedily as circumstances will permit."

Mr. GOUVERNEUR MORRIS said his object was to impress in stronger terms the necessity of calling Conventions, in order to prevent enemies to the plan from giving it the go by. When it first appears, with the sanction of this Convention, the people will be favorable to it. By degrees the State officers, and those interested in the State Governments, will intrigue, and turn the popular current against it.

Luther Marin was so disgusted by the deception and deceit in the ratification debate that he left the convention.

The final version of ratification, adopted on September 15, omitted the text of the amendment, on August 31.

The delegates never had a chance to see the final version of the ratification rules before the ratification rules were engraved as a part of the Constitution.

As in the case of the re-written Preamble, and the last-minute inclusion of the Fugitive Slave Amendment, the delegates approved versions of the final draft that they had not read, or approved.

Rather than the amendment voted on August 31, the text in the Constitution reads:

Article VII.

The ratification of the conventions of nine States shall be sufficient for the establishment of this Constitution between the States so ratifying the same.

Done in Convention, by the unanimous consent of the States present, the 17th day of September, in the year of our Lord 1787, and of the independence of the United States of America, the twelfth. In witness whereof, we have hereunto subscribed our names.

The text about "unanimous consent" was a lie, since New York did not have authorized delegates there, and the text of the amendment to place it before the Congress was omitted entirely.

Madison issued the text to Congress in a series of truncated and different versions, without instructions on what the Congress should do with the various versions of the text.

Having dealt with the ratification method, the delegates then turned to the thorny issue of how to handle the evidence of the notes and official minutes of their deliberations.

From Madison's notes, September 17.

Mr. KING suggested that the Journals of the Convention should be either destroyed, or deposited in the custody of the President. He thought, if suffered to be made public, a bad use would be made of them by those who would wish to prevent the adoption of the Constitution.

Mr. WILSON preferred the second expedient. He had at one time liked the first best; but as false suggestions may be propagated, it should not be made impossible to contradict them.

A question was then put on depositing the Journals, and other papers of the Convention, in the hands of the President; on which, — New Hampshire, Massachusetts, Connecticut, New Jersey, Pennsylvania, Delaware, Virginia, North Carolina, South Carolina, Georgia, aye, — 10; Maryland,4 no, — 1.

The President, having asked what the Convention meant should be done with the Journals, &c., whether copies were to be allowed to the members, if applied for, it was resolved, nem. con. "that he retain the Journal and other papers, subject to the order of Congress, if ever formed under the Constitution."

Part of Madison's deception was submitting the draft of the Constitution and its rules in different documents to Congress, without any instruction to Congress on what it was to do with the drafts.

As a result of the indecision created by the submission of multiple documents, Congress simply sent parts of the documents of the draft Constitution to the states without any instructions on what the states should do.

The self-appointed elites in the various states adopted their own rules to ratify the document, including the force and fraud of arresting delegates in Pennsylvania, who were trying to leave the fraudulent proceedings, to avoid giving assent.

The Federalists in Pennsylvania then sent out deputies to arrest the missing delegates, because without them, the remaining delegates in Pennsylvania would not constitute a quorum.

The Federalists capture them and held them, against their will, so that the Pennsylvania ratification had the patina of a legitimate quorum.

As correctly predicted by Elbridge Gerry, on the last day of the Convention, Madison's Constitution, would precipitate a civil war over the issue of slavery, and would end as Mason predicted, in a centralized aristocratic tyranny that is disconnected from the consent of the governed.

From Madison's notes, September 17.Mr. GERRY described the painful feelings of his situation, and the embarrassments under which he rose to offer any further observations on the subject which had been finally decided. Whilst the plan was depending, he had treated it with all the freedom he thought it deserved. He now felt himself bound, as he was disposed, to treat it with the respect due to the act of the Convention.

He hoped he should not violate that respect in declaring, on this occasion, his fears that a civil war may result from the present crisis of the United States. In Massachusetts, particularly, he saw the danger of this calamitous event. In that State there are two parties, one devoted to Democracy, the worst, he thought, of all political evils; the other as violent in the opposite extreme.

From the collision of these in opposing and resisting the Constitution, confusion was greatly to be feared. He had thought it necessary, for this and other reasons, that the plan should have been proposed in a more mediating shape, in order to abate the heat and opposition of parties. As it had been passed by the Convention, he was persuaded it would have a contrary effect. He could not, therefore, by signing the Constitution, pledge himself to abide by it at all events. The proposed form made no difference with him. But if it were not otherwise apparent, the refusals to sign should never be known from him. Alluding to the remarks of Doctor FRANKLIN, he could not, he said, but view them as levelled at himself and the other gentlemen who meant not to sign.

Madison's notes on the Convention, which he revised throughout his life, and were not published until 1840, four years after his death, and 53 years after the Convention, are the only official records of the proceedings.

As the delegates at Philadelphia had instructed, on September 17, 1787, the official minutes and records of the proceedings had been given to General Washington, for "safe keeping."

In Madison's constitutional rules, the elites (natural aristocracy) had the power to make the laws, and the citizens (hurly-burly) had the duty to obey the laws made by the elites.

As described by Robert Horwitz, in The Moral Foundations of The American Republic, Madison thought that the working class could develop a class consciousness, like the class consciousness of the natural aristocracy.

Horwitz wrote that Madison thought that,

"If all citizens (working class) have the same impulse of passion and interest they would not divide into oppressive and dangerous factions… if (working class) Americans can be made to divide themselves according to their narrow economic interests they will avoid the fatal factionalism."

Madison provided the institutional separation of power that divided the working class into their narrow economic (class) interests. The separation of power was designed to separate the financial interests of the working class from imposing their majority views on the virtuous elites.

All branches of government were safely insulated from the howling masses because the elites occupied all branches of government.

As Madison noted,

"the central function of the legal system is to protect autonomous individuals (elites) from the "tyranny of the majority" (working class).

In Madison's conception, the moral value of Jefferson's individual liberty was not a commercial "faction," worthy of legal status in the constitution, in the same sense that the working class and the elites were a financial faction.

The end goal for Madison was a stable system of rules that would allow the elites to negotiate the spoils of the system with other elites.

In Madison's conception of government, the apparatus of government is a neutral guardian between the two competing class interests that his constitutional separation of power was designed to check and balance.

Individuals are born into the Madison's cultural and institutional arrangement by chance. Individuals did not enter that institutional arrangement by choice, in 1787, and common citizens did not have a legitimate opportunity to modify or vote for other institutional arrangements, after 1788.

The problem with Madison's Flaw of leaving out the rules of justice, in the Preamble, is that the decisions about substantive due process are untethered from the constitution.

There is no logical end to what Marxist Democrat judges deem to be authorized by substantive due process, as it now applies to social groups, not natural persons.

Madison presumed that the Federal representatives obtained the consent of the citizens in the original grant, and then, after that, the common citizens granted the elites the authority to make all the decisions.

In other words, as the anti-federalist Centinel asked about Madison's arrangement,

"If the people are sovereign how does the opinion of citizens direct the policies of government?"

There is nothing in the Federalist constitution, noted Centinel, like the detailed definition of consent in the various state constitutions.

Centinel's observations continue to add to Madison's legacy of the myth of "we, the people."

As a small vignette on the social class dynamics between the aristocracy and the common citizens, Saul Cornell, in The Other Founders, (1999), describes the astonishment of William Maclay, who had converted from being a Federalist to being a Jefferson advocate.

Maclay had been invited to a Federalist dinner party in New York, in 1792. The Federalists were openly boasting that they had pulled a fast one over on the common citizens, in the ratification of Madison's constitution.

Cornell writes,

"Maclay was astonished that the Federalists boasted that they had cheated the [common] people and established a form of government over them which none of them [common citizens] had expected."

Chapter 3. Hamilton's Ruling Class Economic System.

Madison's constitutional rules created the legal framework for elite rule, and Hamilton then added the financial system that permanently benefitted the plutocracy.

The two systems, one political, and the other economic, must be interpreted as working in tandem throughout U. S. history to explain the regularly occurring economic collapses that have plagued American society.

Madison's constitution shifted the King's grant of sovereignty from "We, the people," to the centralized State, where the State power of the plutocracy was not subjected to "the consent of the governed."

Hamilton's economy was based upon debt, credit, and the absence of circulating currency, sufficient to serve as the medium of exchange in commercial and retail transactions.

We argue that the economy that Hamilton created was an unstable economy that ran on elite investment speculation, credit, debt, and not on cash. The ruling class used their crony capitalist unelected political power over the money supply to speculate on investments that did not yield real economic growth.

The macro economic instability of elite rule is caused by the elite's unelected control over the money supply. The elite allegiance to the cultural value of shared plunder held both the political and economic systems together.

Or, to borrow a phrase from bankers at the time, the investments of the Ruling Class did not yield real economic growth based upon "real bills."

One effect of the speculative investments was rapid price inflation, followed by the economic crash, several years later, when the hoped-for economic growth failed to materialize.

Essentially, the real bills doctrine, that guided ruling class bankers for about 200 years, is a rule purporting to link the future money supply to the future value of production, via short term commercial business loans called "bills of exchange," or simply bank loans collateralized by the expected future returns of the investments.

Under Madison's assumption that bankers were smarter than the howling masses, and would always place the public interest above their own private interests in judging the merit of a loan for an investment proposal, real bills was a self-fulfilling economic tautology.

If bankers always based their judgment for a loan on "real bills" of future economic productivity, real productive output in the future would generate a real supply of future money, that would automatically equate the future supply of money with the future demand for money.

Real bills would end up without causing inflation in commodity or retail prices, in the current time period, because, in some prior period of time, the very smart bankers had limited their loans to real investments.

The doctrine states that money supply can never be excessive when issued against short-term commercial bills arising from real investments in goods.

In other words, inflationary over-issue of money is impossible provided credit is issued on loans made to finance real, productive investments, not wildly speculative investments, for example in building railroads on government-secured land.

In his review of the creation of Hamilton's economy, Richard Bernstein posed the basic political question raised by the rules created by Madison and Hamilton:

"Was it dangerous in a democratic government, to have important officers insulated from control by the people, or was it necessary to accept that risk [of aristocratic tyranny] in order to protect fundamental rights from infringement by popular passions or political intrigue?" (The Founding Fathers Reconsidered, Oxford University Press, 2011.)

The basic question raised by Bernstein about American democracy is the same raised by Hobbes: What compels obedience to the rule of law?

In Jefferson and Locke, voluntary obedience to the rule of law is gained by equality of rights in the Constitution, when citizens leave the state of nature. Citizens respect the rights of others that they desire for themselves.

In Hamilton's elite tyranny, the awesome, awful powers of Hobbes' Leviathan compel obedience.

In Federalist #15, Hamilton concluded that,

"...only coercion of individuals was effective in upholding national interests."

Of course, from Hamilton's point of view, the definition of "national interests" was solely to promote the interests of the natural aristocracy.

As Hamilton explained in the Federalist Papers,

"Every community divides itself into hostile interests of the few and the many, the rich and well-born against the mass of people If either of these interests possessed all the power it would oppress the other...we (the well born) need to be rescued from the democracy."

Gordon Wood, in The Creation of the American Republic, cited Hamilton in Federalist #35 on the logical justification of elite rule.

"What justified elite rule, together with the notion of virtual representation," noted Wood,

"was Hamilton's sense that all parts of the society were of a piece, that all ranks and degrees were organically connected...the state was a cohesive organic entity with a single homogeneous interest in a chain in such a way that those on the top were necessarily involved in the welfare of those below them."

In other words, Jefferson viewed society in terms of the welfare of individuals, and Hamilton viewed society in collectivist terms, more akin to the Marxian analysis of the capitalist class, and the working class, based upon the British mixed government model of society.

Under Madison, the State had an independent, collectivist power, untethered from the democratic influence, and fully empowered to make decisions on behalf of the common workers, because the natural aristocracy possessed the moral quality of virtue.

Saul Cornell, in The Other Founders, (1999), cites John Taylor to make the point that anti-federalists, at that time, understood exactly the intent of Hamilton's economic system:

"John Taylor of Caroline, 1795, Hamilton's system of funding was intended to effect accumulation of wealth in a few hands. A political moneyed engine, a suppression of the republican state assemblies by manipulation of paper interest."

Hamilton's observation that the national debt served as a national blessing is correct, viewed from Hamilton's two-social class model. Debt was a blessing to the financial interests of the natural aristocracy.

Debt, in its entire economic function, both for the national government, and for the private interests, was a blessing, for them. Debt and credit, in the absence of currency, placed an irrevocable, undelegated power in the hands of the ruling class because the wealthy could create money out of thin air to pay off their debts, when their speculative investments went bust.

The debt of the United States ... "was the price of liberty," Hamilton said. And, he turned his attention to creating a debt-based economy by placing the debt of the nation in the hands of the plutocracy, and guaranteeing them a profit.

In Federalist #11, Hamilton argued that,

"Commerce is the means by which man's passion and self-interest can be institutionally and organizationally addressed. Commerce is the glue that binds the parts of the system together into a well-ordered whole."

Paper currency was not required in Hamilton's debt-based economy because the Constitution had defined the government's bills of credit to represent a paper medium of exchange intended to circulate, like money, between individuals, and between the Government and individuals, for the ordinary purposes of economic transactions.

At the same time as establishing bills of credit as a substitute for currency, the Constitution eliminated the state government's ability to issue paper currency.

The only social class that had access to bills of credit was the natural aristocracy, who had enough wealth to buy the bills of credit.

Farmers did not have access to bills of credit as a medium of exchange, because they had no wealth or money to buy them, and could not obtain the limited quantity of gold coins that Hamilton's Mint created.

In Madison's rules, First Bank notes, or bills of credit, were the only form of payment accepted when paying federal taxes, which the First Bank was in charge of collecting.

Hamilton proposed that the bank issue notes redeemable on demand for specie. In other words, the wealthy speculators who owned government debt could gain liquidity by converting the notes into gold and silver.

As written by Sean Wilenz, in The Rise of American Democracy: Jefferson to Lincoln (2005)

"Hamilton's fiscal plan would, he believed, ally the federal government to a particular class of speculators, create (through the national bank) a means to dispense political bounties to political favorites and bribes to opponents and introduce what Madison would later describe as the "corrupt influence" of substituting the motive of private interests in place of the public duty."

Part of Hamilton's strategy for using debt to secure the allegiance of the wealthy classes, was that only a very narrow spectrum of elite social class owned the deeply discounted bonds that had been used to finance the Revolutionary War.

According to Klarman,

"As much as 90% of government securities [issued during the War] fell into the hands of speculators ….trading at 12% of face value……In Rhode Island, just 16 people held nearly half of the states securities…In Massachusetts, 35 people held 40% of the state's deeply discounted debt…70% of all taxes raised in Pennsylvania went to just 12 investors."

Hamilton promised the potential investors that he would redeem the discounted bonds at full face value, creating unearned, risk-free, windfall profits for the wealthy investors.

In his analysis of American government finance, created by Madison's constitution, Charles Beard estimated that a quick profit of $40 million was made by wealthy families who had bought the discounted bonds. (An Economic Interpretation of the Constitution of the United States, 1925.)

Beard wrote,

"it seems safe to hazard a guess that at least $40 million gain came to the holders of securities through the adoption of the Constitution."

As he noted, the property rights of the natural aristocracy, protected by Madison's rules, had been placed, "beyond the reach of popular majorities."

As a counter-measure to Hamilton's elitist proposal to reward the Ruling Class, who owned the discounted bonds, Madison proposed that Congress should set aside some money for the original owners of the Revolutionary War Bonds, the farmers and soldiers who tended to be ordinary Americans and not new investors and speculators.

Madison's idea failed to be enacted.

On a political and pragmatic level, Madison's idea of protecting the interests of farmers would have been difficult to implement, through Congress. Nearly half the members of Congress had invested in the deeply discounted bonds.

The elected representatives stood to benefit financially from the enactment of Hamilton's plan.

The institutional lynchpin that held the political and economic systems together was Hamilton's First Bank. The bank served as the depository institution for the U. S. Treasury tax receipts and the cash from selling government bonds, meaning that the First Bank had the nation's supply of capital, under its control.

Albert Gallatin, in his Sketch of the Finances of the U. S. (1796), noted that,

"The Bank had become a political engine and instead of adding to the capital of the U. S. it had actually drained capital away from productive investment."

Gallatin was referring to the gold that migrated, after 1794, from the U. S. to the British banks, who owned the majority interest in the First Bank.

Citing the real bills doctrine, Gallatin differentiated between "productive investment and financial manipulation, attacking speculators who lived to consume, to spend more."

The Bank, however, was privately owned, by both U. S. domiciled investors, and foreign investors, including foreign banks. Two-thirds of the bank stock was held by British interests.

The U. S. Treasury would be a minority stockholder in the bank, authorized to hold up to one-fifth of its initial capital of $10 million, and vote for directors. But the remaining $8 million in stock would be held by private investors—merchants, landowners, speculators or anyone else who possessed the wealth to buy the Bank's stock, and therefore, could direct the Bank's investments.

In fact, one of the foreign banks that owned shares in the First Bank loaned Hamilton the capital in order for Hamilton's Treasury Department to buy shares in the Bank, on behalf of the U. S. Treasury.

There was no legal mechanism, or force, either in the Bank's Charter, or in Madison's Constitution that compelled the credit issued by the Bank, to meet some concept of promoting the commonwealth or the public good.

In other words, the Bank was the repository for the government taxes and also acted as the sales agent to sell the government's bonds. After collecting the revenues, the Bank's officers were then free to make decisions on the merits of the speculative investments of the Ruling Class, both in the domestic U. S. economy, and in Europe.

The Bank loaned money to the U. S. Government to finance government projects and ventures. By the end of 1795, the Treasury, now led by Hamilton's successor, Oliver Wolcott, had borrowed a total of $6.2 million from the bank, more than 60 percent of its capital.

Brian Balogh, in A Government Out of Sight: The Mystery of National Authority in Nineteenth-Century America, (2009), notes that.

"The government borrowed $1 million from the First Bank to fund the Whiskey Rebellion expedition, in 1794."

In this case, Hamilton, in his dual government capacity as Treasurer, and also as an officer in the U. S. military, borrowed money from Hamilton's Bank, to fund the deployment of 13,000 Federal soldiers to march, under Hamilton's command, to end the farmer's protest against one of Hamilton's excise taxes on whiskey.

The farmer's were not living up to their side of Madison's agreement that the natural aristocracy made the rules, which the farmers were then obligated to follow.

The farmer's were obligated, under Madison's rules, to pay their excise taxes in gold and silver, but the farmers did not have gold and silver to pay taxes because the financial system created by Hamilton was based upon debt and credit, not cash.

Farmers in western Pennsylvania had begun holding protest meetings to discuss their opposition to the tax as early as 1792. A mass meeting in Pittsburgh declared that the people would prevent the tax from being collected and one tax collector was even tarred and feathered in protest.

At that time, tax collectors were paid a bounty, or commission, for collecting government revenue. The third-party tax collectors had a financial incentive to extract as much tax from a citizen as possible, because that was how the tax contractor was paid.

The position of tax collector was lucrative, and the person who made the appointment to collect taxes was the Secretary of the Treasury, Mr. Hamilton.

Hamilton had long supported military mobilization to suppress the tax resistance in Pennsylvania, and after Washington declared such meetings unlawful, Hamilton successfully convinced Washington to authorize troop movements to Pittsburgh.

When Hamilton arrived in the Pittsburgh area, the farmer's had dispersed and the federal force had to search hard to arrest twenty men that they prosecuted for their involvement in the Whiskey Rebellion.

This episode, in 1794, evokes memories of a more recent protest, on January 6, 2021, when Federal officers had to search hard to find protestors to prosecute, who had trespassed in the U. S. Capitol.

The reason the farmers did not have currency to pay their debts or taxes, was that Madison's constitution had outlawed states from issuing paper currency.

In 1789, the Constitution prevented the individual states from issuing paper money and Hamilton's Treasury was reluctant to issue paper money due to past experience with fraud and corruption at the state level.

One part of Madison's intent in both the contract clause and the prohibition of state paper currency was that farmers had been paying their debts to the natural aristocracy in state-issued paper currency.

As a further injustice to the natural aristocracy, the state legislatures were very tolerant and lenient to farmers on debt relief, which meant that the natural aristocracy may not ever be paid their debts owed them by farmers.

In Government by Dissent, Robert Martin, (2013) notes,

"In 1791, the Pennsylvania legislature granted speculators their 6th consecutive extension for failing to pay their taxes."

After the Revolutionary War ended, the United States lacked a sufficient quantity of precious metals for minting coins. Thus, Hamilton's 1793 Mint Act, permitted Spanish dollars and other foreign coins to be part of the American monetary system.

Foreign coins were not banned as legal tender until 1857.

Currency was so scarce outside of New York and Boston, that farmers were not able to obtain payment for their goods in the Fall. Many farmers who lacked currency bartered, and traded with merchants or other farmers, and the preferred article of barter was whiskey.

Hamilton's legal charter to form the First Bank included a provision that only the notes on loans issued by the Bank were accepted as legal tender when paying federal taxes, which the First Bank was in charge of collecting.

To review how Madison's rules and Hamilton's economic system worked in tandem to benefit the wealthy families, first Madison eliminated the ability of state banks to issue currency.

Second, Madison adopted a contract clause that made evasion of paying debts in gold or silver illegal. Debts and taxes had to be paid in gold and silver.

Third, Hamilton restricted the issuance of gold and silver coins, and established that only notes issued by his bank were deemed legal tender for paying taxes.

The farmers were left without either gold or paper currency to pay their debts.

According to Michael Klarman, in The Framers Coup, (2016), after the Whiskey Rebellion, in 1794,

"when government cracked down on enforcement of paying taxes in specie, tens of thousands of farmers lost their farms…70% of farmers on some Pennsylvania counties saw their property foreclosed upon…As much as 10% of the population in one Pennsylvania region were in debtors prison."

As a historical note, this same technique of obtaining the land of the farmers worked well, 70 years later, after the Civil War, in the new Slavecracy, in the "debt-lien system" when farmers could not "pay out" at the end of harvest season.

In that later time, there was inadequate currency to pay farmers cash for their crops, in the Fall, or for farmers to pay their loans to the merchant-banker-lawyer Slavecracy in the South.

As was the case in 1794, when the farmers in the 1870s did not pay in gold or silver, they lost their farms to the Sothern merchants and Northern bankers who provided the debt-lien credit. (The Mind of the South, W. J. Cash).

Hamilton's economy was founded on credit and debt. His First Bank controlled the money supply by leveraging its large transaction volume in notes and reserve balances to expand or constrain the money supply.

To rein in credit, the bank promptly presented the First Bank's banknotes to the state banks that had bought them, for redemption in specie, reducing the lending capacity of the entire banking system.

This ability to constrain credit and currency caused massive commodity price deflation for the price for farmer's crops, in the Fall.

To ease credit, the bank lent more to businesses and state banks and treated state banknotes with "forbearance."

The so-called "easing of credit" was the First Bank's response to loans issued to wealthy elites when their prior speculative investments went bust.

In the modern day language, after the Crash of 2008, this "easing of credit" is called government bailouts or "quantitative easing."

In his initial arguments in favor of creating the First Bank, Hamilton argued the doctrine of implied power of the Constitution for the U. S. Government to do any act that was implied under the powers of the Constitution.

Hamilton wrote to Washington, in 1791,

"Every power vested in Government is in its nature sovereign and includes by force of the term a right to employ all means requisite and fairly applicable to the attainment of such power."

Jefferson argued that there was no text in the Constitution that authorized the government to create a bank.

When the constitutionality of the Bank finally reached the Supreme Court, in McCullough, Marshall had previously ruled, in Marbury,

"the framers of the constitution contemplated that the document would establish the rules for the authority of the courts, as well as of the legislature."

In Marbury v. Madison (1803) the Supreme Court announced for the first time the principle that a court, (any Federal court), may declare an act of Congress, or an act of the President, void if the action is inconsistent with the judge's interpretation of the Constitution.

Marshall's ruling contained three parts:

First, Marshall ruled that the judicial power extends to cases "arising under the Constitution."

Second, Marshall ruled that the Supremacy Clause makes the Constitution the "supreme Law of the Land."

Third, Marshall ruled that only federal laws passed by the Legislature, and enforced by the Executive that had been "made in Pursuance" of the Constitution become part of that "supreme Law."

William Van Alstyne, in "A Critical Guide to Marbury v Madison," (1969), suggests that Marshall's 3 part decision in Marbury was something of a judicial coup d'etat that allowed the judiciary to seize a policy making and political role for itself.

Marshall's doctrine of judicial review, directly contradicted what Hamilton had written in Federalist #78:

"the duty and power of judicial review does not mean the judiciary is supreme over the Constitution… the federal courts were designed to be an intermediate body between the people and their legislature in order to ensure that the people's representatives acted only within the authority given to Congress under the Constitution."

Justice Marshall, in his ruling on McCullough vs. Maryland (1819), re-stated Hamilton's words about implied powers, almost verbatim,

"Let the end be legitimate, let it be within the scope of the constitution, and all means which are appropriate are constitutional."

The two rulings, taken together, meant that the all-powerful central government could do anything it wanted. Lincoln used a version of implied powers to justify the Civil War, in order to hold the union together.

Hamilton knew exactly what the role of corruption would be in maintaining elite control over economic policy. Corruption, also known as shared plunder, was the glue that held the economic system together.

Hamilton stated, in his 1792 dinner with Jefferson that,

"Purge the Government of its corruption and give to its popular branch equality of representation and it would become an impracticable government."

The nation's banking system collapsed in 1813, as a result of the First Bank's corruption in speculative investments, and the mal-appropriation of Indian lands in Michigan and Ohio.

Both Madison and President Washington had speculated in the appropriation of Indian lands.

Merrill Jenson points out that during the convention, in 1787, George Mason explained that Maryland Governor Johnston had also entered into land speculation deals on Indian lands, with Lord Dunmore. (The Articles of Confederation, Merrill Jensen, University of Wisconsin Press, Madison, 1970.)

The motive behind Hamilton's promotion of corruption in the financial system was to preserve the benefits of the land transactions by members of the natural aristocracy, which caused the economy to collapse on a periodic basis.

The banking system, and the economy, collapsed again in 1819, as a result of the Second Bank's securities becoming worthless.

As a result of the collapse in 1819, the first wave of ex-appropriation of farm land by the bankers occurred, as farm prices collapsed, and farmers could not pay their debts.

The Tariff of 1824, designed to protect northern financial interests, caused the wholesale price of cotton in the South to drop from 18 cents to 9 cents.

The Tariff of 1824 marked the first phase of the irreconcilable financial split between northern and southern elites, which culminated in the Civil War.

The U. S. banking system collapsed again, in 1836. As a consequence of this collapse, President Jackson was able to muster enough political support to kill the Second Bank.

President Jackson stated, in 1832, that Hamilton's Second Bank,

"makes the rich richer, and prostituted the government to the advancement of the few at the expense of the many."

As written by Sean Wilenz, in The Rise of American Democracy: Jefferson to Lincoln (2005),

"under the set of constitutional rules promoted by Hamilton, the idea that the private banking and business community should have special powers in deciding economic policy was adopted. Without those special powers, according to Hamilton, the wealthy citizens would not have allegiance to the new nation, and without their allegiance, his concept of the free market [crony capitalist] system would not function well."

After McCullough, there was no political force that constrained the power of Leviathan, as long as the Ruling Class was successful in the claim that their unelected power was sanctioned by the implied powers of the Constitution.

The ruling on implied powers served as the legal basis for Lincoln's argument about preserving the Union, for the first two years of the Civil War.

The economic system created by Hamilton served as one of the concepts of the American dream of "rags-to-riches get rich quick."

Madison's constitutional rules did not prohibit common citizens from aiming for this concept of the get-rich-quick American dream. The gold rush, the land speculation in the migration to the West, and the speculation and fraud in railroad building, rampant before the Civil War, were evidence of the attraction of common citizens to this dream.

The major difference between aiming for this dream between the ruling class and the common citizens was the ability of government and banks to bail out the wealthy when their get-rich-schemes went bust.

When the entrepreneurial ventures of common citizens went bust, there was no one there to bail them out.

As Scott Sandidge, in Born Losers: A History of Failure In America, (2005) observed:

"The vicissitudes of capitalism were such that honest dealings and hard work could earn failure… An entrepreneur was faced with inadequate state and federal laws, vengeful creditors, and forced idleness in debtor's prison…Throughout American history the loser bears material witness to the American dream gone wrong."

Throughout American economic history, after each episode of speculative inflation and economic collapse, the Ruling Class re-asserts its control and re-establishes the economic Plantation, in order to begin, again, the cycle of money creation and credit extension.

Get-rich-quick, and shared plunder, were not the only concept of the American Dream. Jefferson's dream of equal rights under the rule of law offered a more fair vision of an American entrepreneurial capitalist society.

Jefferson's version of the American Dream was not codified in constitutional rules. Madison's version of the Dream was.

Chapter 4. George Mason's Anti-Federalist Arguments Against Ratification.

In the aftermath of Lexington and Concord, in April of 1775, America's authentic patriot founders began meeting to discuss what form of government would replace the British monarchy.

We argue that those early discussions were the beginning of the shared cultural value of American liberty, held by all patriots. The term used by Patriots to describe that common value was the "Spirit of '76."

In addition to the discussions about the form of government, the patriots shared a common experience of fighting a war with Great Britain.

The war with King George forged a national identity among the patriots, similar to the shared consciousness of the soldiers who fought in the Civil War, and later, in both World Wars, and the War in Viet Nam.

The soldiers who returned home after those wars shared a collective consciousness about what it meant to be an American.

John Locke had written that shared cultural values, and shared common social experiences, were the necessary precursor conditions for forming a new government, when the citizens left the state of nature.

John Locke had written in his Second Treatise of Government:

"Men all being naturally free, equal, and independent, no one can be deprived of this freedom etc. and subjected to the political power of someone else, without his own consent. The only way anyone can strip off his natural liberty and clothe himself in the bonds of civil society is for him to agree with other men to unite into a community, so as to live together comfortably, safely, and peaceably, in a secure enjoyment of their properties and a greater security against outsider."

Locke's philosophy on government is called the "social contract," which is enacted when citizens leave the state of nature and agree to form a new government.

In Locke's philosophy, individuals entered into a contract with other people to ensure that freedom was equally held by all citizens. The contract was codified in the form of a written constitution, that all parties to the contract agreed to obey.

The emphasis on individual freedom, in Locke and Jefferson, is in direct contrast to Madison's and Hamilton's emphasis on the collectivism of social class conflict between the common citizens and the natural aristocracy.

George Mason, and the other anti-federalists, relied upon this new shared national identity of individual liberty, when they argued against ratification of Madison's document.

The mistake in judgment of George Mason was that he falsely assumed that the Federalists also shared this cultural value of individual freedom.

There was not, in 1787, any commonly-shared cultural values between George Mason and James Madison, similar in concept to today, when there are no shared cultural values held between Democrat Marxists and natural rights conservatives.

Jefferson's concept of equal liberty leads to one version of the American Dream of equal economic opportunity. The shared cultural values of economic and political equality are essential for the operation of a democratic republic because the values establish the condition for voluntary allegiance to obey the rule of law.

Brian Balogh, in A Government Out of Sight: The Mystery of National Authority in Nineteenth-Century America, (Cambridge University Press, 2009.) explained the contrast between Jefferson's Dream and Madison's Dream,

"Jefferson forged a historical interpretation that pitted the interests of the people, expressed through the ballot box – against the will of a small elite. Jefferson's "empire of liberty" thus knit Americans together across a vast expanse by bonds of affection reinforced by material interest."

In the Jefferson American Dream, Balogh writes,

"Jefferson envisioned a republic populated by independent farmers tied to their country and wedded to its liberty and interests by the most lasting bands... a nation of one heart and one mind. The proponents of the Dream argued that enterprising citizens could create value, value that the larger community would ultimatey share. Wealth...produced more wealth in the form of capital."

Balogh's statement about wealth creating more wealth echoes Adam Smith, in The Wealth of Nations, whereas Madison's version of the Dream was based upon the application of the "real bills" doctrine, that stated that the speculative investments of the ruling class would always lead to real wealth.

Madison and Hamilton's American Dream lead to a cultural value of shared plunder of common social assets by the natural aristocracy. The distribution of income and wealth is not distributed widely through the income and employment multipliers of a free competitive market.

In Madison, obedience to the rule of law is enforced by Leviathan, which is currently in the hands of Democrat Marxists.

As written by Gordon Wood, in The Radicalism of the American Revolution (1992.),

"To be an American could not be a matter of blood; it had to be a matter of common belief and behavior. And the source of that common belief and behavior was the American Revolution: it was the revolution and only the Revolution that made them one people."

The point Wood is making is that the first American Revolution forged a common set of national cultural and social values that bound all citizens together into a shared national mission of liberty.

C. Bradley Thompson, in his book, America's Revolutionary Mind, (2019), describes the constellation of common beliefs held by anti-federalists, as the "American Moral Philosophy," and cites Locke's admonition that citizens who adhere to the American civic virtue do not undermine the liberty of other citizens.

Thompson wrote,

"Locke's fundamental law of nature (i.e., to follow right reason) issues two commands: first, each and, every man should pursue his rational, long-term self-interest; and, second, "No one ought to harm another in his life, health, liberty, or possessions."

Prior to 1775, the colonists had been describing their relationship with King George in terms of subjugation and slavery. That earlier period served as the precursor to the Spirit of '76.

The earlier period of oppression, under King George, gave way to the ideology of individual liberty, when the patriots formed their new government.

The moral justification of the first American Revolution was the belief that the British authorities intended to enslave the colonists.

As early as 1765, John Adams raised the alarm in his 'Dissertation on the Feudal Law," in response to the Stamp Art.

Adams wrote,

"Nothing less than this [slavery] seems to have been meditated for us, by somebody in Great Britain. There seems to be direct and formal design on foot, to enslave all America."

In 1767, in response to the Townshend Acts, John Dickinson, of Pennsylvania, raised the same issue of the subjugation of the American patriots by the King's Privy Council, in his Letters from a Farmer in Pennsylvania.

He wrote,

"Some person may think this [tax] act of no consequence, because the duties are so small. A fatal error. That is the very circumstance most alarming to me. For I am convinced, that the authors of this law would never have obtained an act to raise so trifling a sum.... In short, if they have a right to levy a tax of one penny upon us, then they have a right to levy a million upon us."

Jefferson wrote in 1774,

"Single acts of tyranny may be ascribed to the accidental opinion of a day, but a series of oppressions begun at a distinguished period, and pursued, unalterably through every change of ministers, too plainly prove a deliberate and systematical plan of reducing us to slavery."

Patrick Henry wrote,

"There is no retreat but in submission and slavery! Our chains are forged! Their clanking may be heard on the plains of Boston! The war is inevitable — and let it come! I repeat it, sir, let it come... Is life so dear, or peace so sweet, as to be purchased at the price of chains and slavery? Forbid it, Almighty God! I know not what course others may take; but as for me, give me liberty or give me death!"

This common view of the justification for the Revolution shaped Mason's arguments against ratification 12 years later.

Mason emphasized that the fundamental purpose of government was to protect individual liberty. His arguments against ratification echoed Locke and Jefferson that the new nation had been formed by individual citizens who were equally free to conduct one's life as one best sees fit, free from the interference of others.

In 1775, the patriots, meeting as the First Continental Congress, asked Thomas Jefferson to draft the document that expressed the patriot's logic for "taking up arms," against the King.

On July 6, 1775, the Continental Congress approved Jefferson's draft of the Declaration of the Causes and Necessity of Taking up Arms. That 1775 document is the first founding document of America.

The Declaration of 1775 states that the reason for taking up arms against the King, was,

"[The King] altered fundamentally the form of Government established by Charter, and secured by acts of its own Legislature, solemnly confirmed by the Crown; for exempting the "murderers" of Colonists from legal trial, and, in effect, from punishment; for erecting a despotism dangerous to our very existence…

We fight not for glory or for conquest. We exhibit to mankind the remarkable spectacle of a people attacked by unprovoked enemies, without any imputation or even suspicion of offence. They boast of their privileges and civilization, and yet proffer no milder conditions than servitude or death."

As he would write a year later, in the 1776 Declaration, Jefferson outlined a series of abuses perpetrated by the King against the colonists.

Jefferson wrote,

"Our forefathers, inhabitants of the Island of Great Britain, left their [state of nature] native land, to seek on these shores a residence for civil and religious freedom...Government was instituted to promote the welfare of mankind, and ought to be administered for the attainment of that end...We are reduced to the alternative of choosing an unconditional submission to the tyranny of irritated Ministers, or resistance by force. The latter is our choice. We have counted the cost of this contest, and find nothing so dreadful as voluntary slavery...Honor, justice, and humanity, forbid us, tamely to surrender that freedom which we received from our gallant ancestors, and which our innocent posterity have a right to receive from us."

The Patriots objected to the two-track justice system that allowed agents of the Crown to murder Patriots, without consequence.

Back then, the King had said that all the Patriots were traitors and insurrectionists.

The King stated,

"All of them, [deplorables] either by name or description, are rebels and traitors."

According to Jefferson,

"[The Patriots were instructed to] deposit their arms with their own Magistrates, The Patriots accordingly delivered up their arms; but [the King] in open violation of honor, in defiance of the obligation of treaties, which even savage nations esteemed sacred, the British Governor ordered the guns turned over to the King."

Jefferson wrote the Declaration, of 1776, as a social contact between citizens in each state to establish a rightful centralized political power, dedicated to protecting the natural rights of citizens that are left incompletely protected within each state government.

The Declaration of 1776 is America's second founding document.

Jefferson wrote,

"No one is born into moral subjugation to political power."

In the concept of the natural rights republic, Jefferson (1782), thought it was ridiculous to suppose that a man should surrender himself to the state.

"This would be slavery....Freedom would be destroyed by the establishment of the opinion that the state has a perpetual right to the services of all its members."

Jefferson explained the essence of equal rights as the voluntary allegiance of citizens to obey the rule of law. He stated,

"We come to respect those rights in others that we value in ourselves."

Jefferson relied on Locke to express his phrase "deriving their just powers from the consent of the governed."

In other words, "consent of the governed" appears in the Declaration as expressing mutual obligations and duties to both parties to the contract.

Jefferson's use of the term "consent" is connected to citizen sovereignty, natural rights, equality, and self-government, all of which are based upon the social obligation of the parties to the constitutional contract to reciprocate in obeying the rule of law.

Jefferson's main principle of consent is that those bound most tightly by collective rules must be given the greatest say in the making and enforcing of the rules.

Self-government, according to Jefferson, meant allowing citizens a sphere of sovereignty that could not be disrupted by the central government (that which governs the best, governs the least).

As we argued in Chapter 2, the main unsolvable conflict in America today revolves around the fact that Madison shifted King George's grant of sovereignty from individual citizens to the sovereignty of the all-powerful central government, which is not bound by the consent of the governed.

John Adams explained in his resolution of May 10, 1776, this shift in the location of sovereignty. Adams wrote,

"All governments deriving their power from king are replaced by government deriving their power from the people."

Adams correctly perceived that the colonies could either become one consolidated sovereign state, as it did under Madison's document, or it could become a nation of confederated sovereign states, as it did under The Articles of Confederation.

The way that Jefferson used the concept of citizen sovereignty implies a certain type of social reciprocity based upon the citizen's duty to reciprocate equality with other citizens.

Jefferson emphasized this reciprocity in his writings about the civil foundations of the new nation:

"What is here a right towards men is a duty towards the Creator. It is the duty of every man to render to the Creator such homage and such only as he believes to be acceptable to him. This duty is precedent, both in order of time and in degree of obligation, to the claims of Civil Society."

To summarize, Jefferson's natural rights principles were:

- Equality among citizens to participate in government.
- Privacy of citizens from the invasions of agents of government.
- The right to vote in free and fair elections.
- The protection of the natural and property rights of individuals as the supreme goal of government.
- Equal access to the courts and equality before the law.

Mason, in 1787, re-stated Jefferson's argument that Madison and Hamilton had fundamentally altered the form of government established by the Articles of Confederation.

At the end of the Constitutional Convention in Philadelphia, Mason stated,

"This government will commence in a moderate aristocracy. It is at present impossible to foresee whether it will, in its operation, produce a monarchy or a corrupt, oppressive aristocracy, it will most probably vary for some years between the two, and then terminate in the one or the other."

We argue that Madison's form of government ended on November 3, 2020, as a corrupt, oppressive Marxist tyranny, that functions without citizen consent.

Mason falsely assumed, as did Jefferson before him, that all Americans understood this concept of on-going citizen consent.

As a consequence of this false assumption, Mason and the other anti-federalists never convened their own convention, and never offered a written alternative to Madison's document of elite rule, because they continued to believe that the Articles were the only legitimate constitution, formed by the ratification of the 13 independent states.

As noted by Saul Cornell, in The Other Founders, (1999.),

"The anti-federalists never convened their own constitutional convention and never proposed concrete alternatives to the constitution."

The Articles were not on the ballot, to be voted for, or against, by the citizens. The only document on the ballot for ratification was Madison's document.

The only state to allow citizens to vote on ratification, as opposed to ratification by conventions, was Rhode Island. The results of the vote, held on March 24, 1788, was: Vote: 237 for ratification, Vote 2708 against ratification.

In other words, Madison's constitution garnered less than 1% of the vote, a legitimate reflection of the common citizen's opinions in all the other states.

Consent, for Mason, was not a one-time event, where citizens gave their consent to be ruled by the plutocracy, in the fraudulent ratification process, and thereafter, gave up the right of on-going consent.

For Jefferson, on-going consent meant a frequent recurring vote in public elections, upholding the constitution and basic principles of natural rights, (rule of law), and the ultimate, sovereign authority of citizens to influence public policy, once the new government began operation.

The major defect in Madison's arrangement was correctly identified by Centinel, who noted that Madison's constitution was silent on how the on-going "consent of the citizens" is translated into "self-government."

In other words, as Centinel asked about Madison's arrangement,

"If the people are sovereign how does the opinion of citizens direct the policies of government?"

This same flaw of how consent of the governed afflicts the Marxist Democrat version of tyranny. Like Madison's rules, that ended in a corrupt centralized tyranny of rule by the few, the Marxist version of government is rule by the few self-appointed elites.

The anti-federalists thought that the Articles of Confederation accurately conveyed the moral and cultural values of what it meant to be an American.

They had initially assumed that the Convention in Philadelphia was intended to fix the defects in the Articles, not to fundamentally alter the form of a democratic republic government established by the Articles of Confederation.

We argue that The Articles of Confederation are America's third founding document.

Merrill Jensen, in The Articles of Confederation, (1970), noted the linkage between Jefferson's Declaration and the Articles of Confederation.

He wrote,

"The Articles were declared to be the constitutional expression of the philosophy of the Declaration, which limited the central government to the sole power of determining war and peace, rule for capture, of settling disputes between two or more states concerning boundaries, jurisdictions, coining of money and regulating its value, managing affairs with Indians, of fixing the boundaries of new colonies, on the principles of liberty, appointing a Council of State of seven members."

Jensen noted that the final draft adopted August 20, 1776, omitted the article of congressional control of boundaries, charter claims and unallocated lands.

The significance of this omission in the Articles was the subsequent adoption of the Northwest Ordinance, that provided a path toward statehood for the territories, and more significantly prohibited slavery in the future states.

We argue that the Northwest Ordinance is America's fourth founding document, and gives lie to the Black Democrat Marxists allegation that America was founded upon the sin of slavery.

America was founded on the constitutional framework of the Articles of Confederation, which prohibited slavery in the new states. Madison's document, on the other hand, sanctioned slavery in the existing 13 states.

The Articles replaced the insipient slavery of the British monarchy with a decentralized state-sovereignty natural rights republic, under the authority of the Articles of Confederation.

In translating Jefferson's moral values into the Articles, Thomas Burke, of Hillsborough, North Carolina, and the author of the Articles, aimed at resolving six issues.

Burke proposed:

- that all sovereign power was in the states separately.

- that the federal government held "expressly" enumerated powers...that each state retains its sovereignty, freedom and independence.

- that any right which is not by this confederation "expressly" delegated to the United States in Congress assembled is retained by the states.

- Congress is to be made up of two bodies of delegates, the General Council, and Council of State, with one delegate from each state.

- All bills originate in the General Council, and are read 3 times and passed by a majority in the Council of State.

- Every law must be demonstrated to be within the powers "expressly delegated to Congress."

Thomas Paine wrote, in Common Sense, (1776),

"let us hold out the hearty hand of friendship...an open and resolute friend, and a virtuous supporter of rights of mankind and of free and independent states of America, in a non-coercive constitution, with the coercive police powers of the state."

The phrase "mutual friendship" was lifted directly from Paine, and placed, by Thomas Burke, in the Preamble of the Articles, as the basis of the new government.

Burke's intent in his Articles, was,

"to secure and perpetuate mutual friendship and intercourse among the people of the different States in this union."

The Articles declared the purpose of the confederation,

"States hereby severally to enter into a firm league of friendship with each other, for their common defense, the security of their liberties, and their mutual and general welfare, binding themselves to assist each other, against all force offered to, or attacks made upon them, or any of them, on account of religion, sovereignty, trade, or any other pretense whatever."

The Articles placed the new constitution within the context of the philosophy of the Declaration so that the words of the text could be interpreted from the historical context of a strict constructionist perspective.

The words of the Articles meant, as the writers of the Articles used them, as they existed in 1776, as connected in time to the text of the Declaration.

Madison carefully avoided any reference to either Jefferson's Declaration, the prior Articles of Confederation, or any mention of the word "slavery," in his constitution, because he intended to usurp the legality of the prior constitution with his version of a ruling class plutocracy, that preserved slavery.

Thomas Paine explained that when Madison and Hamilton said in their Federalist Papers, that the central government needed more energy, "what they want is energy over the citizens."

"A more perfect union," said Paine, about Madison's flawed Preamble, "meant a nominal nothing without principles."

Paine stated,

"The US Constitution of 1787 is an ill-advised attempt to replicate the British form of mixed constitution...their basis for justice becomes the balancing of particular class interests....they make it difficult for citizens to participate"

The natural rights patriots, aka anti-federalists, objected to five parts of Madison's rules of procedure:

- the Necessary and Proper Clause,
- the Interstate Commerce Clause
- the lack of term limits for Congress,
- the lack of democratic accountability for the Federal judiciary,
- the convoluted rules for amending the constitution,

Mason falsely assumed that Madison also interpreted the meaning of the Articles, as written by Burke, to be a perpetual union of states.

In The Antifederalists: Men of Great Faith and Forbearance, David J. Siemers, summarizes Mason's arguments against ratification.

Siemers noted that Mason said,

"In the [Articles] confederacy, congress represented the states…In the new plan the people will be represented, they ought therefore to choose their representatives."

Siemers noted that on September 15, 1787, the last day of debate at the convention, Mason stated,

"The plan of amendments is exceptionable and dangerous. As the proposing of amendments in both modes to depend in the first immediately and in the second ultimately on Congress, no amendments of the proper kind would ever be obtained by the people, if the Government should become oppressive, as he verily believed would be the case."

Mason wrote,

"Inherent rights" to which all men are born include the enjoyment of life and liberty, with the means of acquiring and possessing property, and pursuing and obtaining happiness and safety."

Mason correctly perceived that Madison' rules on separation of power really were not a separation of power because it elevated the Federal judges above the Executive and Legislative branches.

Mason repeatedly warned the other delegates that Madison's rules would lead to centralized elite tyranny.

As described from Madison's notes:

Mr. RANDOLPH. We have in some revolutions of this plan made a bold stroke for Monarchy. We are now doing the same for an aristocracy. He dwelt on the tendency of such an influence in the Senate over the election of the President in addition to its other powers, to convert that body into a real & dangerous Aristocracy.

Col: MASON. As the mode of appointment is now regulated, he could not forbear expressing his opinion that it is utterly inadmissible. He would prefer the Government of Prussia to one which will put all power into the hands of seven or eight men, and fix an Aristocracy worse than absolute monarchy. The words "and of their giving their votes" being inserted on motion for that purpose, after the words "The Legislature may determine the time of chusing and assembling the electors."

September 6. Mr. WILSON. said that he had weighed carefully the report of the Committee for remodelling the constitution of the Executive; and on combining it with other parts of the plan, he was obliged to consider the whole as having a dangerous tendency to aristocracy; as throwing a dangerous power into the hands of the Senate. They will have in fact, the appointment of the President, and through his dependence on them, the virtual appointment to offices; among others the offices of the Judiciary Department. They are to make Treaties; and they are to try all impeachments. In allowing them thus to make the Executive & Judiciary appointments, to be the Court of impeachments, and to make Treaties which are to be laws of the land, the Legislative, Executive & Judiciary powers are all blended in one branch of the Government.

September 7. Col: MASON said that in rejecting a Council to the President we were about to try an experiment on which the most despotic Governments had never ventured. The Grand Signor himself had his Divan. He moved to postpone the consideration of the clause in order to take up the following:

"That it be an instruction to the Committee of the States to prepare a clause or clauses for establishing an Executive Council, as a Council of State, for the President of the U. States, to consist of six members, two of which from the Eastern, two from the middle, and two from the Southern States, with a Rotation and duration of office similar to those of the Senate; such Council to be appointed by the Legislature or by the Senate."

September 8. A Committee was then appointed by Ballot to revise the stile of and arrange the articles which had been agreed to by the House. The committee consisted of Mr. Johnson, Mr. Hamilton, Mr. Govr. Morris, Mr. Madison and Mr. King.

September 15. Col: MASON. 2ded. & followed Mr. Randolph in animadversions on the dangerous power and structure of the Government, concluding that it would end either in monarchy, or a tyrannical aristocracy; which, he was in doubt, but one or other, he was sure. This Constitution had been formed without the knowledge or idea of the people. A second Convention will know more of the sense of the people, and be able to provide a system more consonant to it. It was improper to say to the people, take this or nothing.

Colonel MASON.

This infernal [slave] traffic originated in the avarice of British merchants. The British Government constantly checked the attempts of Virginia to put a stop to it. The present question concerns not the importing States alone, but the whole Union. The evil of having slaves was experienced during the late war. Had slaves been treated as they might have been by the enemy, they would have proved dangerous instruments in their hands. But their folly dealt by the slaves as it did by the tories. He mentioned the dangerous insurrections of the slaves in Greece and Sicily; and the instructions given by Cromwell to the commissioners sent to Virginia, to arm the servants and slaves, in case other means of obtaining its submission should fail. Maryland and Virginia, he said, had already prohibited the importation of slaves expressly. North Carolina had done the same in substance. All this would be in vain, if South Carolina and Georgia be at liberty to import.

Just prior to the vote to approve Madison's Constitution, on September 15, 1787, Madison inserted the language and sanctions against free states that did not return slaves to their owners.

There was no discussion and no debate about the fugitive slave clause, before the final vote was taken. The other delegates had never seen this text, but had informally agreed to it in private discussions among themselves.

From Madison's notes,

September 15. Took up Article IV, Section 2 (Fugitive Slave clause): Struck out "no person legally held to service or labor in one state escaping into another" and replaced it with "no person held to service or labor in one state, under the laws thereof, escaping into another.

On September 15, 1787, on the day Madison's constitution was published, George Mason stated that the plan was exceptionable and dangerous.

Mason stated,

"As the proposing of amendments (in Article 5), is in both modes to depend in the first immediately and in the second ultimately on Congress, no amendments of the proper kind would ever be obtained by the people, if the Government should become oppressive."

Mason went on to say that Americans had been duly warned about the incipient aristocratic tyranny resulting from the work of the 39 elites who drafted the document, in secret.

Mason described the subterfuge of the Federalist delegates,

"These gentlemen [Federalists] who will be elected senators, will fix themselves in the federalist town, and become citizens of that town more than of your state. This government will commence in a moderate aristocracy. It is at present impossible to foresee whether it will, in its operation, produce a monarchy or a corrupt, oppressive aristocracy, it will most probably vitiate some years between the two, and then terminate in the one or the other.

Mason's language for describing Madison's scheme, on September 15, "take this or nothing," went directly to the heart of Madison's duplicity in creating his constitution.

The entire body of delegates, prior to the appointment of the Committee on Style, on September 8, had not reached agreement on the powers of the Presidency.

The Committee on Style, appointed 3 days before the Convention ended, never released the final clauses of Article II, on the Presidency to the delegates, before they voted on them, on September 17.

Mason stated that,

"Considering the powers of the President & those of the Senate, if a coalition should be established between these two branches, they will be able to subvert the Constitution."

The obvious coalition, today, is a political coalition in the three branches, and the fourth estate of the propaganda news media, that is unified by political ideology of Marxism.

In speaking against Mason's motion in the Bill of Rights, Roger Sherman stated that the reason that a Bill of Rights was not needed, was that,

"the State Declarations of Rights are not repealed by this Constitution and, being in force, are sufficient."

But, of course, it was not the states that created the Constitution, it was "We, the people."

"We, the people," was a national consolidated government that overrode the constitutions of the states, because "We, the people" was the supreme law of the land.

The rights in each state constitution had no significance in the national government.

As Gouverneur Morris stated, on July 23, 1787,

"The Ellsworth amendment erroneously supposes that we are proceeding on the basis of the Confederation. This [Articles] Convention is unknown to the Confederation."

In the Virginia ratification convention, James Monroe cited the differences between the authentic British social class system and the truncated version that Madison created.

Monroe wrote:

"The English constitution is based upon social orders which have a repellent quality which enabled it to preserve itself from being destroyed by the other. The American division of power had no such basis and, indeed, no such intention. There are no real checks in the Constitution that would prevent a coalition of the branches of government and encroachments on the rights of the people."

Mason wrote,

"We are not indeed constituting a British Government, but a more dangerous monarchy, an elective one."

The danger foreseen by Mason proved accurate when the Supreme Court decided Marbury v. Madison that extended the power of the federal judges to rule on both the acts of Congress, and later in times, on the acts of the President.

During the convention in Philadelphia, the Federalists addressed what crimes constituted grounds for impeachment, under Article II. Treason and bribery were obvious choices, but George Mason of Virginia thought those crimes did not include a sufficient definition of punishable offenses against the state.

Mason wanted to insert the term "maladministration."

Madison opposed the term because it was too vague. Mason then substituted "other high Crimes and Misdemeanors" in addition to treason and bribery.

Madison accepted this second suggestion, but the term high crimes and misdemeanors, in the American tradition, has never been defined.

At the conclusion of the Philadelphia convention, Mason predicted that the outcome of Madison's constitution would be an aristocratic tyranny.

As Mason's fellow compatriot, Brutus wrote,

"the judiciary under this system will have a power which is above the legislative, and which indeed transcends any power before given to a judicial by any free government under heaven."

In the The Framers Coup, Michael Klarman, (2016), noted the statement of another anti-federalist,

"The Georgia antifederalist stated that the constitution paves the way for an aristocratical government whereby about 70 nabobs would lord over 3 million citizens as slaves. In "rule by the wealthy."

Melancton Smith, another natural rights delegate to the convention, wrote that,

"The Constitution is radically defective. It vests in Congress "great and uncountroulable powers" that it will use "to annihilate all the state governments, and reduce this country to one single government."

Smith warned that instead of creating a balance of power, Madison's constitution would combine legislative power with judicial power that would eventually destroy the local governments.

He stated that the Supreme Court would interpret the Constitution according to the justices', "spirit and reason, and they would mold the government into any shape they please."

After the Convention ended in Philadelphia George Mason predicted, that Madison's constitutional provisions on federal tariffs would lead to the northern states dominating southern states,

Madison issued a document that falsely refuted Mason about the tariff issue.

Madison's position on tariffs was adopted, and as predicted by Mason, and later confirmed by Clay 40 years later, the tariff provisions led to northern states dominating southern states, the proximate cause of the Civil War.

The next year, in 1788, at the fraudulent ratification convention in Virginia, Madison again argued that the central government "would have only the authority that was explicitly delegated by the states."

Madison lied. He knew when he made this argument in Virginia, that his notes from the Constitutional Convention, in Philadelphia, described an entirely different outcome.

As Madison admitted, in his 1792 essay, A Candid State of Parties,

"...some of the supporters of the Constitution openly or secretly attached to monarchy and aristocracy." As he noted, the Federalists had "debauched themselves into a persuasion that mankind are incapable of governing themselves, and believed that government can only be carried on by the pageantry of rank, the influence of money and emoluments, and the terror of military force."

From the time of ratification of the Articles of Confederation, in 1781, a persistent minority of Federalists argued that state courts must be eliminated. Elimination of the state courts was the intent of the Judiciary Act of 1801.

On the last weekend of March, 1801, the natural rights populists in both Virginia and Pennsylvania called out the state militia, in preparation for a civil war with the Federalists, who were attempting to overthrow Jefferson's election.

Violence was averted at the very last moment, but the debates on the Judiciary Act of 1801, revealed starkly different ideologies between natural rights populists, and the natural aristocracy about the place of the judiciary within a constitutional system of government.

Brutus wrote,

"But the judges under this constitution will controul the legislature, for the supreme court are authorised in the last resort, to determine what is the extent of the powers of the Congress; they are to give the constitution an explanation, and there is no power above them to set aside their judgment... In short, they are independent of the people, of the legislature, and of every power under heaven. Men placed in this situation will generally soon feel themselves independent of heaven itself."

The defect in Madison's constitution originates in the conception of the supreme sovereignty of the central government as a protector of rights. That conception of government is based upon a false premise.

As described by Bernard Bailyn, in The Ideological Origins of the American Revolution, what is the fate of natural rights if Madison's separation of power turns out to be a consolidated central tyranny?

Bailyn asks:

"What if the sense of the constitution (as protector of rights) proved false and it came to be believed that the force of government threatened rather than protected these rights?

Which is exactly where citizens in America find themselves today with the power of the Leviathan in the hands of Marxist Democrats, and the citizens have no way of reclaiming their liberty.

Chapter 5. Madison's Constitutional Plutocracy and Lincoln's Civil War To Save the Plutocracy.

There are currently two competing interpretations of American history, up to, and then, after the Civil War.

One interpretation, which we share, is the interpretation of W. J. Cash, who argues, in the Mind of the South, that after the Civil War, and Reconstruction, the fundamental economic dynamics of the Ruling Class plutocracy, did not change.

In our interpretation, the continuity of history is seen in the regular, observable, continuing series of economic collapse, caused by Ruling Class manipulation of the money supply.

In Cash's interpretation, the Southern slaveocracy reasserted dominance over Southern society, in new forms of slavery. The terms and descriptions of slavery changed, but the oppression and control of the national Ruling Class, initiated by Madison's rules, did not change.

This first interpretation is known as the "historical continuity," thesis. As explained by Gregory P. Downs and Kate Masur, in Notes from The World The Civil War Made,

"The possibility of continuity across the Civil War is not new...From the perspective of southern and African American history, some historians have suggested that war and emancipation did not meaningfully change the larger trajectory of class relations or racial oppression." (in Echoes of War: Rethinking Post-Civil War Government and Politics, UNC Press. 2015.)

The other interpretation of American history is based upon the idea of a fundamental break in the history, that occurred as a result of the outcome of the Civil War, and the subsequent adoption of the 3 Amendments to the Constitution, that, purportedly, ended defacto slavery.

Historians call this second interpretation the "Second Founding," which is interpreted as a national triumph that corrected the original sin of slavery of Madison's immoral constitution.

As William Garrison put it in an 1832 article in his newspaper,

"The Constitution was a compact formed at the sacrifice of the bodies and souls of millions of our race for the sake of achieving a political object, an unblushing and monstrous coalition to do evil that good might come. The compact was not "sacred," but "wicked" and "ignominious." It followed that "such a compact was, in the nature of things and according to the law of God, null and void from the beginning…It was not valid then, it is not valid now."

Scholars of the new founding school suggest that the immoral constitution, cited by Garrison, was replaced by a moral constitution, after the Civil War.

Part of our reliance on Cash is the continued economic importance of cotton as a cash crop, before and after, the Civil War. The U. S. government needed the tax revenues of the cotton trade to pay for the war debt. And, the British Ruling Class needed southern cotton to operate their cotton mills.

Before the Civil War, the plantation elite grew prodigious quantities of cotton, whose exports to England helped Northern elites maintain their financial and economic control over the American economy.

After the Civil War, when, according to Cash, the Slaveocracy "extended the arm" of the land over the entire society, tax revenues from cotton production and export trade, continued to fund the post-war government.

The continued importance of cotton, in other words, provides the one of the basis of our claim of economic continuity between the two historical eras.

During the Constitutional Convention, the imperative of forming the Ruling Class plutocracy overrode the morality of slavery. Slavery, in the South, was an essential component for Northern elite rule in Madison's constitution.

After the Civil War, the northern financial elite needed the Southern plantation elite to continue growing cotton, which is one reason why Sherman's idea of "40 acres and a mule," never got political traction.

The northern elite needed a lot more cotton than 40 acres and a mule could produce. When the northern troops left the South, in the Compromise of 1877, the northern elite permitted the Southern elite to carry on cotton production, just as they had done before the War.

Noah Feldman, in his recent book, The Broken Constitution, is a historian in the "second American Founding" school. Feldman argues that the first constitution was an evil, immoral constitution, which Feldman calls the "compromise constitution."

The second constitution, in Feldman's telling of American history, is the "moral constitution."

Feldman argues against the continuity thesis. He writes,

"Now is the right time to recast the first Constitution as an enterprise that ultimately failed, and to substitute a narrative of a repaired and transformed Constitution for the received narrative of continuity."

The res publica of Madison's representative republic, for Feldman, was simply and exclusively, the creation of "the union." The res publica of the second founding was liberty and equality.

Feldman writes,

"That compromise over slavery was understood by the Constitution's framers and supporters to be necessary in order to achieve the greater goal of union…Without slavery, the Southern slaveholding states would never have agreed to the Constitution. The compromise over slavery was justified to create and preserve the union."

Feldman's use of the term, "to preserve the union," is a euphemism for "to preserve the ruling class aristocracy" that Madison's constitution created.

We use Feldman's argument and logic about "preserving the union," to argue the continuity interpretation of American history.

He states that the compromise over slavery was imperative in order to preserve the union, as if there was no other option, either in 1787, or in 1860.

The obvious "other option," than going to War was offered to Lincoln by General Winfred Scott. According to Feldman, Scott advised Lincoln to just "let them go," which would have also been a better idea in 1787, for Madison, then forcing two alien cultures together in a ruling class plutocracy.

Feldman writes,

"That left Scott with his fourth option to let the South go. The general expressed himself poetically: "Say to the seceded States — wayward sisters, depart in peace!"

The phrase "Go in peace," had also been used by anti-Federalists, in 1787, because letting the slave states go in peace would have allowed Jefferson's version of the American Dream, under the Articles of Confederation, to be realized in the non-slave states, and the Northwest Territories.

But, more importantly, from the perspective of eliminating slavery, the Northwest Ordinance, under the Articles, prohibited slavery in the territories.

If Madison had not been so dogmatic in creating the plutocracy, in 1787, the free states in the new nation would have evolved as the liberty states of America, and avoided the Civil War.

Logically, according to General Scott, the existing government was supposed to let them go, as Jefferson's Declaration urged Britain to let the states become independent.

"Go in peace" would have been a better option, in 1860, than engaging in a Civil War, that killed 750,000 soldiers and 250,000 civilians, up through 1877, that accomplished nothing in altering the terms of elite rule in the compromise constitution.

Feldman spends a great deal of his book trying to explain Lincoln's dictatorial behavior during the War in suspending habeas corpus.

Lincoln had cited Marshall's ruling in McCullough, and also Hamilton's version of implied powers, to argue that the President, under the Constitution, had an implied authority to suspend civil rights, in order to "preserve the union."

Feldman writes,

"The idea was radical because it strongly implied that Lincoln actually had broken the law by suspending habeas. Although Lincoln did not say so, the law he had broken was not just a federal statute but a law contained in the Constitution. By his question, Lincoln was suggesting that he had broken the *Constitution* in order to save it." [emphasis added].

Feldman's treatment of Lincoln's justification for suspending a constitutional right, in order to justify the War, is incorrect.

Lincoln did not argue that he had broken the law in order to save the *Constitution*, rather Lincoln argued that he broke the law to "preserve the union," of the Ruling Class aristocracy.

Eric Foner, agrees with Feldman's interpretation of the Civil War as a second founding.

In his book, The Second Founding: How the Civil War and Reconstruction Remade the Constitution, (W. W. Norton. 2019.), Foner offers a version of the "Let them go," argument.

Foner begins by describing Madison's defect of the "consent of the governed."

"Perhaps the second founding can be seen as a step toward making the Constitution what it might have been if "we the people" had been more fully represented at Philadelphia."

We argue that if the Convention had included common citizens, or, if the ratification conventions had required a popular vote, that Madison's imperative of creating the plutocracy would not have been accomplished.

We further argue, that if the citizens in free states had been offered any other solution than going to War, that the Civil War would have been avoided.

The defect of consent of the governed in Madison's constitution is explained by Feldman,

"The problem [of consent of the governed] was that, except for voting Lincoln out of office in elections that were still two years away, there was no apparent constitutional mechanism for "we the people " to stand up in favor of the Constitution and against either emancipation or the suspension of habeas corpus."

The proponents of the second founding school engage in a type of ritualistic condemnation of Taney's ruling in Dred Scott. For them, Taney's ruling is seen as some monstrous distortion of Jefferson's American promise of liberty.

For example, Feldman writes about the Dred Scott decision this way,

"The first of these [Taney] arguments is the one that remains today so morally offensive and legally indefensible that it continues to stain the court's historical legacy. In order to argue that Scott could not bring a lawsuit in federal court, Taney held that Scott could not be considered a "citizen" under the provision of Article III of the Constitution that gave the federal courts jurisdiction over suits between citizens of different states. To reach that conclusion, Taney held that no one of African descent, whether slave or free, could ever be a citizen of the United States."

Feldman then correctly notes that the Taney decision was a strict constructionist, or originalist, interpretation of the Constitution.

Feldman writes,

"Taney argued that this originalism yielded a Constitution committed to racial inequality."

Prior to the Dred Scott decision, the U. S. Supreme Court had consistently ruled that slaves were property, and could never be citizens.

In 1842, in Prigg v Pennsylvania, Justice Story ruled that,

"The Fugitive slave law was a fundamental article without the adoption of which the Union could not have been formed."

As we noted above, Madison slipped the Fugitive Slave law into the Constitution on the last full day of the Convention, and on September 17, 1787, the last day of the Convention, the other delegates had never seen it, and voted to approve it, without debate.

Feldman describes Lincoln's dilemma of arguing that he possessed legal authority to conduct the War, even in the presence of Taney's ruling.

Feldman writes,

"According to Lincoln, in contrast, loyalty to the Constitution demanded subordinating one's moral instincts to the necessity of compromise. Compromising one's moral principles was the price of union [plutocracy]…But that was not all, Lincoln warned. Once the Supreme Court [Taney] had held that slavery could not be prohibited in the territories, it could go on to hold "that the Constitution of the United States does not permit a state to exclude slavery from its limits." In this scenario, free states would lose their capacity to be free states altogether."

We agree with Lincoln about the implication of Taney's ruling of the extension of slavery into the territories.

In the absence of Madison's constitution, under the Articles of Confederation, if Dred Scott had escaped to a free state, Taney's strict construction of the Articles would have resulted in a ruling that Scott was a free man.

Feldman details Lincoln's mental gymnastics to justify his decision to go to War. Often, Lincoln's logic was contradictory, and varied over the course of the War.

In one case Lincoln argues that citizens have a natural right of revolution.

Feldman writes,

"In Lincoln's account, Texas's claim to territory, and hence the claims of the United States, which had annexed Texas, depended not on a treaty "but on revolution." He explained what he meant: Any people anywhere, being inclined and having the power, have the right to rise up, and shake off the existing government…

In broader terms, Lincoln was articulating a theory of how sovereign political power could be justifiably destroyed, created, and extended. He was embracing a universal human right to revolution. Such a revolution transcended and broke legal and political borders and boundaries."

In another case, Lincoln claims the doctrine of implied powers to justify the war.

Feldman writes,

"If that source of authority did not justify seizure, [of slave property] that left only the more abstract principle of necessity. Necessity, however, was not an established source of constitutional authority."

Feldman gets this part of history wrong. In Marbury, Marshall rules that "necessity, is an implied power of the government.

Feldman writes,

"Lincoln argued that the Constitution should be understood to authorize the president to do whatever he deems *necessary* [added] to preserve the government and enforce the laws…There must be a structural solution to the threat of secession. That structural solution, Lincoln now proposed, was the power of the central government to coerce seceding states to remain in the union. That was why he invoked the "perpetuity of popular government" in his proclamation. Only military force from the federal government could prove that constitutional democracy was a viable form of government."

In a third case of logical contradiction, Lincoln argues that he possesses a type of virtual representation to conduct the War.

Lincoln argued that the Southern states never left the union, and that during the time of their rebellion, they existed under a form of virtual representation, but that the states, which were in rebellion, but had never left the union, would have to be re-admitted to the union, by ratifying the 14th amendment.

Even though the citizens had not voted to allow Lincoln to suspend civil liberties, Lincoln argued, under the premise of virtual representation, that the citizens would probably approve his decisions, at some later time.

Feldman writes,

"Referring to the people's ultimate preferences further suggested that if Lincoln was indeed breaking the Constitution, he was doing so in a way that the people would ultimately vindicate. If that was so, Lincoln was not only breaking the Constitution to preserve it: he was transforming the Constitution into something new. [the second founding]."

Feldman is correct that, after the Emancipation Proclamation, when Lincoln abandoned his "preserve the union argument" to switch to the "abolish slavery argument," the Congress did authorize the legality of Lincoln's virtual representation to suspend civil liberties.

Prior to the Emancipation, Lincoln argued that preservation of the union justified the War.

Feldman quotes Lincoln,

"As for the future of slavery, it was entirely subordinate to saving the union . "My paramount object in this struggle, he wrote, "is to save the Union, and is not either to save or to destroy slavery."

Feldman explains that Lincoln understood that Madison's Constitution was unfair, but that preservation of the union overrode concerns about the unfairness.

Feldman writes,

"Lincoln wanted to be as clear as he could that his objective was to serve the interests of white Americans [the natural aristocracy] by restoring the union, not to liberate African Americans on moral grounds…For Lincoln, there was nothing inherently shocking about saying that the Constitution was both unfair and also settled…The "settled" nature of the compromise was, for Lincoln, the primary reason to maintain it despite its unfairness. "I do not, for that cause namely, [its unfairness], or any other cause, propose to destroy, or alter, or disregard the constitution," According to Lincoln, loyalty to the Constitution demanded subordinating one's moral instincts to the necessity of compromise. Compromising one's moral principles was the price of union."

After the Emancipation Proclamation, Lincoln argued that slavery had to go but the power of the Plutocracy would remain.

As Feldman noted,

"If liberty and equality were true and universal goals for the nation, then slavery would have to go and the [immoral] Constitution would have to be replaced by something different."

Part of our argument about the historical continuity of American history is that those laws to suspend habeas, which Lincoln claimed provided him with virtual representation and implied consent, are still on the books, and are now in the hands of Democrat Marxists.

As we noted above, in the issue of on-going consent of the governed, Lincoln agreed with Thomas Hobbes that when the citizens left the state of nature, and gave their initial consent to form Madison's new government, the consent was a one-time, and irrevocable consent.

Lincoln saw the central government as a sovereign power, which existed independent of the consent of the governed. For Lincoln, preserving the union meant preserving the unchallenged power of Hobbes' Leviathan.

Feldman explains,

"In Hobbes's understanding, the structure of government constitutes the sovereign state. The sovereign state, first of all, exercised its coercive power to make all its citizens obey [the rule of law]. Once their obedience to the state was in place, it could be argued that the citizens "consented" to it, on the grounds that they [the citizens] were much better off under the state's protection than they would have been under anarchy...Lincoln's position required him to insist that the Constitution did not allow the withdrawal of [original] consent by the people of the states, even when they [the Southern states] had withdrawn consent through the same kinds of conventions they had used to consent to the Constitution in the first place."

As we noted above, Madison's constitution is immoral, not simply because it promoted slavery, but because the citizens never consented to ratify Madison's rules, in the same way that the election of November 3, 2020, is immoral because the citizens did not consent to the coup that overturned the election.

We agree with the historical continuity thesis interpretation of Edward Ayers, that the Second Founding-New South thesis was a myth, perpetrated by the progeny of the plantation, after the War ended.

"Southern farmers thought that public policy and private enterprise favored almost everyone in America, other than themselves...farmer's voices seemed to go unheard. Farmers felt abused by both of the major parties and exploited by every level of business. Disenfranchisement had removed the great majority of black voters from the rolls, and a large portion of poor and illiterate white men." (The Promise of the New South: Life After Reconstruction, Edward Ayers. Oxford University Press, 1992.)

Ayers argues that the myth of the New South ended in a bloody race riot in Atlanta, in 1906, that belies the entire Second Founding thesis.

He writes,

"In the year of 1906, a race riot culminated the racial biiterness of the preceeding three decades...The White mobs broke into one black business after another, assaulting and killing black people, male or female, who happened to be inside....Whites felt no more secure after the riot of 1906...The Atlanta riot marked a pause, a symbolic culmination in the history of the New South."

Madison's constitution was not replaced by a constitution that was a "government of the people, by the people, for the people, that must not perish from the earth," because, as Feldman explains, the new constitution would have had to create a government that somehow incorporated the on-going consent of the people.

We agree with the strategy of Stephan Douglas that a better solution to the slavery issue would have been to let the citizens of each new state vote to join the union as either free or slave.

Feldman explains that during the Lincoln-Douglas debates of 1858, that,

"Douglas asked the audience to imagine that Lincoln had been present at the Philadelphia convention. If he had convinced others of his claim that the union could not endure half-slave and half-free, Douglas asserted, there would have been no Constitution formed at all."

Feldman gets wrong his next interpretation of the strategy of popular sovereignty strategy of Douglas.

Feldman writes,

"The truth is that there was nothing historical about Douglas's popular sovereignty theory or Taney's theory that there was a constitutional right to hold slaves in the territories."

The historical basis of Douglas' voting strategy was not in Madison's constitution. It was in the Articles of Confederation.

But, then, Feldman embraces our interpretation of the immorality of Madison's constitution by noting that the citizens had never voted to ratify Madison's constitution.

He writes,

"Douglas was correct about popular sovereignty [in new states] because the people of the states never voted to ratify the compromise constitution."

Douglas was also correct about the immorality of Madison's constitution because it permanently elevated the financial interests of the natural aristocracy over the interests of common citizens.

During the debates, Feldman writes,

"No, Mr. President" Douglass rejoined, it is not the innocent horse that makes the horse thief, not the traveler's purse that makes the highway robber, and it is not the presence of the Negro that causes this foul and unnatural war, but the cruel and brutal cupidity of those who wish to possess horses, money and Negroes by means of theft, robbery, and rebellion."

Feldman explains that after the Emancipation Proclamation, neither the "go in peace" option, or the Douglas 'popular sovereignty" option were viable options for Lincoln.

Feldman writes,

"The only option that emancipation logically allowed was to defeat the Confederacy and impose new norms on Southern society by force, a determined police system." [Leviathan].

As we argue in the next chapter, after the Civil War, Leviathan was an economic disaster for Black people, farmers, Indians, industrial workers, and West Coast Chinese immigrants.

Leviathan was not "a rising economic tide that lifts all boats," rather Leviathan was "mint juleps for the few, and pellagra for the crew." In order for some people to get rich quick, other people would suffer economic loss.

Eric Foner, in another book, Reconstruction: America's Unfinished Revolution,1863 – 1877, (Harper & Row, 1988.), describes what happened to common citizens after the War.

Foner writes,

"For large numbers of northern workers the war was an economic disaster. A flood of paper money [Green Backs] and regressive tax led to a decline in real income… the railroad boom nourished postwar [economic] growth, paid for by an outpouring of speculative credit, which created a financial house of cards..by 1876 over half the nation's railroads had defaulted on their bonds…nearly half the nation's iron furnaces had suspended operation …10000 businesses failed… [the economic depression of 1873] 65 months remains the longest period of uninterrupted economic contraction in American history."

Foner cites the collaboration between northern elites and southern elites in maintaining the culture of shared plunder, both before, and after, the Civil War.

Foner writes,

"A community of interests among eastern merchants, financiers, cotton manufacturers, foreign governments and southern slaveholders. Lords of the Loom,[northern] and Lords of the lash [southern]…Lincoln enriched northeastern capitalists at the expense of farmers and laborers… protective tariffs, high rail freight state and federal aid to private corporations [crony capitalism]."

The economic continuity between Madison's constitutional plutocracy and Lincoln's Civil War, is evidenced by the banking and fiscal policies adopted by Lincoln, in addition to his assertion of tyrannical powers to control the economy.

Lincoln flooded the economy during the War, with Green Backs, and restricted their circulation in Southern States, after the War. The increase of the money supply, in the North, during and after the War is the proximate cause of the depression of 1873.

At the outbreak of the Civil War, the Federal Treasury realized that a new paper money system was needed, because Jackson had killed the Second Bank, which operated on credit and gold and silver, not cash.

New methods for raising the supply of money were established, including the creation of a permanent Federal system of paper currency.

Congress authorized the issuance of regular circulating paper money in 1861 for the first time since the Revolution. Known as "demand notes," these were redeemable in gold and silver, on demand, by their holders. Mostly, their holders were financially wealthy citizens who had the wealth to buy the notes.

In 1862, demand notes were replaced by Legal Tender notes, and, in 1863, by Compound Interest Treasury notes.

In 1863, the National Banking Act was introduced to replace the former Second National Bank, which had been killed by Jackson.

The National Bank's manipulation of the money supply, along with the corruption of the culture of shared plunder, plunged the lives of common citizens into a series of economic depressions, which lasted through the beginning of World War I.

Our argument of the historical continuity between Madison's constitutional plutocracy and Lincoln's Civil War is not simply the historical continuity of elite rule.

The argument is also based upon the enduring legacy of Madison's constitutional ascendancy of the natural aristocracy, in the absence of any on-going consent of the governed.

We agree with the continuity interpretation of V. O. Key, in Southern Politics in State and Nation (Knopf, 1949.). Key noted that the system of economic and political apartheid imposed on the South [after the Civil War] by the Democrats was not simply about "white supremacy."

He said, "the issue of Negro suffrage is a question not of white supremacy but the supremacy of which whites." [the Ruling Class].

The constitutional system of special interests created by Madison enabled this political arrangement and allowed it to function unchallenged because the constitution was silent on the issue of on-going consent.

After the War, what the farmers wanted was equal access to capital to make investments in their farms and to finance the next crop. What they found, according to Stephen Hahn, was a territorial financial monopoly, "which prevented competition in the extension of credit, and a monopoly over the sources of necessary credit in a system increasingly dominated by staple agriculture." This last element of monopoly had a handy title of "no cotton, no credit." (A Nation Under Our Feet: Black Political Struggles in the Rural South from Slavery to the Great Migration, Belknap, 2005.)

Our continuity thesis of the Ruling Class is summarized by Heather Cox Richardson, in The Death of Reconstruction: Race, Labor and Politics in Post-Civil War North, 1865 – 1901. (Harvard University Press, 2001.)

Richardson cites the 1869 comments of Elihu Washburne, a Republican, in the administration of President Grant.

She quotes Washburne,

"The demoralization of the government thanks to the expenditures of vast and unheard of amounts of public money giving out immense contracts by which sudden and vast fortunes were made…the intense desire to get suddenly rich out of the government and without labor…"

"Get rich quick" using crony capitalist connections to government, in conjunction with the unelected power of bankers to manipulate the money supply, continues to be the main operational principle of Madison's constitutional plutocracy, and Lincoln's justification of preserving the union.

Chapter 6. The National Plutocracy of Crony Corruption and the Culture of Plunder During the Gilded Age.

The rise of the Republican Party, before the Civil War, was due to the compelling political slogan "free labor."

The common citizen voter's attraction to the free labor slogan was based upon their allegiance to Jefferson's American Dream of hard work, in an economy of equal rights, where everyone had a free opportunity to obtain financial success.

In The Death of Reconstruction: Race, Labor and Politics in the Post-Civil War North, 1865 – 1901, (Harvard University Press, 2001.) Heather Cox Richardson, explains that in the Jefferson Dream,

"Individual prosperity did not depend on birth, wealth or anything but a willingness to work, the ability to work intelligently, and the virtue of frugality."

Richard White, in his book, The Republic for Which It Stands: The United States During Reconstruction and the Gilded Age, 1865 – 1896, (Oxford University Press, 2017.), explains part of the political attraction of the free labor ideology.

White writes,

"Prosperity formed part of free labor's promise but not its goal...Despite corruption and their own racism, most Republicans sincerely embraced free labor and continued to believe in its transformative capacity and its egalitarian assumptions...Free labor began as an argument for equal rights and homogeneous citizenship, but [later] became an argument for exclusion. Free labor demanded self-ownership and freedom of contract."

Lincoln used the free labor political argument in the debates against Stephen Douglas, who replied with his own version of free labor, for Whites only.

White explains,

"The Republicans [Lincoln] had intended to create a free labor republic of independent producers who shared a homogeneous national citizenship with rights guaranteed by the federal government...

the republic Lincoln imagined at the end of the Civil War had not been realized...Reconstruction had not achieved its larger ambition...Contract freedom quickly revealed itself a delusion when those negotiating contracts were so incommensurate in wealth and power [with the Ruling Class].

In other words, the "free labor" slogan had both a political component, which was successfully used by Republican politicians to win elections, and a mythical component which was a delusion.

Free labor, as an ideology, formed the basis of Jefferson's American Dream of an entrepreneurial capitalist society.

White notes,

"The core idea of individualism that a person's fate should be in her own hands and that freedom gave citizens the opportunity and responsibility to make themselves what they could."

In practice, during the Gilded Age, the ideology of free labor turned out to be something completely different...the Ruling Class could compel poor people to perform labor for free.

White cites the statement, from an article in North American Review, of a poor person in the South, who translated the practical meaning of the myth of free labor.

"What I agree to do in order to escape from starvation or to save my wife and children from starvation, or ignorance of my ability to do anything else, I agree to do under compulsion, [labor contract] just as much as if I agreed to do it with a pistol to my head..."

White describes the practical application of free labor myth in the Gilded Age with this anecdote,

"John Henry was arrested under the Black codes which turned what was a misdemeanor [loitering] into a felony. The judge sentenced him to 10 years...and he was leased to the Chesapeake and Ohio Railroad, [to work for free]."

James M. McPherson, in Ordeal by Fire: The Civil War and Reconstruction, (Alfred Knoph, 1982.), explains the widespread use of the convict leasing system,

"In the convict leasing system …leasing convicts to private contractors [the plutocracy] meant that cheap convict labor that could be worked like slaves."

The myth of preserving the union of free labor became Lincoln's initial justification for the Civil War.

Eric Foner, in The Second Founding: How the Civil War and Reconstruction Remade the Constitution, (W. W. Norton. 2019.), describes how Lincoln used the myth of free labor for the War's justification.

In order to preserve "the union," Lincoln described his idea of what would happen to the slaves, under the delusion of free labor, after the Civil War ended.

Foner writes,

"The free labor vision [of the Republicans] was that slaves would enjoy the same opportunities for advancement as northern workers and [slaves] motivated by the same quest for self-improvement [as Whites]…the South would eventually come to resemble the free society of the North, with public schools, small towns, and independent producers."

After Reconstruction ended in 1877, the Republican Party abandoned the political slogan part of free labor, and withdrew support from the civil rights policies of the reconstruction era.

Beginning with the Compromise of 1877, and the compromised election of Republican President Hayes, the Republican Party switched from a focus on reconstruction in order to embrace a more intensive culture of shared plunder that benefitted the plutocracy.

As Richardson notes, in The Death of Reconstruction, after 1877,

"Hayes stopped using U. S. troops to protect southern freedmen. Instead Hayes turned the military might against workers engaged in America's first national strike [and against Indians]."

Mark Twain called this new era the "Gilded Age."

During the Gilded Age, the old adage that the "rich got richer," is accurate.

The economic factor that changed, after the Compromise of 1877, in the Gilded Age, is that the improvement in Ruling Class welfare came at the expense of the welfare of common citizens.

In economics, this outcome, during the Gilded Age, is called "zero-sum," where the gain in social welfare for the Ruling Class comes at the expense of the social welfare of the common citizens.

The adage changed to the "rich got richer, and the poor got poorer." We describe, below, the welfare of 5 social groups during the Gilded Age, whose welfare declined, while the incomes of the plutocracy rose.

We make the additional allegation that the welfare of the Ruling Class could not have improved without the increased immiseration of the common citizens.

Up to the Civil War, the social welfare dynamics of Madison's plutocracy was characterized as crony capitalist shared plunder, where the rich got richer, without necessarily requiring that common citizens suffered economic loss.

Eric Foner, in Reconstruction: America's Unfinished Revolution, 1863 – 1877, (Harper & Row, 1988.), writes that, prior to the Civil War,

"Planter rule did not interfere with yeoman's self sufficiency."

After the Civil War, the rich got richer because they caused the poor to get poorer by the manipulation of the judicial system, in combination with their unelected power to manipulate the money supply, and their concentrated, unelected power over the banking system.

Our argument about the rich getting richer is based upon a coordinated power, not Madison's separation of power, between economics, politics, and the judiciary that combined to direct the flow of financial benefits to the Ruling Class.

The three systems worked in tandem to deliver the benefits to the wealthy, without on-going consent of the governed.

The banking system, the investment speculation, and the crony capitalist corruption of the Ruling Class caused the welfare of the Ruling Class to improve, while that combination of power caused the welfare of common citizens to decline.

Lawrence Goodwyn, in the: A Short History of the Agrarian Revolt in America, (Oxford University Press, 1978.), explains how the three systems worked in tandem.

He writes,

"The underlying entire structure of commerce was the national banking system, rooted in the gold standard …dominated by the House of Morgan…the currency was so constricted that virtually every year the calls on the eastern money market by Western banks at harvest brought the nation dangerously close to financial panic….the [constriction of currency] had a strong downward pressure upon commodity prices at harvest time…The ultimate monopoly was the money trust, a banking system of private plunder anchored in a metallic currency and assured of political power because it owned both sound money parties [and the banks]."

White, in his book, The Republic for Which It Stands, explains that,

"The Republicans created a national banking system that simultaneously funded the [government's war] debt and created the nation's first standard currency [Greenback]…the government levied a prohibitive tax on state-chartered banknotes…the national banks bought government bonds with greenbacks, and collected interest paid in gold on the bonds and then used the bonds as collateral to issue bank notes, which they then used for loans to collect additional interest. In 1875 the US government bonds formed 63 percent of the investments of New York City national banks."

The institutional capacity of the banks to both manipulate the money supply, and issue debt, placed the banks in the middle of a golden financial triangle. The banks, the plunder of the Ruling Class, and the crony capitalist exploitation of government contracts and patronage were coordinated by the agencies of the government, which operated beyond the consent of the governed.

To paraphrase Madison, the government controlled the people, but the people had no power or authority to control the government.

The banking power was concentrated and centralized in New York. White notes,

"By 1870 New York banks contained nearly a quarter of all American banking resources and the national banks controlled 87% of all the financial assets."

White explains the essential role of gold in the money system. He writes,

"[Republican], at their simplest, thought of the gold standard as self regulating…[real bills]. The Treasury Dept had to monitor trade, the tariff, and the national banks to make sure that it always had enough gold to redeem paper currency…By limiting the supply of money…the gold standard led to deflation which transferred wealth from debtors [farmers and industrial workers]to creditors…wealthy creditors gained premiums beyond interest payments …because the dollars paid to them were always more valuable than the earlier dollars they had lent [inflation]…The gold standard also allowed a much smoother integration of NY and London capital markets." [nascent corporate globalism].

Goodwyn, in the Populist Moment, explains,

"At the heart of the banker's approach was an understanding of gold and silver money not as a medium of exchange, but as a commodity that had "intrinsic" value…the government t had contracted the currency, which had depreciated [farmer commodities] and having purchased government bonds [in fiat paper money] the bankers looked forward to windfall profits to be made from redeeming their [bonds]in gold, valued at prewar levels."

In our explanation of Cash's return to the plantation thesis, the first step in the golden triangle is the banking control over the money supply, which leads to speculation and corruption, which ends in economic collapse.

Goodwyn writes,

"The contraction of the fiat money supply spread the economic pain over a longer period of time…

forcing the price levels down to a point where it was no longer profitable to redeem paper dollars in gold to finance imports…contraction of the money supply was a mass tragedy for the nation's farmers."

Prior to the economic collapse, the plutocracy engages in plunder, which is described as the power to obtain resources and wealth from others in immoral actions, and crony corruption, which means using the agencies of government to obtain wealth.

The economic collapse is caused by prior investment speculation which did not yield real economic growth.

White explains how corruption worked when Jay Gould cornered the gold market, in New York. He writes,

"The gold exchange took place in the Gold Room..If Gould and Fisk cornered the market in gold they could hold the merchants for ransom…The success of the scheme depended on the U. S. Treasury [to stop selling gold]. Gould and Fisk recruited President Grant's brother in law then Grant's private secretary Orville Babcock…and then an assistant treasury secretaty in charge of gold sales….Black Friday ruined thousands who lacked access to a relative of the President."

In another case of Ruling Class corruption, White explains the railroad corruption, called Credit Moblier. He writes,

"Charles Danan of the New York Sun broke the Credit Moblielier scandal in the midst of the presidential campaign of 1872…It was the King of Frauds because it linked the private corruption of the railroads with public corruption…The railroad investment company, [Credit Moblier] had come to Congress offering stocks, bonds and land…"

White estimates that about 50% of the U. S. Congress bought in on the Credit Moblier corruption. The proximate cause of the Panic of 1873, was the corruption of Credit Moblier, and the subsequent collapse of Jay Cooke & Co., America's premier banking house, that facilitated the sale of Credit Moblier bonds to the members of Congress.

Corruption and investment speculation were tied together by the ability of the elite to manipulate the money supply to suit their own interests. After each episode of corruption and speculation, the economy collapsed.

White notes,

"The panic of 1873 began September 18, 1873, and lasted until 1879...25 railroads defaulted in 1873, 71 defaulted in 1874, and 25 in 1875. By 1876, roughly half the railroads had gone into receivership... Railroad stocks lost 69% of their value...Half the iron foundries closed within a year of the crash....there were 5183 bankruptcies in 1873...in 1878 there were 19478 bankruptcies...25% of workers in NYC were unemployed in 1874...The 65 month contraction was the longest in American history."

White links the economic collapse of 1873 to the Silver Crime of 1873, both events of which caused by Ruling Class plunder and crony corruption. The first step in the corruption for the plutocracy was to manipulate the money supply to benefit the Ruling Class.

White explains,

"In January, 1873, Congress voted to demonetize silver...Silver would no longer be a legal standard. [later the Congress changed its mind]The crime of 73...began with the remonetization of silver...gold dollars would disappear from circulation [if silver fell below par with gold....silver was not worth as much and the country was gripped by a depression...the outcry for that materialized emanated from debtors, farmers, laborers and others most vulnerable to the hardship of the depression."

The judicial system played an important part in the creation and maintenance of a consolidated power during the Gilded Era by modifying the purported intent of the three Civil War Amendments from equality for slaves to concentrated economic power for the Ruling Class.

White, in The Republic for Which It Stands, describes,

"Cruickshank, in 1875, and Slaughterhouse 1873, were part of a parade of disastrous decisions that ruled the Reconstruction amendments did not protect freedmen from actions of one citizen against another or from actions by the states."

Eric Foner, in The Second Founding, explains the strange path of the 14th Amendment, from protection of slaves to protection of corporations. He writes,

"Increasingly, The Court construed the 14th Amendment as a vehicle for protecting corporate rights…The Court employed a state-centered approach in citizenship matters and a nation-centered approach in affairs of business."

In The Burden of Southern History, C. Vann Woodward, (LSU Press, 1968.) writes,

"By a series of opinions beginning in 1873, the Supreme Court constricted the 14th Amendment by a narrow interpretation which proclaimed that privileges and immunities [for citizens] that we call civil rights were not placed under federal protection at all…the commitment to equality had never really been made."

As Supreme Court Justice Oliver Wendell Holmes lamented in 1903, after the prior decisions on the 14th Amendment, there was nothing the Courts could do, because precedent in civil rights cases had elevated the rights of corporations over the rights of citizens.

Holmes, in Giles v Harris, 1903, wrote:

"If the great mass of the white population intends to keep blacks from voting there was nothing the justices could do…relief from a great political wrong could only come from the people of a state."

We explain the social welfare dynamics of Madison's plutocracy with the aid of three social welfare diagrams, which describe the "before and after" era of the Gilded Age.

The first diagram is called Pareto Optimality, which describes a social welfare function where the economy expands to a certain theoretical maximum point, where no citizen can be made better off, without decreasing the welfare of any other citizen.

The common way of saying this social welfare function is that a rising tide of economic growth lifts all boats. Economic growth is seen as a social benefit that improves the welfare of rich and poor, alike, at the same time.

Diagram 2. describes this social and economic state of affairs, which is consistent with Jefferson's American Dream of an entrepreneurial capitalist economy, where hard work is rewarded by financial success.

Diagram 2. Pareto Optimality in Jefferson's American Dream.

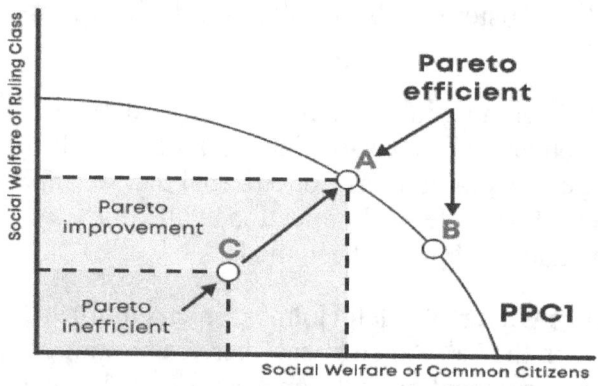

The outward shaped concave curve represents the best possible production outcomes in an economy, given the economy's production resources, at a certain point in time.

Under the economic conditions of a free competitive market, price-based system, marginal theory predicts that this Pareto social welfare optimum would be achieved by the marginal adjustments of supply and demand to a point of equilibrium, caused by the competitive price system.

Diagram 1 describes two different possible points of social welfare, at Point A, and Point B, along the production possibilities frontier.

Either point could be a Pareto Optimum because both points are along the maximum frontier of economic growth. Economists would say that the social welfare outcome, at either Point A or Point B, would represent two points of "indifference" because either point could be a social welfare maximum.

Point C, on the interior of the production possibilities frontier, describes an inferior point of economic growth, which could be improved by moving economic resources to a more efficient use.

The economic force that possibly could move the economy from Point C to Point B, for example, could be entrepreneurial capitalism, where entrepreneurs find new ways to deploy underused resources in order to make a profit.

Point A represents the social welfare outcome of both social classes obtaining equal maximum income and benefits, at the same moment in time. The shaded green area represents maximum social welfare for both social classes.

Point B represents a movement, along the production possibilities frontier, where the welfare of the common citizens is improved, without damaging the economic production of the entire economic system.

The movement from Point A to Point B could be achieved by a constitutional system where taxes are used to improve the welfare of common citizens, without damaging economic efficiency of the entire society.

We argue that this Point B represents Jefferson's concept of the American Dream.

We describe a second diagram that shows the case of economic growth that benefits the Ruling Class, without damaging the economic welfare of the common citizens.

In this second case, the rising tide of economic growth lifts the boats of the Ruling Class, without sinking the boats of the common citizens.

Diagram 3. shows a social welfare along the production frontier heavily skewed to the benefit of the Ruling Class, where the constitutional rules force the social welfare maximum from A to Point Á, to the benefit of the Ruling Class.

The shaded tan area under the curve represents the improvement in social welfare of the Ruling Class, which resulted from increased economic growth, between 1792 and 1860.

Diagram 3. Social Welfare in the American Society, Between 1792 and 1860.

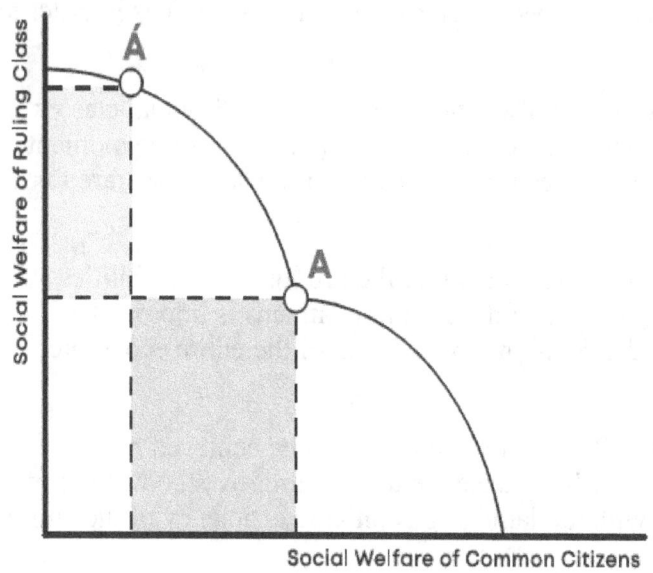

Social Welfare of Common Citizens

The benefits of economic growth favored the welfare of the Ruling Class, while the benefits of economic growth were not distributed to the common citizens.

We argue that this point Á, of social welfare in Diagram 2, describes the American economic system, before the Civil War.

The original point A on the production possibilities curve reflects the idea that social welfare for common citizens did not change, as a result of the social welfare improvements of the Ruling Class.

The shaded blue area under the curve, at point A describes a static, unchanging social welfare for common citizens, during a time of aggregate economic growth.

In other words, the cultural value of shared plunder allowed the Ruling Class to obtain greater economic welfare, for themselves, without damaging the social welfare of the common citizens, between 1792 and 1860.

Diagram 4. depicts the American economy in the Gilded Age, where the economic growth, between 1877 and 1907, benefitted the Ruling Class, by causing economic despair and income loss of common citizens.

The production possibilities frontier expanded outward, from the previous point A, and the tan area, under the curve, at Â represents the improvement in Ruling Class social welfare.

The production possibilities curve for common citizens inverted from concave to convex, to reflect that the improvement in social welfare for the Ruling Class caused social welfare declines for common citizens.

Common citizens, in the five social groups below, did not benefit from the economic growth, from 1877 to 1907. The shaded purple area, at point C, in Diagram 4, reflects the loss of social welfare, for common citizens, which was caused by the improvement of social welfare of the Ruling Class.

Diagram 4. Social Welfare in the American Society in the Gilded Age, Between 1877 and 1907.

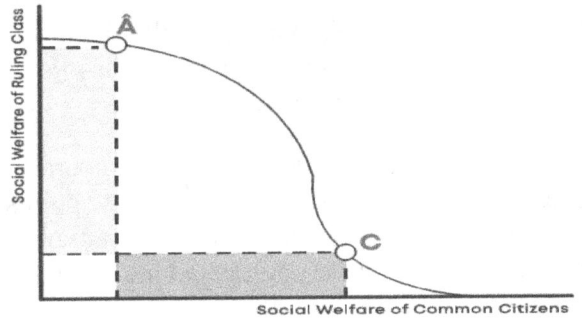

Diagram 4, at point Â, represents Madison's constitutional concept of the American "Get-Rich-Quick" dream for the natural aristocracy.

The periods of economic growth were disrupted by economic collapse, especially in 1873 and 1893.

The economic collapses acted as a social welfare ratchet downwards for common citizens.

The economic collapses acted as a social ratchet upwards for the Ruling Class. The economic collapses did not damage the social welfare of the Ruling Class because the banks controlled the money supply and the agencies of government bailed out the Ruling Class.

The ability of the Ruling Class to extract greater benefits, while damaging the economic welfare of common citizens is due to Madison's defect in the Preamble of his constitution, after the Civil War.

Diagram 4., at point Â, describes how Ruling Class control over prices, and money supply, shifts the social welfare utility frontier to the benefit of the Ruling Class, while damaging the economic welfare of common citizens.

As a result of monetary manipulation, the increase in money supply causes inflation. During an inflationary period, the social welfare of the Ruling Class improves, while the incomes and social welfare of the common citizens is damaged.

A decrease in money supply causes asset prices and commodity prices to decline, and eventually results in an economic collapse. During price contractions, the incomes of farmers and other producers decline.

We rely on Kenneth Arrow's book, Social Choice and Individual Values, (Yale University Press, 1951.), to describe why Madison's constitutional defect leads to recurring economic collapse.

Arrow's work begins with an analysis of how a nominally democratic society can avoid the logical problem of infinite regress. Arrow points out that in creating a constitution, the constitutional rules must explain the process of how individual preferences are aggregated into social decisions.

Arrow's point is that the concept of on-going "consent of the governed" in the constitution must be able to translate political decisions into economic policy and laws.

Arrow is raising the same question as the anti-federalist, Brutus, about Madison's defect of how on-going citizen consent in his constitution is translated into policy and law.

Arrow's initial concern of infinite regress means that the economy returns to a prior point, time after time, [Nash equilibrium] because the constitution does not provide the unambiguous mission statement in the Preamble.

Early computer programming experts called this infinite regress a "do-loop", because the specified programming conditions are never obtained.

The 3 social welfare functions we describe above are mathematical formulas used to describe the end goals of society. The 3 welfare functions mathematically specify and define the term "public purpose," also known as the "res publica."

Arrow went on to show, from a mathematical point of view, that, in the absence of an unambiguous public purpose, for every known method of making collective political decisions, there was no possibility of arriving at a social welfare optimum that would be consistently valued, from one time period to the next.

Consistency in the ranking of end goals of a democratic society, Arrow concluded, was impossible, given an existing written constitution, if the Preamble did not contain a clearly defined objective to determine the public purpose.

For example, in Diagram 2, above either Point A or Point B, could possibly be a social welfare maximum. Arrow's argument is that the constitution must provide a political way to solve the point of indifference between A and B.

For example, in Madison's nominal nothing of a Preamble, a "more perfect union" could be anything the elites and judges decide it is, at the moment that they decide.

Consistency, according to Arrow's theorem, of Madison's "more perfect union" could only be achieved in a dictatorship.

What Arrow meant by the condition of dictatorship is the ability of one dominant social preference function becoming the social preference ordering for all of society, regardless of the preference functions of the other individuals.

The preference functions for Madison's constitution are represented in Diagrams 3. and 4., above, where the social welfare at the new points, Á and Â, are obtained through the power of the Ruling Class, not through democratic procedures of on-going consent of the governed.

The only way out of the Arrow Paradox, in a democracy, is to assume that only individuals, and not social classes, have welfare functions, and to require that the constitution contain an explicit statement of the ultimate goal to be achieved via the constitutional rules on translating the individual consent of the governed into laws.

If the constitution fails on either condition then Arrow's condition of non-dictatorship is violated.

Arrow's insight is roughly the difference between a constitution based upon individualism and a society based upon social class collectivism, as is the case for Madison's constitution that elevated the welfare of the natural aristocracy over the social class of common citizens.

If the end goals of society cannot be made subject to individual preference rankings, [individualism] as Kenneth Arrow suggests, than upon the same logic, social welfare outcomes cannot be subject to social preference rankings, and consequently, the social class welfare goal must be imposed in a dictatorship.

The importance of Arrow's insight explains part of the cause of recurring, observable economic collapses, about every 10 years, in American history.

The U. S. economy collapses because Madison's defective constitution is not based upon consent of the governed, and contains no mechanism for aggregating individual preference functions into a social welfare function that obtains Pareto Optimality.

In other words, applying Arrow's insight, the U. S. economy is subject to the paradox of infinite regress of economic collapse because Madison's rules result in a cycle of corruption and speculation, which results in economic collapse, not real, sustained, economic growth that is fairly distributed to individuals, according to Jefferson's American Dream.

The significance of this insight by Arrow is that constitutional rules and laws must contain a priority ranking based upon their contribution to obtaining the most important social value contained in the constitution, through on-going consent of the governed.

That ultimate constitutional value could be national economic prosperity, or it could be maximum individual freedom, or, as the case of Madison's constitution, it could be rule by the Ruling Class, without on-going consent of the governed.

Arrow suggests that the social welfare function to be maximized in a democracy, given by the theory of general economic equilibrium, is the highest level of consumption of goods possible, given society's available income.

In other words, Arrow suggests the end goal of the democratic constitution is Pareto Optimality, which binds individual citizens into a voluntary allegiance to the rule of law, in common defense of equal liberty.

Amartya Sen extended the implications of Arrow's work in his book, Collective Choice and Social Welfare. (Harvard University Press, 1970.)

In tracing out all the implications resulting from Arrow's paradox, Sen wrote that "...nothing whatever is said as to who provides the ends represented by the Bergsonian social welfare function."

The "who" that Sen refers to are the social classes of the natural aristocracy "who" were parties to the initial constitutional contract, [39 self-selected elites] and the "ends" are the goals of the constitution [Lincoln's preservation of the union], that the "who" agree to.

Without the "who" and the "ends," clearly stated in the constitution, Sen affirms Arrow's conclusion that the "what" to be maximized [wealth of the natural aristocracy], cannot be decided in a democratic process.

The surrogate public purpose of Madison's constitution, as argued by Lincoln in the justification of the Civil War, is the preservation of the "union," which means the preservation of the plutocracy [the ends] and the maximization of their wealth [the what].

In the case of Madison's constitution, the individual preference functions, contained in Jefferson's Declaration, were replaced by the social class preference functions of the Ruling Class, in Madison's rules of civil procedure of 1787.

In the earlier period of time, Madison assumed that the virtue of the natural aristocracy would translate into better social welfare decisions than allowing common citizens an on-going democratic voice in political decisions.

In the current period of time, this same argument is made by Democrat Marxists, who believe that they are smarter than common citizens, and, therefore, they know better what is good for common citizens, than the citizens, themselves.

Lawrence Goodwyn, in The Populist Moment, explains that the current Democrat Marxist ideology of elite rule is the same as the ideology of Vladimir Lenin to implement Soviet Communism.

Goodwyn writes,

"The answer reached by Lenin was to entrust the advent of the new day [communism] to a small intellectual elite, tightly organized as a revolutionary party.'

Madison's American Dream of "Get-Rich-Quick" contains no adhesive glue that binds individuals to defending each other's freedoms in the current period, [plunder] and does not have adhesive power for generating loyalty to the a democratic political system in future generations. [dog-eat-dog law of the jungle].

Given Madison's defective Preamble, and Hamilton's defective banking system, after each economic collapse, each generation of common citizens, are subjected to starting over, economically, in an imaginary renegotiation of the benefits to be obtained from continuing the constitutional contract, without the benefit of being able to leave the constitutional contract.

In the era of the Gilded Age, that social renegotiation occurs after each economic collapse, and ends in a further economic decline of welfare of common citizens, achieved by the increase in social welfare of the Ruling Class.

Our economic analysis of the cycle of economic collapse in the Gilded Age is similar to the French economist, Clement Juglar, who described the American business cycle, during that era, as a series of economic collapses.

According to Douglas Steeples and David Whitten, in Democracy in Desperation: The Depression of 1893. (Greenwood Press, 1998.), Juglar had concluded that,

"Business cycles [were a part of a continuum of economic development] comprised of three phases prosperity, crisis, and liquidation., which always followed in the same order....for the US circumstances [in the Gilded Age] pointing to imminent contraction typically included excessive spending on luxuries, rising prices, a proliferation of speculative ventures, and many loans and discounts with a very small reserve in specie."

With Madison's political civil rules of procedure, and Hamilton's Ruling Class banking system, the U. S. economy has a built-in malfunction that causes economic collapse, about every ten years, which is devastating to the incomes of common citizens, but leaves the financial welfare of the Ruling Class untouched because the agencies of government [Leviathan] bail them out.

We describe the social welfare of five social groups, during the Gilded Age, whose incomes were permanently damaged by the operation of the plutocracy.

The five social groups are:

Black People in the Gilded Age, After the Failure of Republican Reconstruction.

The Gilded Age for Farmers in the South and West.

The Gilded Age for Native American Indians.

The Gilded Age for Working Class Industrial Workers in the North and Midwest.

The Gilded Age for West Coast Chinese Immigrants.

We apply the analysis of W. J. Cash, in The Mind of the South, to explain that, in each case of increasing immiseration, in each social group, the collapse of the economy is preceded by Ruling Class corruption and speculation, followed by common citizen protest, followed by a restoration of elite rule, which Cash called the restoration of the plantation society.

As we describe below, the restoration of the plantation society in the Gilded Age, after each collapse, is accomplished through violence by the Ruling Class police State, to compel common citizen obedience to Leviathan.

In our analysis of the Gilded Age, we raise the question: Why did this economic misery for the five social groups in the Gilded Age happen?

Our argument is that this misery for common citizens did not have to occur. There was no logical economic justification for these five social groups of citizens to endure economic hardship.

As was the case for the "Let Them Go In Peace," argument for letting the slave states go, in either 1787, or 1860, rather than engage in the Civil War, there was a better option available, in 1865, to avoid the economic misery of the five social groups.

The constitutional configuration of rules of Pareto Optimality in Jefferson's American Dream, would have produced a better social welfare outcome for all social classes, after the Civil War.

In other words, a better social welfare outcome of Pareto Optimality, specified in the 3 new constitutional amendments, would have avoided the economic misery of the five social groups, during the Gilded Age, if only the constitution, after 1865, had contained a goal of economic growth, consistent with equality under the law.

Geoffrey Brennan and James M. Buchanan, in The Reason of Rules: Constitutional Political Economy, (Liberty Fund, 2000.), explain that the remedy for the special interest tyranny is based on the potential for changing the constitutional rules or institutions of social order.

They write,

"These constitutional rules provide the framework within which patterns of distributional end states emerge from the interaction of persons who play various complex functional roles."

"Just conduct," writes Buchanan, "consists of behavior that does not violate rules to which one has given prior consent."

As we noted above, Madison's constitution is immoral because citizens were never provided an opportunity to give prior consent to be ruled by the Ruling Class.

The two essential conditions for Buchanan's constitutional system to work are the belief that individuals pursue their rational self-interest, and that the constitution identifies the pursuit of the rational self-interest as the goal, in the Preamble, of a democratic republic.

The initial conditions of inequality in property distribution, in 1787, led to a permanent political inequality in the ensuing civil society of Madison's constitution.

When property rights are given Madison's constitutional priority in rules, rather than economic growth, then the social function served by free market exchange, which is to provide a vehicle for rational self-interested individuals to pursue their life's mission, does not work.

With regard to their opinion of Madison's constitution, they write,

"To the extent that this (Madison's) constitution commands little respect, in part because it is seen to fail in its function of limiting the scope of both governmental and private intrusion into what are widely held to be protected spheres of activity."

Madison's constitution allows the privileged classes to change the rules as it may suit their needs, and to apply business and economic rules that apply to others, but not to themselves.

Our argument about the cause of the misery of the five social groups in the Gilded Age is that the scope of intrusion of the Ruling Class into the protected spheres of individual activity increased after 1865, because the permanent res publica of Madison's constitution was preservation of the plutocracy, whose centralized, national, power increased, as a result of the Union winning the Civil War.

As Foner explains, in Reconstruction: America's Unfinished Revolution,

"The civil war wedded a new conception of the powers and potentialities of the national state…carrying into reconstruction the conviction that federalism and state rights must not obstruct the sweeping national effort to define and protect the rights of citizens."

Black People In the Gilded Age, After the Failure of Republican Reconstruction.

The banking and financial environment during Reconstruction affected the lives of all common people, but was particularly devastating to former slaves, who had become farmers.

As Lawrence Goodwyn wrote, in The Populist Moment,

"The commercial world possessed a monopoly of the money supply and effectively withheld credit" [from farmers both Black and White."

The entire national economy ran on debt and credit, so that the access to credit for farmers in the South and West was essential. As we noted above, the banking system limited the circulation of money [Greenbacks} in the South after the War.

The Farmer's Alliance, in 1886, had identified the lack of credit and money in their Cleburne Report, which called for national banking reform.

The Cleburne Report called for,

"A federally administered national banking system embracing a flexible currency to be achieved through substitution of legal tender treasury notes for existing private national banks...the currency would provide for "per capita" circulation that shall increase as the population and business interests of the country expand."

Both Black and White farmers were denied credit, on a type of plutocratic equal opportunity basis.

Goodwyn notes, the denial of credit to farmers was not due to poor credit risk, rather it was due to Ruling Class hostility to common citizens. He writes,

"The farmer's cooperatives encountered trouble because of the implacable hostility of the financial and commercial world...the bankers refused to take the notes offered by the Alliance state exchanges because the bank's mercantile clients wanted the exchange to go under..."

There was no logical economic or financial reason for the banker's to deny farmers the credit that they needed to finance the harvesting of their crops.

The motivation of the bankers was rooted in the dynamics of Madison's social class conflict. The bankers wanted the farmers to go under, and they caused them to fail, and the failure eliminated competition, which enriched the plutocracy.

The welfare of the Ruling Class bankers could not have improved without causing the increased immiseration of the common citizens by denying credit and restricting access to cash.

In addition to denying Black people credit, the Ruling Class decided that the 14th and 15th Amendments, giving Blacks the right to vote, was a bad idea because Black voters were trying to implement civil rights through legislation.

In The Death of Reconstruction, Richardson writes,

"Republicans agreed that Blacks would have to lose the vote before they destroyed American society [plutocracy]…Blacks represented those who threatened to commandeer the government [voting]…Blacks should be segregated to protect the sensibilities of the "better classes."

The preservation of the union, in the Gilded Age meant allegiance to the myth of free labor, and preservation of the privileges of the Ruling Class.

Richardson explains,

"Northerners [Republicans] turned against freed people [slaves] after the Civil War because Blacks came to represent a concept of society and government that would destroy the free labor world. Blacks threatened the core of American society. [plutocracy]… [Republicans] rejected free labor in favor of exploiting government for their own ends. [crony capitalism]… The American system of free labor [the myth] based on individual enterprise would collapse as the government became a broker between different interests." [Leviathan].

In other words, the social welfare of Blacks, obtained through voting, had to be destroyed in order for the Ruling Class to gain greater wealth, than if Blacks had been able to continue to vote.

The myth of free labor and the preservation of the plutocracy is consistent with the second interpretation of the American Dream of "Get-Rich-Quick."

In The Death of Reconstruction, Richardson cites the Madison conception of the American Dream:

"Republican Elihu Washburne: the demoralization of the government thanks to the expenditures of vast and unheard of amounts of public money, giving out immense contracts by which sudden and vast fortunes were made…the intense desire to get suddenly rich out of the government and without labor…[crony capitalism]… By the mid 1870s, almost every one accepted the argument advanced by Democrats in 1867, that politicians used the monies garnered from taxation to give government jobs to or even bribe their worthless constituents."

In Splendid Failure: Postwar Reconstruction in the American South, (Ivan R. Lee, 2007.), Michael Fitzgerald laments that perhaps nothing could solve the problems of Black people in the Gilded Age. He writes,

"Yet, the former Confederates prevailed, through fraud and violence and in obvious violation of the laws, while the public looked away….perhaps nothing could have sustained egalitarian commitments of Reconstruction."

We agree with Fitzgerald that nothing could sustain egalitarian commitments, under Madison's constitution. Egalitarianism in economic opportunity is only possible under the Jeffersonian American Dream version of the constitution.

Under Madison's constitution in the Gilded Age, "Get-Rich-Quick," came at the expense of Black people getting poorer and poorer.

As Fitzgerald writes, in the Gilded Age,

"Illiterate freedmen had limited job opportunities and they were ill-situated to negotiate contracts. [free labor contracts]…Black codes forced contracts upon laborers on pain of arrest….the freed people seldom made much beyond food and housing for their year's labor."

Fitzgerald notes that the Freedman's Bureau suggested that Blacks be paid a cash wage of $10 per month. Of course, the Freedman's Bureau over looked the small difficulty that there was no cash to pay Blacks, because the banking system ran on credit, and restricted the circulation of cash.

However, Fitzgerald's, observation of a cash wage of $10 per month is useful for making our argument that the rich got richer because the poor got poorer.

The wage of $10 per month equates to a total wage payment for roughly 4 million former slaves, of about $480,000,000 million per year, which was not paid out to Black people.

On a yearly basis, the rich got richer because the poor Blacks got poorer to the tune of about $480 million, per year. The restoration of the plantation, after the end of Reconstruction, took a long time to accomplish.

The restoration of the plantation took about 35 years, during the Gilded Age. [35 years x $480 million per year].

The Ruling Class could not have gotten richer without damaging the welfare of Blacks, during the Gilded Age.

The restoration of the plantation was accomplished by police state violence.

Eric Foner, in Reconstruction: America's Unfinished Revolution, writes,

"The opponents of reconstruction launched a campaign of violence that made a mockery of political convergence …and a threat to their [Blacks] very physical survival."

In The Republic for Which It Stands, Richard White notes,

"The election of 1868 was one of the most violent in Americanc history…In Albany Georgia the Young Mens Democratic Club had ordered 5 cases of repeating rifles…They fired at nearly point blank range into the Black rally on the town square…Black Republicans had a choice: flee be killed or vote Democratic…In St Landry Parish, Louisiana, as many as 200 blacks in the course of the campaign were killed…A congressional investigation put the state's election too at 1081 dead."

H. Leon Prather, in We Have Taken A City: The Wilmington Racial Massacre and Coup of 1898, (Dram Tree Books, 2006.), describes how the Democrat Party leaders brought a howitzer and a Gatling gun to Wilmington, N. C., to overthrow the Black City Council.

Prather notes that the Cape Fear River was swollen with the carcasses of Blacks killed in the coup.

Prather quotes Furnifold Simmons, Chairman of the State Democratic Party, who chortled "We have taken a city."

Simmons stated,

"North Carolina is a White Man's State, and White Men will rule it, and they will crush the party of Negro domination beneath a majority so overwhelming that no other party will ever dare to establish Negro rule here."

Some historians cite the Atlanta riot of 1906, as the end of Reconstruction, and the restoration of the national plantation. Other historians cite other dates and other riots.

For example, in The Promise of the New South: Life After Reconstruction, (Oxford University Press 1992.), Edward Ayers cites the 1906 Atlanta riot as the end of Reconstruction. He writes,

"In the year of 1906, a race riot culminated the racial bitterness of the preceding three decades...The White mobs broke into one black business after another assaulting and killing black people, male or female, who happened to be inside....The Atlanta riot marked a pause, a symbolic culmination in the history of the New South."

Paul Escott, in Many Excellent People: Power and Privilege in North Carolina, 1850 - 1900, (University of North Carolina Press, 1985.), notes that in North Carolina, after the 1898 race riot in Wilmington,

"The Democratic Party resorted to fraud and force to safeguard its power and then designed a final, undemocratic political and social solution. This solution - segregation and disfranchisement - eviscerated the coalition of poorer whites and blacks and insured that established interests would not be threatened in the future."

Our argument about Black People in the Gilded Age, After the Failure of Republican Reconstruction, does not require a specific end date for the restoration the plantation by the Ruling Class.

We rely on the accuracy of the thesis of W. J. Cash, in The Mind of the South, that for Blacks, after the Gilded Age, the economy and society in the South and Western United States, looked just like it did in 1860.

As Mark Summers notes, The Ordeal of the Reunion, the violence to restore the image of the plantation periodically reoccurs.

He writes.

"[The violence} flares up especially whenever the ruling faction felt its tenure of office in danger."

The Gilded Age for Farmers in the South and West.

In our analytical framework of the golden triangle of banks, Ruling Class plunder, and crony corruption, the combination of power was successful in establishing both a monopoly over banking, and a monopoly of economic power over manufacturing production and commercial transportation.

As Goodwyn notes, in The Populist Moment,

"The ultimate monopoly was the money trust, a banking system of private plunder anchored in a metallic currency and assured of political power because it [Ruling Class] owned both sound money parties…The destruction of the cooperatives by the banks was a decisive blow, for it weakened the interior structure of democracy."

The destruction of democracy for the farmers was part of the strategy of restoring the plantation for the Ruling Class, during the Gilded Age.

As Goodwyn notes, it was an all-out coordinated attack by all segments of the Ruling Class plutocracy against the farmers.

"All important sectors of commercial America opposed the cooperative movement, not only the banks, and commission agencies, but grain elevator companies, railroads, mortgage companies, and furnishing agents…… the cooperatives were destroyed by the raw application of commercial power … the futility of the [economic] cooperative effort, in the absence of a fundamental restructuring of the monetary system [was not possible]… Corporate America simply possessed far too much economic and political influence …the courts, the press, the National Guard, governors, legislators and the Pinkertons all worked in harmony to defeat the workers."

In Plain Folks Fight: The Civil War and Reconstruction in Piney Woods Georgia, (UNC Press, 2005.), Mark Wetherington, describes the Ruling Class as a coordinated, national plutocracy, which was different than the regional dynamics of the plutocracy, before the Gilded Age.

"There was collaboration between New South boosters, Northern industrialists, and real estate speculators who delivered the wealth of the region to deals struck in Atlanta and New York...But the question of which white men ruled at home lingered as new political and economic realities shaped the area's identity. Increasingly, key economic and political decisions affecting plain folks lives were being made in places far from their neighborhoods and counties....lending credence to Governor Brown's warning that defeated Confederates would become "slaves to Northern avarice and Northern insolence."

Phillip Wood, in Southern Capitalism, cites the case in 1895, of a southern industrial recruiter making a pitch to northern textile manufacturers to move south.

"In his appeal to the New England Cotton Manufacturing Association, Edmonds told the manufacturers that they could not overcome the major southern advantage, "...a large, and at that point, mostly untapped supply of poor white workers, who were docile, not given to strikes, and as a class, were anxious to find work and willing to accept much lower wages than northern operatives."

The farmers would become slaves to Northern avarice as the Ruling Class reasserted the image of the plantation on farmers, but this time in a nationally coordinated golden triangle.

In the chronology of events for farmers in the Gilded Age, the Ruling Class obtained the land from the farmers, and then drove the farmers into a new type of neo-slavery system of textile manufacturing, where the entire family could work for free, under the same type of company store debt-peonage that existed on the farms.

As described by Sydney Nathans, in The Quest For Progress, the farmers soon found themselves,

"...clashing head-on with bankers, merchants, railroads and warehousemen, none eager to sacrifice their profits to the cooperative competitors...Credit and the currency supply of the entire nation, it became evident, were in the viselike grip of the county's largest bankers, who, in the name of "sound currency" had dictated two decades of deflation and tight money."

This was Madison's American Dream of a nation-wide plutocracy, writ large.

The Federal monetary policy had the effect of assisting the Ruling Class political coalition of bankers and furnishing merchants in schemes to obtain title to the land of the farmers.

The dual effect of taking land away from farmers was a greater concentration of land ownership in the hands of the Ruling Class, and greater number of formerly free-holders forced into the neo-slavery debt-peonage system of low wage, low skill, textile manufacturing.

As described by C. Vann Woodward, in Origins of The New South,

"In their attack on the national banking system, the agrarian economists were on solid ground in contending that private privilege was exercising a sovereign power, a [unelected] power of regulating national currency, for private gain rather than for meeting the needs of the country."

It was during this Gilded Age era that farmers and White textile workers realized that Jefferson's American Dream was not exactly the American Dream they thought that they were living under.

Goodwyn writes,

"A large number of people in the U. S. discovered that the economic premises of the society were working against them…farmers by the millions found that this claim [of equal rights] was not supported by the events governing their lives. The American political system was not seen [by farmers] to be democratic, but hierarchical: business lobbies governed the legislative process on vital issues….the Democratic Party "of the people" revealed itself as a business party… It does not require an excessive leap of the imagination [to understand] that when the Alliance leaders spoke of "centralized capital allied to irresponsible corporate power"…that this power was a menace to individual rights and popular government."

Goodwyn cites the Agrarian leader Tom Watson, who described the economic farming system in place during the Gilded Age.

"The [farming] system tears a tenant farmer from his family and puts him in chains and stripes because he sells cotton for something to eat and leaves his rent unpaid."

The farmer's rent was unpaid because the farmer did not have cash. The farmer did not have cash because the banking system ran on credit, not cash.

As James M. McPherson, in Ordeal by Fire: The Civil War and Reconstruction, (Alfred Knoph, 1982.), explains, the entire economic system in the South ran on credit. He writes,

"The [Sothern] merchant received his goods on credit from an urban wholesaler who was financed [obtained credit] by a northern bank. The [Southern] merchant charged 50 -60% above the cash price for goods sold to the tenant on credit….[secured by a contract to grow cotton]…The increased supply of cotton [grown under the contract] drove the price [of cotton] down."

When the farmer did not pay his bills, or taxes, his lands were confiscated by the Ruling Class, and the farmer was forced into debt-peonage, not a system of free labor, but a system of laboring for free.

Part of the collaboration between the government and the bankers to inflict economic damage on the farmers concerned the ability of the government to impose taxes on the farmers, which the farmers could not pay, because they did not have cash.

Eric Foner, in Reconstruction: America's Unfinished Revolution, 1863 – 1877, explains,

"By 1875 in Natchez over 150 farmers forfeited all or part of their lands for debt or non payment of taxes….many small farmers saw their holdings pass into the hands of owners of larger estates. By 1877, the tax system had become increasingly regressive with the least able to pay property taxes bearing the heaviest proportional burden…many planters had thousands of dollars in property excluded from taxes."

This treatment of taxation by the Ruling Class, where the tax burden was shifted from the wealthy, onto the backs of common citizens, is what William Graham Sumner was describing in his speech on The Forgotten Man. Sumner stated,

"Now, the plan of plundering each other produces nothing. It only wastes. [resources]. All the material over which the protected interests wrangle and grab must be got from somebody outside of their circle. [zero-sum].The talk is all about the American laborer and American industry, but in every case in which there is not an actual production of wealth by industry there are two laborers and two industries to be considered, the one who gets [Ruling Class] and the one who gives. [common citizens]. Now, who is the victim? He is the Forgotten Man."

White notes, in The Republic For Which It Stands, that, in addition to property taxes, the taxes were also imposed on the farmer's export crops, primarily because the excise taxes on cotton were the single most important source of revenue for the national government.

White writes,

"Between 30 -40% of the tariff burden fell on exports of agricultural products."

The tax on cotton increased the retail price of cotton, and caused a decline in demand, and the price paid to the farmers.

The decline in the price of cotton and tobacco was particularly severe when the Ruling Class deliberately contracted the money supply, as they did in the economic collapse of 1893.

White explains,

"In 1890, the federal government reduced national bank notes in circulation by 55%, between 1882 and 1891…since the money supply depended on the gold supply, the gold standard provided insufficient currency and contributed to deflation… By limiting the supply of money…the gold standard led to deflation [of farm products] which transferred wealth from debtors [farmers] to creditors [plutocracy]…wealthy creditors gained [unearned] premiums beyond interest payments …because the dollars paid to them [on debt] were always more valuable than the earlier dollars they had lent…The gold standard also allowed a much smoother integration of N. Y. and London capital markets. [banking globalism]."

Goodwyn notes, in the Populist Moment,

"The crop lien system became for millions of Southerners little more than slavery... Farmers, caught between high interest rates and low commodity payments, lost all hope of ever being able to pay out. Every year more and more of them lost their land to the furnishing merchant and became his tenants...The commercial world possessed a monopoly of the money supply and effectively withheld credit from the farmers."

In Man over Money, Bruce Palmer writes,

"By 1900, the farmers decline into debt peonage through the crop-lien reached 50% of all farmers, since the end of the Civil War."

Beginning in 1876, the Democrats throughout the South began passing a series of laws, known as "anti-enticement laws" that made it illegal to entice a farmer from the land of his landlord, or to "aid or abet" the farmer in transportation from the land.

In conjunction with the Landlord-Tenant Acts, which made it a felony to remove crops from the land without the landlord's approval, the system of laws in the South were effective at eliminating opportunities for economic advancement or escape to freedom.

As noted by Wood, the combination of laws,

"Allowed the planters to create a labor force whose freedom was severely curtailed by the indebtedness arising from the operation of the lien system and reinforced by the actions of the State."

Farmers were held in a form of debt slavery by legal and political contracts from which they could not escape. Adherence to the rules of the free labor contracts were enforced by the Leviathan of the police power of the state.

If farmers attempted to escape from the debt-lien contracts by fleeing from the region, they were captured and prosecuted. If they were convicted, they were shipped off to the convict labor system to work for free.

As the case of debt peonage shows, it is quite possible, under Madison's rules, to have a nominally democratic constitution wherein the rules of procedure are followed perfectly but whose outcomes do not provide for justice in the political exchanges between individuals, because common citizens do not have an opportunity to provide on-going consent of the governed.

Under Madison's constitution, once the Ruling Class established their neo-slavery system, there was no constitutional pathway of reform of the system, and there was no pathway of escape from the system.

According to Paul Escott, the

"Elite Democrats did more than beat back the challenge of the Populists, disfranchise black people, and stigmatize cooperation between Tar Heels of both races. They imposed an undemocratic electoral system, so complete and effective that all future political discourse had a restricted character."

In some historical accounts, that undemocratic system was called "Jim Crow." We think a more accurate description of the system is Economic Apartheid.

The debt-lien system for farmers occurred during the Gilded Era that featured two economic collapses, and following Cash, in The Mind of the South, after each collapse in 1873, and 1893, the plutocracy restored the image of the plantation.

After each economic collapse, the rich got richer, because the poor got poorer.

Goodwyn writes about the economic collapse of 1893.

"But however bad things looked,[for farmers in 1892] things soon got worse. In 1893 America plunged into a severe economic depression …which occurred during the annual financial squeeze caused by the autumn agricultural harvest….Grover Cleveland was forced to sell massive gold bond issues through the syndicate organized by J P Morgan, which saddled the country with a debt of over a quarter of billion dollars,..the bankers paid for the bonds with gold they had withdrawn from the US Treasury."

Goodwyn quotes a farmer from Mendot, Kansas, who wrote to President Cleveland,

"I take my pen in hand. We are starving…I have not had nothing to eat today…"

There is no logical economic justification for this level of suffering of the farmers. The root cause of the suffering is the defect in Madison's constitution that created a plutocracy, which cannot be reformed because citizens have no power over the Leviathan that Madison created, and because common citizens have no way to escape from the system.

The Gilded Age for Native American Indians.

In The Ordeal of the Reunion: A New History of Reconstruction, (UNC Press, 2014.), Mark Summers, captures the essence of Ruling Class plunder of the Indians.

Summers writes,

"Nathaniel Taylor, Andrew Johnson's Commissioner of Indian affairs explained, 'Members of Congress understand the negro question, but when the progress of settlement reaches the Indian's home, the only question is how best to get his lands"

Francis Prucha, in the Great Father, quotes Bishop Whipple, on the issue of plunder of Indian land.

"Bishop Whipple, 1864, "the politically appointed men entered their duties with only one thought, and that is plunder…the only human beings in the U. S. who has none of the restraints or protection of the law is the treaty Indian."

Members of Congress figured out that the best way to get the lands of the Indians was to combine Ruling Class plunder with the crony corruption of the police power of the state.

Part of the crony corruption was to use the U. S. Supreme Court to establish the precedent that Indians were not citizens, using the same logic that Dred Scott was not a citizen.

Eric Foner, in The Second Founding, writes,

"The 14th amendment did not explicitly exclude Native Americans...but the amendments requirement that citizens be "subject to the jurisdiction of the United States was meant to leave out those living within Indian nations...Not until 1924 did Congress extend birthright citizenship to Native Americans."

A second part of the crony corruption was to use the agencies of government as a funnel for graft and corruption to private third parties, who conducted the formal policies of subduing the Indians, in order to take their land.

In The Great Father: The United States Government and the American Indian, (University of Nebraska Press, 1984.) Francis Paul Prucha, writes,

"Supplying goods to Indians was a multimillion dollar business in the 1870s. It was the chief area of illegal and unjust economic gain...George Stuart, of the Board of Indian Commissioners, said, "I soon discovered how it was that the "Indian Ring" was enabled to make such an immense profit..."

The "Indian Ring" Stuart refers to was a component of the golden triangle of plunder, corruption and banking, which combined forces to plunder the Indian land.

In this part of the plunder, private third party contractors to the government performed two valuable functions. First, they withheld their supplies from Indians, in order to starve Indians or freeze them to death.

Second, they performed as an auxiliary militia, with the U. S. Army, to kill Indians, and more importantly, to kill all the Buffalo. The contractors killed the Buffalo, skinned them, sold the skins for a profit, and consequently destroyed the food source for the Indians.

Prucha writes, in The Great Father,

"Secretary of the Interior Delano, in 1874, said "The buffalo are disappearing rapidly but not faster than I desire. I regard the destruction of such game as facilitating the policy of the Government."

Part of the coordination of plunder of the land with the crony corruption of government occurred because of laws which restricted the movement of Indians, similar in logic to the laws in the South that made it illegal to entice a Black person from the land of his landlord, or to "aid or abet" Black people in transportation from the land.

In the case of Indians, it was illegal for Indians to leave the reservation, or for White people to aid or abet their movement.

White, in The Republic For Which It Stands, writes,

"In the West, the whites could move around freely…Indians could not…Between 15 – 25% of the Piegans starved and died on their Montana reservation during the winter of 1882 and 1883[because they could not legally escape]."

White describes the long forced marches of Indians, by the U. S. Army, to various forts and reservations.

He writes,

"[On one march], when the Indians reached the Platte River …they were imprisoned at the fort…when they refused to continue [on the march] to the Indian territory, Army officers attempted to freeze and starve them into submission."

The plunder, the corruption, and the violence worked in tandem to obtain the land, under Madison's American Dream of Get-Rich-Quick."

The logic of national Ruling Class plunder was described by Prucha, in The Great Father:

"James Henry Carleton [American Army Indian fighter} was not unmindful of the rich possibilities of the land vacated by the Indians… the riches could not be mined unless the Indians were removed to reservations…Why should the nation [Ruling Class] be deprived of its immense wealth?"

Prucha cites Henry Teller, Secretary of the Interior, as providing the same logic of national plunder. He writes,

"Henry Teller, former senator from Colorado, followed Kirkwood as Secretary of the Interior strongly advocated for reservation reduction...the surplus land not needed [by the Indians] would be opened to the operation of the homestead law."

Prucha notes,

"In 1881, Kirkwood counted 102 reservations occupied by 224,000 Indians....he believed that if all the Indians could be gathered together into four or five reservations the savings [plunder] would be great...Columbus Delano, began to play a numbers game trying to fit all the Indians into one large reservation...Inside the Indian territory he found one person per 558 acres...he decided "there would be 180 acres of land per capita...he admitted that the acres given up by the Indians would be thrown open to white settlement [plunder]."

Richard White notes,

"In 1887, Congress passed the General Allotment Act, that allowed distribution of Indian lands ...without Indian consent...In 1881, Indians held 155 million acres. By 1890 Indians held 104 million acres...By 1900, Indians held 77 million acres. Thomas Jefferson Morgan, Commissioner of Indian Affairs said, "the tribal relations should be broken up, socialism destroyed...Indians would conform to the white man's ways peaceably if they will, forcibly if they must."

And, forcibly, it was. The restoration of the plantation, for Indians, was violent, brutal and permanent.

White quotes General Philip Sheridan, on the violence against the Indians,

"General Sheridan: "We [the royal We, the people] took away their country and their means of support, we broke up their mode of living, their habits of life, and we introduced disease and decay among them...Sheridan's instructions to Custer were to find the Cheyenne's and destroy their villages, and ponies, to kill or hang all warriors and bring back all women and children."

White notes,

"On November 29, 1864, at Sand Creek, in the territory of Colorado, Colonel. John Chivington, attacked a camp of Cheyennes, and slaughtered 200 Indians, mostly women and children...The Indians thought that they were protected by a prior military treaty..."

The restoration of the plantation, for the Indians, took about 35 years.

Prucha notes that Indian policy fluctuated between two extremes, with the central question being how best to obtain the Indian lands.

He writes,

"U. S. Indian policy represented a movement between two extremes: the idea of assimilating the Indians into white American society...and the idea of segregation outside the limits of white society."

Segregation meant moving the Indians to smaller and smaller reservations, under the violent police power of the state. The land obtained from the Indian removal was obtained for free.

The final, violent restoration of the plantation, for the Indians, occurred in 1890, at Wounded Knee.

By that time, as White notes, the Gilded Age was coming to a close, the election of Democrats to the U. S. Congress was over, and all the land that could plundered from the Indians had been obtained.

The Board of Indian Commissioners, in 1869, wrote,

"The history of government connections with the Indians is a shameful record of broken treaties and unfulfilled promises... a sickening record of murders, outrage, robbery, and wrongs..."

Our argument is that the social welfare of the Ruling Class could not have improved without the devastation of the social welfare of the Indians.

The slogan "Free Labor," was paired with another favorite slogan of the Republicans in the 1850s, "Free Soil."

Like Free Labor, the interpretation of Free Soil could vary, depending upon the context. In one interpretation, Free Soil meant limiting slavery to where it already existed, as was Lincoln's initial position, in 1860.

In the Gilded Age, Free Soil had a second interpretation: How to get the Indian lands for free.

The unearned profit gained by the Ruling Class in obtaining the Indian lands for free, and then selling it for a capital gain, constitutes the basis of our argument that the social welfare of the Ruling Class improved, at the permanent cost to the social welfare of Indians.

There is no logical economic, or moral, justification for inflicting misery on the Indians. If the 13th, 14th, and 15th Amendments had granted birthright citizenship to the Indians, in 1868, the Indians would not have been left defenseless, without civil rights, to defend themselves against the brutality of the Ruling Class, under Madison's conception of the American Dream.

The Gilded Age for Working Class Industrial Workers in the North and Midwest.

Our argument about the rich getting richer during the Gilded Age, is based upon a coordinated power, not Madison's separation of power, between economics, politics, and the judiciary that combined to direct the flow of financial benefits to the Ruling Class.

The banking system, monetary manipulation, the investment speculation, and the crony capitalist corruption of the Ruling Class caused the welfare of the Ruling Class to improve, while that combination of power caused the welfare of industrial workers to decline.

In the case of the first three social groups we reviewed, above, the use of debt and credit by the banks, in the absence of cash, was the major component of economic control in the golden triangle of power that caused the social welfare of common citizens to decrease.

In 1880, according to Heather Cox Richardson, for the first time in American economic history, nonagricultural, industrial workers outnumbered agricultural workers.

The shift to wage work caused the Ruling Class to shift the methods of control in the return to the plantation thesis, described by W. J. Cash.

The use of debt and credit declined, as a tool of control, while the corruption of the plutocrats in obtaining wealth through crony capitalism increased.

Rather than debt or credit, the banker's manipulation of the money supply worked in tandem with the increased use of the coercive police power of the state, to deal with working class protests against the monopoly power of the plutocracy.

Richardson explains that in the 20 years between 1880 and 1900, 6.5 million workers launched 23,000 strikes. The increase in strikes and civil unrest occurred during each economic collapse, caused by Ruling Class speculation and corruption, which did not yield economic growth that benefitted the working class.

Gross domestic product increased that benefitted the Ruling Class, as we described above in Diagram 3, with the inverted convex social welfare curve for industrial workers describing that the workers did not obtain the benefits of economic growth.

In our application of the Cash return-to-the-plantation thesis, as the Ruling Class corruption intensified, the crony capitalist use of government agencies increased, and as the common citizen protests increased, the return to the plantation was accomplished by increased use of violent police state coercion.

Economic collapse was still a regular occurrence during this part of the Gilded Age, but each collapse was now paired with labor strikes that occurred every time the economy collapsed.

In 1890, the Baring Brothers bank collapsed. In February, 1893, the Philadelphia and Reading Railroad collapsed. In 1893, 360 national and state banks collapsed and 119 railroads went into receivership. By 1895 25% of all railroads were in receivership, and 15000 businesses failed. In 1895, in Fall River Mass unemployment was 85%. Average unemployment in all industries was 21%. In Michigan, 2066 factories had dismissed 43.6% of their workers, at the end of 1893.

Richard White writes,

"In 1886, more than 600,000 American workers walked out of shops, factories and work sites. There were 1400 separate strikes, affecting 11,516 businesses..."

The National Bureau of Economic Research cites nine economic downturns between 1873 and 1907. Out of a total of 420 months, during that time period, the U. S. economy was in recession 211 months, or 50% of the entire time.

Diagram 5. provides an overview of the correlation between economic collapse, and increased citizen and industrial worker strikes, from 1873 to 1907.

The unstable economy was due to monetary manipulation, investment speculation, corruption, and crony capitalism, followed by economic collapse.

The new factor during this era was the increased violence surrounding citizen protest and industrial worker strikes. In each economic downturn, the industrial workers lost social welfare, and the Ruling Class benefitted from the misery inflicted on the industrial workers.

Diagram 5. Monetary Manipulation, Investment Speculation, Corruption, Economic Collapse and Labor Strikes Duri Gilded Age

Begin Date	End Date	Duration	Description	Strikes and Protests
1873-10-01	1879-03-01	5 years 5 month	Failure of Jay Cooke & Company, the largest bank in the United States, which burst the post-Civil War speculative bubble.	The deflation and wage cuts of the era led to labor turmoil, such as the Great Railroad Strike of 1877.
1882-03-01	1885-05-01	3 years 2 months	The recession of 1882–85 was a price depression. From 1879 to 1882, there had Ruling Class investment speculation in railroad construction.	Haymarket Riot, 1886 (40,000 to 60,000 citizens participated). Six strikers were killed at the McCormick Reaper Manufacturing Company.
1887-03-01	1888-04-01	1 year 1 month	Investments in railroads and buildings weakened during this period	Coeur d'Alene Mining Strike of 1892. The owners of the Coeur d'Alene mining district decided to curtail labor organization by creating an owner's militia.
1890-07-01	1891-05-01	10 months	International monetary disturbances, such as the Panic of 1890 in the United Kingdom.	The Homestead Strike occurred at the Carnegie Steel Company's Homestead Steel Works in 1892. The strike culminated in a gun battle between unionized steelworkers and a group of men hired by the company to break the strike. The steelworkers ultimately lost the strike.
1893-01-01	1894-06-01	1 year 5 months	Failure of the United States Reading Railroad and withdrawal of European investment led to a stock market and banking collapse. And a run on the gold supply.	The Pullman Strike of 1894 started outside Chicago at the Pullman sleeping car manufacturing company
1895-12-01	1897-06-01	1 year 6 months	Production shrank and deflation reigned	
1899-06-01	12/1/1900	1 year 6 months	Production declined	
9/1/1902	8/1/1904	1 year 11 months	downturn lasted for nearly two years and saw a distinct decline in the national product. Industrial and commercial production both declined	
5/1/1907	6/1/1908	1 year 1 month	A run on Knickerbocker Trust Company deposits on October 22, 1907, set events in motion that would lead to a severe monetary contraction.	

Sources: NBER for dates of economic recession. Internet sources for descriptions.

The five strikes highlighted in Diagram 5. are the major strikes during this era. There were hundreds of strikes and thousands of workers involved in the protests.

Eric Foner notes,

"In January, 1874, city police violently dispersed a crowd of 7000 people. The strikes denoted a

"transition period in the nation's history." The depression had brought European style class conflict to America...and strengthened the antagonism between rich and poor."

Leviathan was supposed to act as an independent, objective power broker to mediate the conflict between the natural aristocracy and common citizens.

As Richardson notes, in Death of Reconstruction,

"The struggle between the theory of a society based upon free labor [Jefferson] and one based upon class conflict [Madison], mediated by [central government], profoundly affected race relations."

The two conceptions of the American Dream were summarized by James Truslow Adams, in The Epic of America, (Simon Publications, 2001).

"It is not a dream of motor cars and high wages merely, but a dream of a social order in which each man and each woman shall be able to attain to the full stature of which they are innately capable and recognized by others for what they are."

Scott Sandidge, in Born Losers: A History of Failure In America, (Harvard University Press, 2005.), describes how industrial workers in the Gilded Age interpreted Jefferson's version of the American Dream, for themselves. He wrote of a new ideal of freedom for industrial workers, seeing the workers as individuals.

[There was] a new ideal of freedom: every citizen an entrepreneur...every worker enjoyed unfettered choices to sell his labor or not, to accept the boss's terms or not, to incur debts or not....contract law presumed that individuals freely chose their situations. [free labor].

The Ruling Class had their own, different, interpretation of the American Dream. Their interpretation of the Dream was not based upon individualism. It was based upon Madison's conception of a two-class society, the natural aristocracy and common citizens.

The two-class society allowed the Ruling Class to view common citizens as a sociological collective entity, not as individuals. This collectivist perspective explains much of the plunder and violence of the Ruling Class against industrial workers in the Gilded Age.

The industrial workers were not seen by the plutocrats as individual citizens, rather they were the proletariat. Just like Black people were a social class, just like farmers were a social class, just like Indians were one monolithic social class, as seen from the eyes of the Ruling Class.

Madison had suspected that common citizens would form their own social class awareness, or consciousness, to match the existing class consciousness of the Ruling Class, in 1787.

As described by Robert Horwitz, in The Moral Foundations of the American Republic, (University of Virginia Press, 1986.), Madison thought that, if the working class could develop a class consciousness, that they would adopt the culture of shared plunder of the system, just like the elites.

Horwitz wrote that Madison thought that,

"If all citizens (working class) have the same impulse of passion and interest they would not divide into oppressive and dangerous factions… if (working class) Americans can be made to divide themselves according to their narrow economic interests they will avoid the fatal factionalism."

In Madison's conception of the Dream, individual liberty was not a financial "faction," worthy of legal status in the constitution, in the same sense that the working class and the elites were commercial factions, each with a distinct social class financial interest.

If the common citizens did form a class consciousness, as Madison predicted, then the Leviathan of Madison's constitutional rules of checks and balances would effectively mediate conflict between two groups, one of which had been permanently empowered over the other.

The end goal for Madison was a stable system of rules that would allow the elites to negotiate the spoils of the plunder, with other elites.

In Madison's rules, there are only two social classes, the elites and the working class. His system of politics would only require, forever, two political parties to represent the commercial interests of these two factions.

One political party, the elites, would have unfair advantages in contract law and property rights, and the other political party, would represent the interests of the working class, but without the burden of on-going consent, or actually participating in democratic rule making and enforcement.

In An Economic Interpretation of the Constitution of the United States, Charles Beard explained that, for Madison,

"The primary objective of [Madison's] government is the making of rules which determine the property relations of members of society, the dominant classes whose rights are thus to be determined perforce obtain from government."

There is a sense of equality among elites, in Madison's constitutional rules, because the elites, of either political party, all shared the cultural value of plundering the system.

The essence of the rule of law in Madison's arrangement is special financial group interest negotiation over the distribution of the spoils of the plunder.

As Madison noted,

"the central function of the legal system is to protect autonomous individuals (elites) from the "tyranny of the majority" (working class)."

The Ruling Class had the power to increase or decrease the money supply, at any time during the business cycle, which suited their investment speculation and plunder interests.

In Ordeal by Fire, James M. McPherson explains that sometimes the elites tried to do both things, at the same time.

McPherson writes,

"In 1874, congress passed a bill to increase the amount of Greenbacks and national banknotes by about 10%...Grant vetoed the bill...[and instead] Congress passed the 1875 Specie Resumption Act."

The effect of the Species Resumption Act was to give the Ruling Class an instant profit by being able to convert their worthless Greenbacks into either gold or silver.

At the same time, the contraction of the supply of Greenbacks, in 1875, had the effect on farmers and industrial workers of causing an economic collapse, beginning in 1873.

The Sherman Sliver Purchase Act (1890) required the U. S. Treasury to purchase silver and issue paper currency for the silver it bought. The paper currency was convertible to either silver of gold.

Astute plutocrat investors immediately began converting the paper currency into gold, for an immediate profit. The increased demand for gold caused the U. S. Treasury to run out of gold.

Government gold reserves were reduced from $192 million, in 1990, to below $100 million, in 1993. The Government had issued $350 million in paper currency, under the Sherman Silver Purchase Act, and $100 million in gold reserves, in 1893, was not sufficient to cover the Government's obligations to convert paper to gold.

Rather than allow the Government to default, President Cleveland went to J. P. Morgan, one of the most vaunted plutocrats, and had The Bank of Morgan loan the Government $65 million, in gold, in exchange for an agreement to sell U. S. Gold Bonds, in Europe, for a tidy commission of $7 million.

The effect of this transaction caused a monetary contraction, which damaged the social welfare of workers and farmers, and was the proximate cause of the economic collapse of 1893.

The partnership between government and private corporations was a component of crony capitalism that allowed agencies of government to protect the social welfare of the Ruling Class.

Before his empire collapsed, Jay Gould recognized that the most critical government interventions to help him solve labor unrest would come from the least democratic sector of government, the courts.

According to Richard White, this intervention of the courts, in the form of injunctions to halt labor protests, shifted the existing power of the Ruling Class to an even more repressive use of the police power of the state.

White writes,

"The influence of the courts in support of private corporations shifted the balance of power between workers and employers... In 1886, Gould stopped negotiations [with workers] because court injunctions from federal and state courts ..forbade strikers to persuade other workers to join the strike. The courts permitted the railroads to recruit gunmen, who were deputized to act against the strikers...On May 3, the police opened fire, killing 6 strikers."

As was the case of Anti-Enticement laws against Black people and Indians, which restricted the freedom of movement to escape oppression, the government enforced Anti-vagrancy laws against industrial workers, making it a crime to be wandering around, while unemployed.

According to Foner,

"The vagrancy laws made unemployment a crime...[when workers were convicted of vagrancy] they were leased out as convicts [free labor] to manufacture railroad cars [for Gould and Rockefeller].

The courts also used Madison's rules on contract law to intervene in labor disputes, on the side of employers. The legal precedent of the contract law had been successfully used by the U. S. Supreme Court to protect slave property, and to enforce the free labor contracts of Black people during Reconstruction.

In the Gilded Age, the courts ruled that labor strikes were a form of conspiracy against the state [Ruling Class].

The logic of the courts was that a labor conspiracy was a crime, and thus, the crime could be enjoined [stopped] by injunctions, and by the use of the police power of the state.

As was the case of converting the due process provisions of the 14th Amendment from protection of Black people to protection of corporations, the 1890 Sherman Antitrust Act, ostensibly designed to limit monopoly capital, was generally more successful in prosecuting labor unions than industrial combinations.

The national legal power of the Ruling Class corporations changed forever in 1889, when New Jersey permitted corporations to purchase and hold shares of other corporations, as a combined corporate entity.

The effect of that change made the provisions of the Sherman Anti Trust law moot against monopoly power because the courts ruled that conglomerates were not the same legal beast as a business trust, which was the object of the Sherman Act.

Between 1895 and 1904, nearly 4,000 companies merged with rivals, creating conglomerates such as DuPont, General Electric, and US Steel, which ushered in the modern era of Big Business.

In Labor Market Institutions in the Gilded Age of American Economic History, (National Bureau of Economic Research, 2016.), Suresh Naidu and Noam Yuchtman, describe the intervention of the government of behalf of the Ruling Class against industrial workers.

They explain that contract law, inherited from English common law, prohibited a worker from leaving the employment contract of the "Master."

They write,

"The common law of employment, inherited from England, was heavily influenced by the doctrine of Master and Servant, which restricted the ability of most employees to leave their employers. In extreme cases, apprenticeship, indentured servitude, and especially slavery, these restrictions allowed colonial American employers to extract greater labor effort without paying market wages. [free labor]"

Naidu and Yuchtman describe how the courts reinterpreted the injunctive powers of the Sherman Act against industrial workers in the Gilded Age.

They write,

"The institutional innovation that most effectively pacified labor violence was the labor injunction. At the behest of employers, judges issued injunctions ordering employees to return to work and allowing government forces to break up pickets and other activities that prevented replacements from working. In laying the groundwork for the injunction, the judiciary confronted legal dilemmas that were fundamental to the American constitution, pitting rights to property and contract against rights to freedom of association and speech. [Jefferson's American Dream vs. Madison's American Dream] For example, three powerful tactics for strikers were picketing, the sympathy strike and the secondary boycott. Judges issued injunctions against all of these tactics, arguing that picketing violated employer property rights, that sympathy strikes constituted enticement, and that secondary boycotts violated the Sherman Act."

They describe how violence was used by the Ruling Class to force a return of industrial workers to Cash's plantation. The court ordered injunctions legitimized the use of force by the police power of the state.

They write,

"Employers also hired the Pinkerton National Detective Agency ("the Pinkertons") to break strikes: Brecher (1972) notes that "[The Pinkertons'] had 2,000 active agents and 30,000 reserves totaled more than the standing army of the nation." Pinkertons could infiltrate and sabotage unions, and could also be used in direct physical conflict with strikers, as in the Homestead strike… data shows that between 1877 and 1892, the modal use of American militia was to quell labor unrest was 8 times the number of uses in response to natural disasters."

Our argument about the rich getting richer during the Gilded Age, is based upon a coordinated power, not Madison's separation of power, between economics, politics, and the judiciary that combined to direct the flow of financial benefits to the Ruling Class.

The banking system, monetary manipulation, the investment speculation, and the crony capitalist corruption of the Ruling Class caused the welfare of the Ruling Class to improve, while that combination of power caused the welfare of industrial workers to decline.

There is no logical economic reason why industrial workers were killed by the Ruling Class during the Gilded Age. The Ruling Class killed workers because they viewed workers as a sociological collectivist entity, not as individual citizens, inured with equal natural and civil rights as the Ruling Class.

The explanation for the violence against the industrial workers, in the Gilded Age, lies in Madison's constitutional configuration of the rules, which elevated the financial interests of the Ruling Class over the interests of common citizens.

As was the case of the argument "Let them go in peace," to avoid the Civil War, and "birthright citizenship for Indians," in the 14th Amendment, this violence against the workers could have been avoided with a different Preamble, and a different configuration of rules in Madison's defective constitution.

That new, and better, configuration of constitutional rules would embrace the goal of Pareto Optimality, where economic growth benefits all citizens, not just the Ruling Class.

We note, in passing, that the unchecked power of the Leviathan government, created by Madison, is not constrained, or limited in any way by the consent of the governed.

That powerful, independent government is now in the hands of Democrat Marxists, who conduct government in collusion with the Big Business crony corporations, created by law, in 1889, to allow corporate consolidation.

West Coast Chinese Immigrants During the Gilded Age.

In Closing the Gate: Race, Politics, and the Chinese Exclusion Act, (UNC Press, 1998.), Andrew Gyory asks a question very similar to the question that we raise about the Gilded Age for the first four social groups we reviewed, above.

Gyory writes

Why did the United States pass the Chinese Exclusion Act in 1882? This Gilded Age statute, which barred practically all Chinese from American shores for ten years, was the first federal law ever passed banning a group of immigrants solely on the basis of race or nationality."

Gyory reviews two historical explanations about the treatment of West Coast Chinese immigrants, and the enactment of the Exclusion Act, both of which he finds inadequate.

Gyory writes,

"Historians have ascribed two theories to explain the origins of the Chinese Exclusion Act: The California thesis and the national racist consensus thesis.

The California thesis, advanced by Mary Roberts Coolidge in 1909, posits California and its working people as the key agents of Chinese exclusion.... the `California thesis,' does not stand up under close scrutiny and should be substantially modified, if not completely altered..."

The American White Racist thesis that combines racism with the emerging social class consciousness of the white labor union movement... "Historians Philip Taft, Joseph G. Rayback, and Gerald N. Grob stressed the national labor movement's opposition to Chinese inmnigration in the 1870s, a point echoed by Herbert Hill, who has argued that nationally, "organized labor took up the anti-Chinese litany after 1870" and formed "the vanguard of the anti-Asian campaign."

Gyory is especially harsh in his criticism of Gwendolyn Mink, of the White racist thesis.

He writes,

"The historian who most forcefully connects the national labor movement with the Chinese Exclusion Act is Gwendolyn Mink. In her 1986 study, Old Labor and New Immigrants in American Political Development: Union, Party, and State, 1875-1920, ...

Mink argues that after the Civil War, immigration, rather than immigrants, played the decisive role in formulating an American version of labor politics…Although the 'Chinese menace' was geographically contained, [in California] the anti-Chinese movement must be viewed in a national [White Supremacy] context. It invigorated national union solidarity." In providing "a peculiar bridge between unionism and national politics," she adds, Chinese exclusion became the dominant issue uniting the labor movement after the Civil War."

Gyory explains that Mink's analysis of the American labor movement is deeply flawed. He writes,

"By placing anti-Chinese politics at the heart of the national labor movement, and the national labor movement at the heart of the anti-Chinese campaign, Mink profoundly distorts the evolution of working-class ideology and organized labor after the Civil War. Like countless historians before and after, she misunderstands the positions of workers… By misrepresenting workers' attitudes toward Chinese immigration, Mink seriously skews the development of the labor movement after the Civil War and presents a thesis on the origin of the Chinese Exclusion Act that is patently invalid."

According to Gyory, Mink's analysis is deeply flawed, not because she promotes American institutional White racism as the cause of Chinese immigrant mistreatment, but because Mink does not emphasize the national political dynamics between Republicans and Democrats.

Gyory explains that his own, preferred, historical thesis of the Exclusion Act, is based upon political competition at the national level.

"Racist as white workers may have been in this era, they were neither much more nor much less racist than other segments of American society. [everyone is racist] … neither thesis explains the process by which Chinese exclusion came to be enacted. Nor does either thesis explain how national politicians appropriated and packaged the issue… The single most important force behind the Chinese Exclusion Act was national politicians of both parties who seized, transformed, and manipulated the issue of Chinese immigration in the quest for votes. Chinese immigrants became pawns in a political system characterized by legislative stalemate and presidential elections decided by razor-thin margins."

We offer W. J. Cash's return to the plantation thesis as a more compelling and accurate historical thesis of the mistreatment of Chinese immigrants in the Gilded Age.

In our explanation of Cash's return to the plantation thesis, the first step in the golden triangle is the banking control over the banks and the money supply, which leads to speculation and corruption, in this case railroad corruption, which ends in economic collapse.

Prior to the economic collapse, the plutocracy engages in plunder, which is described as the power to obtain resources and wealth from others in immoral actions, in this case, from the Indians, and crony corruption, which means using the agencies of government to obtain wealth, in this case, unlimited and unchecked land grants to build the railroads on Indian lands.

The economic collapse is caused by prior investment speculation which did not yield real economic growth. In this case, fraudulent and corrupt bond offerings on railroad investment ventures, which eventually collapsed the national economy, in both 1873, and 1893.

We place the mistreatment of Chinese immigrants into the historical framework of the Ruling Class natural aristocracy, which gained unchallenged political power, after the Civil War.

Madison's constitution worked in tandem with Hamilton's banking system to direct financial resources to the Ruling Class, before, during, and after the Civil War.

Nothing about the constitutional privileges of the Ruling Class has changed in America.

To answer Gyory's question, our thesis of historical continuity explains the Exclusion Act.

Our historical thesis is easy to understand: After the Ruling Class used Chinese labor to build the railroads, they enacted the Exclusion Act to strip Chinese citizens of their citizenship, and sent them back to China.

In this case, Cash's return to the plantation was in China.

Our thesis begins with the corruption associated with the railroads.

We rely on Richard White to place the corruption of the railroads in the center of Gilded Age history. While we acknowledge other national corrupt acts, we emphasize that the railroad corruption ties together all of the mistreatment of Black people, Southern farmers, Indians, industrial workers, and West Coast Chinese immigrants, in the Gilded Age.

In "Information, Markets, and Corruption: Transcontinental Railroads in the Gilded Age, (The Journal of American History, June 2003.), White describes the extensive and pervasive corruption of the railroad Ruling Class.

He writes,

"Corruption is a species of fraud that involves violation of public or private trust. A covenant of some sort, either implied or explicit, [Jefferson's promise of liberty] is violated. Corruption involves betrayal, often of a third party. The corrupt buy or sell what was not supposed to be for sale, a vote, for example, or public property. They turn to personal advantage and their legal status as trustees of persons or property. Or they grant only to a privileged few what is purportedly available to all or available only through open and fair competition." [Jefferson's American Dream of an entrepreneurial capitalist economy].

White is describing Madison's American Dream of "Get-Rich-Quick," for the privileged few of Madison's natural aristocracy.

He cites the corruption of the railroads as the single most important act of corruption in the Gilded Age. He writes,

"At the center of national corruption, both financial and political, were particular corporations: the railroads. They were the major corporate consumers of capital…"

White describes crony capitalism, as the access of the Ruling Class to the agencies of government.

He writes,

The Gilded Age was a key moment in that history not just because the issue of corruption dominated politics but because the rich, who now controlled corporations,...

used them to infiltrate the state [Leviathan] and to turn parts of it to their own purposes. They also did something equally important: they moved to take control of the mass circulation of financial information in order to manipulate financial markets."

During the Gilded Age, the railroad companies received, from the U. S. Congress, between $16,000 and $48,000 per mile of track in land grants and cash subsidies. In all, the railroads received 131 million acres from the US Government.

White notes the influence of the Ruling Class in national government.

He writes,

"The early transcontinentals were speculative endeavors run by men who were essentially financiers. Early owners usually hoped for a quick gain. [Madison's American Dream]. The railroads sought friends in both parties… it was not focused on democratic elections, [destroys Gyory's thesis] which were expensive and hard to control…Lobbyists were common enough, but the Washington lobbies of the Central Pacific and Texas and Pacific railroads operated on a scale far greater than that of most of their counterparts."

In addition to crony capitalism, White describes the banking and money component of Madison's Dream of Ruling Class plunder, which was based upon credit and debt, not cash.

He writes,

"The paradox of Gilded Age financial corruption was that its goal was to accrue debt; how, then, did the corrupt turn debt into riches." The first way is well known. Its most famous manifestation was the insider contracts that funneled money, in the case of the Union Pacific, from stockholders and lenders into the pockets of the inner clique who controlled the Crédit Mobilier, which systematically overcharged to build the road while selling shares in the company at below-market prices to leading politicians… The whole scandal of the Crédit Mobilier was based, after all, on the widespread conviction that insiders had corrupted both the [railroad] corporations and Congress."

As a result of the corruption on bonds, and on railroad over-building, the economy collapsed in 1873. White explains,

"The corruption endemic to the transcontinentals played its part in the panic of 1873, which within a year was being described as a "railway panic" caused by the "overconstruction of railways." The failure to recover from the panic was blamed on the paralysis of the enormous amount of capital invested in railroads. The railways, in the South as in the West, were planned and constructed with borrowed funds. The interest on those funds was often paid by more borrowing. Bankers had realized even before the panic that the ability to draw in new funds [pyramid scheme] to keep this cycle going was coming to an end. The specie shortage that afflicted the economy in 1873 was the result partly of monetary policies and partly of a large negative trade balance that the United States had with Great Britain."

The Chinese immigrants were an important labor source for the railroad Ruling Class. We slightly agree with Gyory that the Chinese immigrants were pawns, in a gigantic corrupt plundering scheme of investment speculation on railroads.

The immigrants booked their passage to the United States using what was known as a "credit-ticket," an arrangement in which their passage was paid in advance by U. S. businessmen to whom the immigrants were then indebted for a period of work, similar in concept to the first indentured servants in Virginia.

Andrew Gyory, in Closing the Gates, explains that bringing Chinese workers to America was part of the plunder and corruption of the Gilded Age. The coolie brokers made substantial profits from the global trade in Chinese labor.

He writes,

"[Railroad] speculators often hired "coolie brokers" to recruit illiterate Chinese men and induce them to sign contracts. [free labor contracts] Speculators then transported them on a grueling "middle passage" (under conditions approaching the African slave trade) to Peru and Cuba and sold their contracts to the highest bidder…Former Confederate general Nathan Bedford Forrest, president of the New Selma, Marion, and Memphis Railroad (and grand wizard of the Ku Klux Klan), subscribed five thousand dollars to procure a thousand workers from China to lay track across Tennessee."

White notes,

"Manufacturers from Ohio and Missouri placed orders for Chinese workers, and Chicago businessmen invited two Chinese traders to discuss similar ventures. Merchants Choy Chew and Sing Man accepted and visited cities further east in July and August. With excitement building in the Northeast, Koopmanschap "will employ all available vessels," the New York Times reported, "and his agents in China will be prepared to fill them with human freight as fast as they arrive."…A Chinese emigrant agency agreed to provide "75 steady, active, and intelligent Chinamen" who would work eleven hours per day in spring and summer and ten and a half hours in fall and winter. Sampson would pay them twenty-three dollars a month—about ninety cents a day—for the first year, and twenty-six dollars a month for the second and third years…One thousand Chinese workers arrived in Alabama to lay track toward Chattanooga. Railroad directors in Virginia, West Virginia, and Pennsylvania placed orders, and Koopmanschap soon claimed that "eastern capitalists" had signed contracts for over two hundred thousand "coolies."

The sociological description of Chinese immigrants as "coolies," fits our analysis that the Ruling Class viewed the Chinese immigrants as a collectivist, undifferentiated proletariat, not as individuals with natural rights.

Two years prior to the enactment of the Exclusion Act, the railroad work was petering out, and the Chinese immigrants left the railroads to look for work in the big metro regions of the West Coast.

They found work in tobacco, textiles, agriculture, and leather goods.

In 1880, the Chinese, representing 8.7 percent of California's population, composed 33 percent of woolen-mill operators, 34 percent of domestic servants, 39 percent of fishermen, 44 percent of brick makers, 48 percent of gardeners, 52 percent of boot and shoe makers, 80 percent of launderers, and 84 percent of cigar makers.

In The Road to Chinese Exclusion: The Denver Riot, 1880 Election, and Rise of the West, (University Press of Kansas, 2013.), Liping Zhu, describes part of thelegal oppression of Chinese immigrants, before the passage of the Exclusion Act.

He writes,

"California's Criminal Proceedings Act, provided that "no Black or mulatto person, or Indian, shall be permitted to give evidence in favor of, or against, any white person." Although the statute did not specify "Chinese," the [state's Supreme Court] justices agreed that American Indians and Mongolians came from the same stock. Thus, the court ruled that a lower court could not accept the testimony of Chinese. [California] Chief Justice Hough C. Murray even politicized his ruling, writing that if the Chinese were allowed to testify in court, the country would soon "see them at the polls, in the jury box, upon the bench, and in our legislative halls!"

Initially, the U. S. Supreme Court endorsed the collectivist view of the Chinese immigrants, when various provisions of the California law, and the Exclusion Act made their way to the Supreme Court.

Zhu notes,

"U.S. Supreme Court Justice John Marshall Harlan asserted that the Chinese were "a race so different from our own that we do not permit those belonging to it to become citizens of the United States"

In the absence of civil liberties and legal protection of the Civil War Amendments, thousands of Chinese workers were killed on the job building the railroads.

The Chinese workers were not viewed as individuals, worthy of dignity and respect by the railroad Ruling Class, and consequently no records were kept when a Chinese worker was killed, on the job.

The normal and ordinary treatment of the dead worker was to place his carcass in a shallow grave, by the tracks, and move on down the line.

The estimates of the number of Chinese workers killed building the railroads comes primarily from the work of a single Chinese Aid Association, whose members walked along the various rail lines counting the shallow graves.

In their article, "Verily the Road was Built with Chinaman's Bones": An Archaeology of Chinese Line Camps in Montana, Christopher W. Merritt, Gary Weisz & Kelly J. Dixon, (International Journal of Historical Archaeology, 2012.) write,

"Many of the Chinese who died were buried in simple, unmarked graves along the grade (Fullerton 1961; Helterline 1984, pp. 33) in order to prevent slowing the construction effort, and to allow for easier relocation and disinterment for shipment to China…Between 1879 and 1883, it is estimated that over 1,000 Chinese workers died while assisting in the construction of the NPRR, leading to reporters to note that "verily the road was built with Chinaman's bones" (Helena Independent 1884, p. 3). Lewty (1987, p. 96) notes that as the backbone of the NPRR construction effort, the Chinese suffered most from the work as they were killed in falls, explosions, and some even from scurvy due to poor diet afforded them on the front."

In our treatment of the social welfare dynamics of the Gilded Age, the social welfare of the railroad Ruling Class improved, while the social welfare of the Chinese workers, especially the ones who were killed on the job, declined.

The social welfare of the Ruling Class could not have improved without the social welfare loss of the Chinese workers.

The Ruling Class made effective use of the political tool of race hatred in the West, between Whites and Chinese, as they did in the South, between Black textile workers and White textile workers.

The tool of race hatred was used by the railroad Ruling Class to maintain social control and to obtain cheap labor.

In Gilded Freedom: U. S. Government Exclusion of Chinese Migrants, 1848-1882, (University of Hawaii Press, 2016.), Robert Villanueva, writes,

"Evidence arguably proves that Gilded Age politicians used this race-baiting tactic to undermine the rising economic mobility of this Asiatic group. In the 1860's after goldmine owners threatened to replace white miners with Chinese laborers, after union delegates refused to use dynamite to quarry rocks. Under enormous pressure, union bosses hesitantly agreed to use the lethal explosives, and take salary cuts as well."

After the railroad work petered out, the Chinese workers returned to San Francisco, where they competed with White workers, mostly Irish, for low wage jobs.

The tool of race hatred was effective in causing race riots during the end of the 1880s.

The Irish workers organized themselves into White vigilante units, similar in concept to the KKK, in the South.

Denis Kearney was the leader, and his group was called Kearneyites.

A news report at the time stated,

"Complete havoc erupted in the city, in which 250 Chinese migrants were stoned by hostile whites on San Francisco's Front Street Wharf."

The Chinese immigrants were caught between two versions of the American Dream.

In Madison's version of "Get-Rich-Quick," American Dream, the Ruling Class needed cheap Chinese labor to work in mines and build the railroads.

Both the Knights of Labor, and Chinese immigrants thought that they were laboring under the illusion of Jefferson's Dream of equal liberty.

According to Richard White, in The Republic for Which It Stands

"The Knights of Labor thought of the Chinese not as workers, but as coolies, virtual semi-slaves, who undermined free labor…The Knights considered the Chinese as tools of the corporations…When widespread violence erupted in the autumn of 1885, the Knights were at the center of it."

In other words, both the Ruling Class, and the Knights of Labor adopted a sociological, collectivist view of the Chinese immigrants.

The Knights of Labor thought that the Chinese immigrants were tools of the Ruling Class, which is accurate.

The Ruling Class viewed both Chinese immigrants and the Knights of Labor labor as collectivist social classes.

In other words, the Ruling Class viewed Chinese immigrants, and White workers as the Lumpenproletariat, an unthinking underclass devoid of class consciousness.

We argue that the Chinese immigrants never adopted a social class consciousness that would have confronted both the Knights of Labor and the Ruling Class view of them.

As White notes, the accurate sociological view of Chinese immigrants posed a dilemma for both the Knights of Labor and the Ruling Class, because the immigrants were not exactly like Black slaves, but they were not exactly like free White labor, either.

White notes,

"What counted as coerced labor and what to do about it became a central political question in the Gilded Age…The accusation that the Chinese were coolies, servile labor brought in by employers to drive down the wages of free labor, had been prevalent in the West since the California Gold Rush."

The partial solution to the Chinese problem was described by Eric Foner as the unintended consequence of the Civil War Amendments as they were applied to the immigrants.

Foner writes,

[The unintended consequence of 13th amendment], "In California, the movement against Chinese immigration, led to Chinese Exclusion Act, in 1882, promoted as a part of fulfillment of the 13th Amendment."

According to Foner, the solution for the Chinese immigrants was similar to Lincoln's idea about how to handle slaves. The first part of the solution was to stop importing the Chinese, and the second part was to send the ones who were already here, back to China.

Eventually, beginning around 1885, about ½ of the Chinese immigrants in the U. S. were eventually sent back to China.

The Exclusion Act Law made it illegal for Chinese immigrants to come to the U. S., and the law revoked the status of citizenship for Chinese immigrants already in the U. S.

The Exclusion Act was eventually repealed, by Congress, in 1943, as a part of Roosevelt's war strategy of forming an alliance with China, to defeat the Japanese Imperial Army.

In 1898, the Supreme Court ruled that Exclusion Act provision of revoking the status of Chinese citizenship was unconstitutional, but by that time, a majority of the immigrants that had been in the U. S., in 1882, had already been sent back to China, and the Ruling Class had already turned its attention to importing Japanese immigrants to replace the Chinese workers..

We argue that the Chinese immigrants understood Jefferson's American Dream of equal opportunity under equal rights.

What the Chinese immigrants wanted, in coming to America, was to live under Jefferson's Dream of an entrepreneurial capitalist society.

Robert Villanueva, in Gilded Freedom, summarizes this aspiration of the Chinese immigrants by citing the testimony, during hearings on the Exclusion Act, of a White owner of a shoe manufacturing plant.

"A white shoe manufacturer testified that "[f]or businessmen to employ Chinese is simply putting nails in their [White owner's] coffins, because they [Chinese] gain the experience, then go off into their own businesses and compete against us."[White owners].

In other words, the Chinese immigrants wanted to come to America, work hard, learn a trade, and then start their own small business.

What they got, instead, was Madison's American Dream of a Ruling Class plutocracy, created by Madison's constitution.

Gyory asks, "Why did the United States pass the Chinese Exclusion Act?"

We ask a slightly different question: "Why did this suffering of the Chinese immigrants occur? There was no logical economic, or moral, justification to inflict suffering on the Chinese immigrants.

A different configuration of constitutional rules, and a different Preamble, would have avoided this suffering, and the need for the Ruling Class to enact the Exclusion Act.

Chapter 7. The Emergence of the Global Corporate American State.

In her American Bar Association article, "Does "We the People" Include Corporations?" Ciara Torres-Spelliscy asks the right question about the legal treatment of corporations, under Madison's constitution.

She asks, "Who counts as a member of "we the people?" (ABA Groups, Volume 43, Number 2, 2021.)

A better question to ask is not about whether corporations are persons, under "We, the People," [which they are], it is about Madison's defective constitution, and his vacuous Preamble that suggests that a mythical, imaginary, collectivist "We, the People," created the constitution, and that the "people," maintain an ultimate, mythical, sovereignty to alter or abolish the government.

We argue that when King George surrendered to the United States, that he transferred sovereignty from the Crown to the individual citizens in each of the 13 states.

Under the logic of Jefferson's Declaration, the makers of the Articles of Confederation maintained the location of sovereignty in individuals, as the ultimate source of authority, who delegated specific enumerated powers to the central government.

When Madison usurped the Articles of Confederation, he re-located sovereignty away from individuals, to an all-powerful collectivist central state, consistent with Hobbes' characterization of the Leviathan.

In The Doctrine of Sovereignty Under the United States Constitution, (Indiana University School of Law, 1929.), Hugh Evander Willis, explains Hobbes' description of Leviathan, as it applies to the United States.

He writes,

"Hobbes assumed, first, that there was a pre-civic state of war, and, second, that each individual contracted with every other [individual] to surrender irrevocably [emphasis added] to one body of men (or a man) the natural right of each individual to govern himself…

Law, according to him, was the creation of the State. The ruler [the King] was not a party to this contract and therefore could not break it."

Willis then asks the same question about corporations being a person, in Madison's constitution, as Torres-Spelliscy.

Willis asks,

"Is the State a person? Yes, in just the same way that a corporation is a person. But, it may be said, that corporate personality is a fiction and if the personality of the state is no more, it [the state] is a fiction... Yet it [corporation] can own property, contract in its own name, be guilty of personal crimes, and sue and be sued in its own name. It has a reality distinct and apart from that of its shareholders or shareholder, even where one man buys up and owns all the stock, or where it is a subsidiary. It may have a citizenship in one country though all its shareholders are citizens of other countries. It, and not its shareholders, is liable for the torts of its servants and for breaches of contracts...There is no escape from the conclusion that the notion that a corporation is a fiction must go. It is a reality. It is an entity and a personality. It is not a natural person but an artificial person, but with just as real a [legal] entity as a natural [human] person."

The better question to ask, than the one Torres-Spelliscy asks about corporations being a member of "We, the People," is about where corporations fit in the location of ultimate sovereignty, under Madison's constitution.

Willis asks,

"Where does sovereignty reside in the United States? Who is sovereign under the United States Constitution?"

"The concept of a sovereign State, separate from and independent of its government on the one hand and of its people [We, the People] on the other, has been a metaphysical juggernaut, whose end [the state's end] apparently has been its own existence; whose purpose, its own preservation and aggrandisement; whose power, is without limit or control..."

We argue that Madison transferred the sovereignty of individual people, under the Articles, to the irrevocable sovereignty of a metaphysical state, not constrained, in any way, by the consent of the governed.

The American Leviathan has the unchecked power to admit any group it wishes to the Constitution, [illegal aliens], under the vacuous, mythical entity of "We, the People," and citizens have no recourse against the power of the Leviathan.

Our descriptive term for the American Leviathan is "the deep state," of intelligence agencies, the military, and corporate lobbyists who maintain unchecked power in Washington, D. C.

Willis comes down on the side of "We, the People," as the ultimate source of sovereign authority in Madison's constitution.

Willis writes,

"But the whole people as organized in government to express and adjust their will either directly or through representatives. They ["We, the people,] have created no artificial personality to correspond with the people as a whole viewed as a political unit. They can make and unmake constitutions, states and agents. They [We, the People"] are sovereign. As a practical fact the sovereignty is vested in those persons who are permitted by the Constitution of the State to exercise the elective franchise…but in the people as a whole as organized at present in our dual form of government.'

The flaw in the sovereignty logic of Willis is seen in his admission that "We, the People," did not create a competing artificial personality to exercise consent over the artificial personality created by Madison's transfer of sovereignty to sovereign state.

The "whole people," seen as "as a whole," do not exist as a political entity, organized as a political personality. Only individual humans exist, in reality.

And, to jump ahead in time, to the coup of November, 2020, the individual citizens must be able to vote in fair elections, or the government is illegitimate because the deep state usurps the sovereignty of "We, the People."

In An Economic Interpretation of the Constitution of the United States, Charles Beard, (MacMillan Co, 1925.), discusses the flaw in the logic of Willis.

Beard states,

"The only effectual method to secure the rights of the people and promote their welfare is to create an opposition of interests between the members of the two distinct bodies [the natural aristocracy and the common citizens], in the exercise of the powers of government, and balanced by those of a third….that these interests be so distinct as to prevent a coalition of any two of them [the natural aristocracy and the state] for the destruction of the third [We. The People]….rather he advocated a government whenever the people feel a grievance they cannot mistake the authors of their grievance and will apply the remedy with certainty and effect, discarding them at the next election."

The only check the common citizens have on the power of Leviathan, under Madison's document, is to vote every four years on the Ruling Class representatives, who will rule them for the next four years.

That check on power by voting is subject to fraud and corruption, as it was in November, of 2020. After November, 2020, the Ruling Class began selecting themselves, to rule.

After Leviathan is created, "We, the People" do not control Leviathan, because Leviathan is disconnected from the consent of the governed, and from the initial grant of authority [1788] to Leviathan, which is irrevocable.

The description of the deep state, by Willis, is accurate. The mission and end goal of the American deep state, under Madison's rules, is the perpetuation of its own existence; whose purpose, is to exercise power, on behalf of the natural aristocracy, without limit or control by "We, the People."

The artificial, imaginary, "We, the people," in Madison's text suffers from the same logical defect as Rousseau's volonté générale.

As Brutus noted, in his arguments against ratification, there is no mechanism for the consent of the governed to influence law or policy under Madison's rules, any more than there is a mechanism for consent of the governed to influence volonté générale.

Both concepts, "We, the people," and "the general will" are imaginary concepts, with no legal enforcement mechanisms.

The constitution of "We, the people," was created by 39 self-selected elites, in a type of fraudulent, secret, virtual representation, where the elites claimed that they constituted "We, the people."

In Madison's replication of the British social class system, he transferred the sovereignty of the Crown to the sovereignty of the State, which appeared to him to look like the Crown.

His constitutional rules empowered one social class, the natural aristocracy, over the interests of the other social class. To Madison, the unelected Senate looked like the House of Lords, in England.

Under Jefferson's American Dream, sovereignty would continue to reside in individuals, because individuals were provided constitutional rules to provide on-going consent, under the Articles of Confederation.

The answer to Torres-Spelliscy's question about corporations being persons, under "We, the People," makes sense in the historical context of the Gilded Age.

Corporations are creatures of the State, created for the benefit of the natural aristocracy to raise capital and conduct business operations, with limited legal liability to the individual investors, or for the majority owners of the corporations.

The legal and political logic of corporations attempting to be viewed as "persons," or as "citizens," during the Gilded Age, was to limit legal liability from wrongful acts, and to extend civil law protections to the individuals who are associated, and manage, the corporations, in other words protection for the Ruling Class, who own the corporations.

In some cases, the U. S. Supreme Court rules that corporations are citizens, and in other cases, the Court rules that corporations are persons. And, sometimes, the Justices rule that corporations are not covered under "We, the people."

Alex Park, in his article, "Supreme Court Rulings That Turned Corporations Into People, (Mother Jones, 2014), noted that,

"Justice John Paul Stevens argued in his dissent to Citizens United that "Corporations…are not themselves members of 'We the People' by whom and for whom our Constitution was established."

As Willis noted above, the treatment of corporations as citizens, and persons, under "We, the people," has been a "metaphysical juggernaut."

It is just a small logical step, in American jurisprudence, to go from the logic of corporations as persons, to corporations, as citizens, with all the privileges and immunities of human citizens.

The Privileges and Immunities Clause of Article IV, Section 2, of the Constitution states that "the citizens of each state shall be entitled to all privileges and immunities of citizens in the several states."

In contrast to privileges and immunities of "citizens," the 14th Amendment 14th guarantee that states, like the federal government, cannot "deprive any person of life, liberty or property, without due process of law; nor deny to any person within its jurisdiction the equal protection of the laws."

Due process ensures that all levels of government operate within the law and provide fair procedures for everyone, including corporations, who are defined, by the U. S. Supreme Court, under the 14th Amendment, as "persons."

Corporations are not specifically mentioned in the Constitution, nor in the 14th Amendment. But from 1809 to 1882, corporations sought many of the same constitutional rights guaranteed to individual citizens, including the rights to own property, enter into contracts, and to sue and be sued, in Federal Courts, just like individuals.

In Bank of the United States v. Deveaux (1809), the Court ruled,

"The jurisdiction of this court being limited, so far as respects the character of the parties in this particular case, "to controversies between citizens of different states," both parties must be citizens, to come within the description…A corporation aggregate, is certainly not a citizen; and, consequently, cannot sue or be sued in the courts of the United States, unless the rights of the members, in this respect, can be exercised in their corporate name."

According to Alex Park, in his article, "Supreme Court Rulings That Turned Corporations Into People,"

"Deveaux argued that, because corporations weren't people, [citizens], they couldn't sue in federal court. Chief Justice John Marshall agreed. This meant businesses could only sue or be sued in federal court if all the shareholders, and at least one member of the opposing party, lived in the same state."

Park continues,

"Thirty-five years later, after hearing the Louisville, Cincinnati, and Charleston Railroad case, the Supreme Court shifted course, ruling that corporations were "citizens" of the states where they incorporated."

In 1853, according to Park,

"In Marshall v. Baltimore and Ohio Railroad, the Supreme Court upheld the notion that corporations were citizens, but only for the purposes of court jurisdiction; [standing], they did not have the same constitutional rights as actual people. [citizens].The court also ruled that, for litigation purposes, shareholders would be considered citizens of their company's home state."

We argue that the American Ruling Class partnership between corporations and Leviathan, after the Civil War, would not have been as effective without the Civil War Amendments, which allowed the U. S. Supreme Court to make corporations "persons," under the "We, the People," Preamble of Madison's constitution.

The pathway of corporations to become "persons" is almost as fraudulent and illegitimate as the so-called "convention" ratification process of Madison's constitution.

We rely on Adam Winkler's article Corporations Are People' Is Built on an Incredible 19th-Century Lie: How a farcical series of events in the 1880s produced an enduring and controversial legal precedent. (The Atlantic, 2018.), to make our case about the illegitimate rulings that made corporations "persons."

The judicial farce began in 1882, and, according to Winkler, the farce,

"Involved a lawyer who lied to the Supreme Court, an ethically challenged justice, [a corrupt court recorder who modified the text of the opinion] and one of the most powerful corporations of the day." [a railroad].

The corrupt attorney, who lied to the Supreme Court, represented the Southern Pacific Railroad. Roscoe Conkling had been a member of Congress, and served on the committee that drafted the text of the 14th Amendment [in 1868].

Conkling both represented the railroad in the case before the Supreme Court, and also provided direct testimony, and introduced evidence, based upon his work in drafting the 14th Amendment.

According to Winkler,

"The head lawyer representing Southern Pacific was a man named Roscoe Conkling. Conkling told the justices that the drafters had changed the wording of the amendment, replacing "citizens" with "persons" in order to cover corporations too. Laws referring to "persons," he said, have "by long and constant acceptance ... been held to embrace artificial persons as well as natural persons." Conkling buttressed his account with a surprising piece of evidence: a musty old journal he claimed was a previously unpublished record of the deliberations of the drafting committee. [that Conkling stated supported his contention about changing the word "citizens" to the word "persons"] . According to historians, Conkling was simply lying. Nonetheless, the Supreme Court embraced Conkling's reading of the Fourteenth Amendment."

The corrupt court reporter modified the text of the opinion, and added his revised rendition at the top of the Court's ruling. Davis was also an attorney and had represented railroads, before he became a Supreme Court recorder.

According to Winkler,

"By tradition, the reporter writes up a summary of the Court's opinion and includes it at the beginning of the opinion...

The reporter in the 1880s was J. C. Bancroft Davis, whose wildly inaccurate summary of the Southern Pacific case said that the Court had ruled that "corporations are persons within ... the Fourteenth Amendment."

The corrupt Supreme Court Justice was Stephen Johnson Field. According to Winkler, Field used the fraudulent document, prepared by the Court recorder, as legal precedent to be followed by subsequent Courts.

"A few years later, in an opinion in an unrelated case, Field wrote that "corporations are persons within the meaning" of the Fourteenth Amendment. "It was so held in Santa Clara County v. Southern Pacific Railroad," explained Field, who knew very well that the Court had done no such thing." [Field had prior knowledge of Conklin's strategy and knew at the time, in 1882, that Conkling was lying to the Court].

In 1886, in Santa Clara County v. Southern Pacific Rail Road, the Court cited the legal precedent, established by Field, in an unrelated case, that corporations were "persons" under the 14th Amendment.

In the 1886 case, Chief Justice Morrison Waite, stated,

"The Court does not wish to hear an argument on the question whether the provision in the Fourteenth Amendment to the Constitution which forbids a state to deny to any person within its jurisdiction the equal protection of the laws applies to these corporations. We are all of opinion that it does...The defendant Corporations are persons within the intent of the clause in section 1 of the Fourteenth Amendment to the Constitution of the United States, which forbids a state to deny to any person within its jurisdiction the equal protection of the laws."

Winkler concludes his article by noting that the 14th Amendment, purportedly passed to protect the civil rights of Black people, had instead been turned into a political weapon to protect the civil rights of corporations.

He writes,

"Between 1868, when the 14th amendment was ratified, and 1912, the Supreme Court would rule on 28 cases involving the rights of African Americans and an astonishing 312 cases [affirming] the rights of corporations."

In the crony capitalism of the Gilded Age, corporations were in a partnership with the government to build railroads, and sell worthless bonds to unsuspecting investors.

The partnership between corporations and the State, in America, was not exactly like Mussolini's partnership, where the State was the senior partner, and gave instructions to the corporate junior partners.

In the American partnership, the senior partner was the consolidated political power of the corporations, who told the junior partner what to do.

According to Alex Park, in his article, "Supreme Court Rulings That Turned Corporations Into People,"

"In 1898, (Smyth v. Ames): Building on the Santa Clara decision, the court voided a Nebraska railroad tax, ruling that it [the tax], was akin to the government taking a corporation's property without due process—a violation of its 14th Amendment rights."

"1906 (Hale v. Henkel): Having blocked unlawful seizures of corporate property, [taxes], the court went on to shield companies from other kinds of intrusion. Writing for the majority, Justice Henry Billings Brown found that corporations, like people, [citizens], are protected from unreasonable searches and seizures under the Fourth Amendment." [in the Bill of Rights for "citizens" not persons]."

As a result of the Court rulings, granting civil rights to corporations, the unchecked political and economic power of corporations over common citizens increased, after the Civil War.

During the period of time, from 1882 to the creation of the Federal Reserve Act, in 1913, U. S. corporations began the transition from a national monopoly power to a global imperial power, fueled by their new domestic monopoly power legal rights.

As described by James Livingston, in Origins of the Federal Reserve System, Money, Class, and Corporate Capitalism, 1890-1913., (Cornell University Press, 1986.), the transition to a global imperial power required a new, and different type of banking system, than the "free banking" system that existed during the Gilded Age.

The type of banking system required by corporations to be a global imperial power looked exactly like Hamilton's First Bank, and the subsequent Second Bank.

He writes,

"The federal reserve system was a product of the crisis of the 1890s...the market investment [banking] system was reorganized and stabilized...The banking and monetary reform movement of 1894 must be understood as the context in which a corporate business elite began to work on [creating] a world view and a program appropriate to its control over an emergent modern industrial society."

The movement to a global imperial power was accomplished with political propaganda that viewed small business and entrepreneurial capitalism as the main economic problem that was acting as a barrier to global greatness.

The corporation's line of political attack on entrepreneurial capitalism, according to Livingston, was that unlimited capital investments in small businesses was unproductive, and lead to "over production in the economy, which caused prices to decline because there was a glut of too many products in the market."

Livingston notes, that the faux public purpose of the corporation's propaganda was to,

"prevent "unproductive" investments...They [the corporations] did not want to give small entrepreneurs the opportunity to convert redundant currency [i.e. small business profits] into capital, [investments] to undertake "unproductive" enterprises and thus [create] chronic overproduction....The creators and proponents of the new corporate order based their defense of industrial consolidation on a critique of the competitive-entrepreneurial regime....because it produced chronic overproduction...."

The logical solution to the economic problem of small business "overproduction," for the corporations, according to Livingston was "centralization of financial responsibility," whose power over the money supply would eliminate capital investments by small businesses.

Livingston explains, that from the perspective of corporations,

"If individual banks were granted the power of note issuance on their general assets, [called free banking] small or regional entrepreneurs would be able to convert currency [profits] into capital…a central bank that had a monopoly on the right of note issuance was critical to the restriction of unproductive capital investments [by entrepreneurs]… the overthrow of the competitive entrepreneurial regime could not be completed unless the banking system, which converted the savings of society into investments was managed by the large corporations." [the Third National Bank].

During the early period of the Gilded Age, before corporations became "persons," the Ruling Class business elite had allegiance to the domestic economy, because most of their investments were in physical capital, like railroads and steel mills, located in the geographic territory of the United States.

What changed, during the corporation's transition to a global imperial power, after they gained the legal rights of persons, was that monopoly capitalism shifted its allegiance from the U. S. markets to making money in the global market.

In other words, the corporations were becoming citizens of the "world," and did not exist to promote the general social welfare of American common citizens.

The corporations gained legal rights, in 1882, without any concomitant responsibility or obligations to promote the "general social welfare," under Madison's vacuous statement in the Preamble, to "promote the general Welfare, and secure the Blessings of Liberty," because "We, the People" did not have a constitutional enforcement mechanism to control Leviathan.

The new "third national bank" was necessary to provide the supply of capital to monopoly capital corporations, unhindered by diversions of capital to small businesses.

According to Richard Franklin Bensel, in The Political Economy of American Industrialization, 1877 - 1900, (Cambridge University Press, 2000.),

"To understand the relationship between industrialization and the financial system...the high rate of capital investment [in U. S. corporations] depended on the stability of the American financial markets, which in turn rested on the stability of the dollar and the relative absence of political uncertainty with regard to taxation, military adventures... Adherence to the international gold standard minimized the political risk associated with American investment...As a result, both domestic and foreign investors could hold American securities, without worrying whether central state exchange rate policies would unpredictably affect their value...Investment capital thus moved into and through the US in two distinct streams investment from across the Atlantic, and investment capital from the relatively developed and capital rich East into the developing [Western] regions."

We argue that the transition to global imperialism of corporations, at the end of the Gilded Age, changed, permanently, the structure of the U. S. economy, by disintegrating the supply chains and small business inter-industry relationships that existed prior to the transition to global imperialism.

In the earlier period, the more integrated supply chains of the domestic economy tended to transmit income and employment multipliers to a greater proportion of the economy, which benefitted small companies, and common citizens.

As the transition to monopoly capitalism occurred during the end of the Gilded Age, the large corporations internalized the flow of income multipliers within their own monopoly corporate structures, leaving out income and employment multipliers for small companies, who were not plugged into the monopoly corporations supply chains.

In other words, as we argued in Diagram 4, in Chapter 6, above, the economic growth benefitted the social welfare of the Ruling Class, and did not benefit the great majority of the U. S. population, at the turn of the century.

Douglas Steeples and David Whitten, in Democracy in Desperation: The Depression of 1893, (Greenwood Press, 1998.), write,

In 1904, more than a third of the combinations were monopolistic in intent…319 firms controlled 40 % of all manufacturing assets in the US…a single firm generated 60% or more of output in one industrial sector.

The economic concentration of production and capital increased the severity and duration of the economic depressions that were a recurring feature of monopoly capitalism.

To reiterate the argument of Kenneth Arrow, made in Chapter 6, the defect in Madison's constitution caused infinite regress of economic collapse in the American economy, because Madison's Preamble did not contain an unambiguous goal of economic growth.

As Livingston notes,

"Throughout the nineties, the business cycle operated as a catalyst accelerating the process of social transformation. …The nation that emerged from depression in 1897 was distinctively different from that of 1893….depression was so conspicuous in the timing, amplitude, and content of those changes."

The term 'business cycles" used by the National Bureau of Economic Research (NBER), is accurate to describe the pattern of economic collapse, about every ten years. Business cycle is the same descriptive term as Arrow's infinite regress because the economy cycles from boom to bust, on a regular basis.

There is no logical economic reason, or theoretical justification, of the American boom-bust economy. A different Preamble, and a different configuration of constitutional rules would produce better economic outcomes, where no person could be made better off, without harming the welfare of another person.

The monopoly capitalism caused by Madison's constitution, in conjunction with the treatment of corporations as "persons," is contrasted with Jefferson's American Dream of entrepreneurial capitalism, in A Government Out of Sight: The Mystery of National Authority in Nineteenth-Century America, by Brian Balogh, (Cambridge University Press, 2009.).

Balogh notes,

"The conceptual conflict between a nation of independent yeoman who required little or no government hierarchy and a state bent on consolidation for the benefit of the few…[Jefferson's Dream] argued that enterprising citizens could create value, value that the larger community would ultimately share. Wealth…produced more wealth in the form of capital investment…Jefferson envisioned a republic populated by independent farmers tied to their country and wedded to its liberty and interests by the most lasting bonds… a nation of one heart and one mind."

The glue that held Madison's Dream together was the cultural value of shared plunder by the Ruling Class, now emerging as a corporate imperial power, which required a new national bank to reach the full potential of global greatness.

Or, as Balogh notes, in Madison's Dream,

"[Financial] Interest replaced virtue as the glue that connected citizens to their government." [plunder].

Chapter 8. The Creation of the Federal Reserve Bank.

Our argument regarding American economic history is that there is a historical continuity about the power and privileges of the Ruling Class, which we describe as W. J. Cash's thesis of the return to the plantation.

We argue that the creation of the Federal Reserve Bank, in 1913, fits into our historical economic continuity thesis. The members of the Board of Governors of the Federal Reserve are private wealthy citizens, who manage a private corporation, for the benefit of private banks, large corporations, and wealthy families.

This set of the Ruling Class has a social class awareness of their power and privileges gained under Madison's constitutional rules that created a plutocracy.

Middle class and working class common citizens do not have a social class awareness of their own financial interests, and thus, the Ruling Class has no comparable competitor, or any other organized competitor political interest group, such as the Ruling Class' American Bankers Association, to promote their group financial interests.

According to C. B. MacPherson, in The Political Theory of Possessive Individualism: From Hobbes to Locke, (Oxford University Press, 1962.),

"It was not that the interests of the laboring class were subordinated to the national interest. The laboring class was not considered to have an interest; the only interest was the ruling-class view of the national interest."

During the plunder and investment speculation phase of the U. S. economy, the Board of Governors are directly responsible for causing the economic conditions of inflation and easy credit by their manipulation of interest rates and bank reserve requirements.

Their poor economic decisions, over the past 110 years, have caused the economy to collapse, on a regular, periodic basis. After each collapse, the Board of Governors act to restore the banks and corporations to their former economic social status by bailing them out.

We apply the theory of public choice, of James Buchanan, to argue that the social welfare that the Board of Governors maximizes is the social welfare of the Ruling Class.

Our argument about the Board of Governors social welfare preferences are very easy to understand. All of them were born in the Northeast, all of them attended Ivy League colleges, and all of them were employed by private banks, before their tenure at the Federal Reserve Bank.

All of them view the world and the U. S. economy from the perspective of doing what is good for the Ruling Class. Not one of them is an ordinary, middle class American citizen, and none of them were elected.

Our argument is not about who "owns" the Fed.

Our argument follows the logic of Madison that the Ruling Class, back in 1787, had a coherent vision of themselves, called a social class consciousness.

Because of their social class consciousness, Madison ascribed to the natural aristocracy a social class moral characteristic of "virtue," that meant that if the Ruling Class obtained disproportionate constitutional power, that their virtue would allow them to put the public's interest above their own personal financial interests.

We argue that the Ruling Class does, in fact, have a coherent world perspective of themselves. Our argument is that the Ruling Class does not possess virtue, and that their decisions on the Federal Reserve Board of Governors reflect their social class preferences.

Further, we argue that middle class, and working class American citizens never developed a class consciousness of their own financial and political interests, which Madison had expected the common citizens to develop.

In the constitutional framework of the plutocracy, the only preferences that count are Ruling Class preferences, because they are the only social class in American history that is organized politically to seek their preferences.

The creation of the third national bank followed the creation of the first National Bank, called the Bank of the United States in 1791, which obtained a 20-year charter, granted by the U. S. Congress.

The Second National Bank was chartered by Congress in 1816, and was killed by Andrew Jackson, in 1833. When Jackson killed the Bank, he stated,

"Many of our rich men have not been content with equal protection and equal benefits, but have besought us to make them richer by act of Congress [the Bank]…we can at least take a stand against all new grants of monopolies and exclusive privileges, against any prostitution of our government to the advancement of the few at the expense of the many."

The period of time, from 1833, to the creation of the third national bank, in 1913, was called the "free banking era" because there was no powerful central bank to control the issuance of debt and credit by the state banks, or nationally-chartered, banks.

In other words, banks were "free" to issue whatever loans they wanted to, which was a proximate cause of the plunder and investment speculation in the Gilded Age, which caused the recurrent economic collapses during that period.

Unlike the creation of the third bank, in 1913, the creation of the first two banks involved transparent political debate about the social class privileges obtained by the Ruling Class in the operation of the national banks, and the role that the banks played in the credit and debt economy, on behalf of the Ruling Class.

The third bank was created in secrecy, at a remote island, off the coast of Georgia, appropriately called "Jekyll Island."

The participants in the secret meetings were bank owners of the four biggest banks in the nation, a powerful Ruling Class U. S. Senator, and a senior officer of the U. S. Treasury Department.

The creation of the third bank fits the story line of the book, "The Strange Case of Dr. Jekyll and Mr. Hyde," because the bank's public purpose had a dual personality: outwardly good, but sometimes shockingly evil, behind the scenes.

Our historical analysis of the creation of the third bank begins when Madison left his meeting, in Annapolis, in 1786, with the trade commissioners of five states.

Ostensibly, the meeting in Annapolis was to solve problems of interstate trade, and national commercial transactions, under the Articles of Confederation.

Madison, and Hamilton, who attended the Annapolis Convention, agreed that the Articles of Confederation were hopelessly inadequate to meet the financial purposes of the natural aristocracy.

Hamilton had prepared a long document, in 1780, explaining the need for a national central bank, which would serve the interests of Madison's natural aristocracy.

Hamilton was particularly fond of the Bank of England, as a model for the first national bank.

Hamilton wrote,

"The Bank of England unites public authority and faith with private credit, and hence we see what a vast fabric of paper credit is raised on a visionary basis."

Hamilton described national debt as a "blessing," and he was correct.

The debt of the nation was a blessing for England's ruling class, who owned most of the American debt, and for the natural aristocracy in America, who used the national debt to speculate on worthless investments.

National debt, and the credit system of the banks, was not a blessing for common citizens because common citizens did not have circulating currency, or access to credit, to pay their taxes and debts.

Hamilton revised his 1780 document into a political document, in 1791, to convince George Washington to support the creation of the First National Bank.

Jefferson did not prepare a competitor document against the creation of the Bank, and lost the political battle with Hamilton over the first Bank.

When they left Annapolis, Madison and Hamilton intended to overthrow the Articles, and replace the Articles with a government that was ruled on behalf of the natural aristocracy.

Hamilton knew, in 1787, that the new government required a central national bank to be an effective agent of the Ruling Class, and he and Madison both knew that they needed some big-time propaganda strategy that would justify the creation of a national bank.

Both Madison and Hamilton also knew that they would have to disobey the resolution of Congress, in 1787, in order to overthrow the Articles at the Philadelphia convention.

Congress had instructed Madison to preserve the Articles of Confederation, and the instructions included the provision that any revisions to the Articles must be approved by the legislatures of the states.

Congress had resolved, on February 21, 1787,

"Resolved that in the opinion of Congress it is expedient that on the second Monday in May next a Convention of delegates who shall have been appointed by the several States be held at Philadelphia *for the sole and express purpose of revising the Articles of Confederation* and reporting to Congress and the several legislatures such alterations and provisions therein as shall *when agreed to in Congress* and confirmed by the States [legislatures] render the federal Constitution adequate to the exigencies of Government and the preservation of the Union." [emphasis added].

They found their propaganda justification to overthrow the Articles, in Shay's Rebellion.

One of the purposes of the new government, according to Madison's Preamble, was to "insure domestic tranquility."

In August of 1786, farmers in western Massachusetts began to take direct action against debtors' courts, who were issuing court orders to confiscate the land of the farmers, who had failed to pay their debt and taxes.

The farmer's first strategy was to prevent the judges from entering the court houses, so that the judges could not issue their orders to take the farmer's lands.

The farmer's revolt was very threatening to the status quo political privileges of the Ruling Class, because the social class conflict arguments being made by the farmers were similar to the class conflict arguments being made by common citizens in Europe to overthrow the monarchies.

According to the internet website, History.com,

"Henry Knox, an artillery commander during the Revolutionary war and the future first U.S. Secretary of War, wrote to George Washington in 1786 to warn him about the rebels [farmers]:

"[T]hey [the farmers] see the weakness of Government and they feel at once their own poverty compared with the opulent, [Ruling Class] and their own force, and they are determined to make use of the latter in order to remedy the former."

The farmers in Massachusetts were engaged in a tax revolt against the Ruling Class, in Boston, for the same causes that Southern farmers, during the Gilded Age, were engaged in a revolt against the southern neo-Slaveocracy.

Not only were the northern farmers, in 1786, refusing to pay taxes, even worse they were attempting to pay taxes and debts with worthless state-issued paper currency, and not in gold and silver, the preferred medium of exchange of the Ruling Class.

After the Civil War, farmers in the South, could not pay their debts and taxes because there was no currency, and there was no gold or silver for the farmers to obtain to pay taxes and debts because the economy ran on debt and credit, not on cash.

When the farmers in the South did not pay their taxes, because there was no currency, their lands were confiscated by the elite, and the farmers entered a new form of Cash's return to the plantation called "debt-peonage."

In the North, about 80 years earlier, when the farmers could not pay their taxes and debts, their farms were confiscated by the elites. In the North, the farmer's return to the plantation was called "debtor's prison."

We argue that there is historical continuity for the causes and the consequences of for farmer's revolt in both eras. In both eras, the solution to the farmer's revolt, for the Ruling Class, was the creation of a powerful, privately-owned bank corporation.

Madison turned Shay's Rebellion into a propaganda tool for the natural aristocracy to instill panic in the society that the "Union" was imperiled by the farmer's revolt.

The use of propaganda panic, in 1787, by the Ruling Class elite is very reminiscent of the Covid panic and the panic of the January 6, 2021, protest over the election coup, by the deep state elite, today, to accomplish the transition to a global Marxist tyranny.

Back then, the Ruling Class called the farmers "insurrectionists," and many of the elite, then, called for the traitors to be executed. The goal, then, was to overthrow Jefferson's constitutional natural rights republic, in order to transition the government to Madison's aristocratic Leviathan.

Today, the January 6 protesters are deemed insurrectionists, and the protesters are held, without due process, in solitary confinement.

The goal of the panic propaganda of the Marxist Democrats, today, is to overthrow Madison's representative republic, in order to obtain control over Madison's deep state Leviathan.

As we have noted in our argument in favor of Cash's historical continuity thesis, the pattern of events, for the Ruling Class aristocracy in creating the Federal Reserve, follows a historically observable path.

First, banks and the U. S. Treasury Department create too much money, and too much loose credit.

The era of loose credit causes the Ruling Class to plunder national financial resources, and make worthless investments that do not create "real" economic growth. But, the loose credit does allow the Ruling Class to rack up incredible profits during the bubble part of the era of plunder.

The era of plunder, and investment speculation, ends in economic collapse, where common citizens suffer social welfare declines, while the Ruling Class escapes unharmed, because crony capitalism allows the government to bail them out, and make them "whole" again from their losses.

The period of economic collapse is preceded by a sharp contraction of both credit and the money supply, which causes commodity prices of farmers to collapse, and the income of common citizens to decline.

The return to the plantation occurs when the elite resume their former positions in the economy, and restore the social class status quo ante by further impoverishing the common citizens.

Then, the entire process renews, again, in what Kenneth Arrow called "infinite regress."

The creation of the Federal Reserve Bank fits into this economic pattern.

The economy collapsed in 1893, and the depression, called "one of the worst" in U. S. economic history, lasted about 4 years.

Then, about 10 years later, in 1907, the economy collapsed again, and the depression lasted about 7 years, to around 1914.

The panic of 1907 started when the credit issued by Knickerbocker Trust to commercial businesses turned out to be worthless. Knickerbocker's bank debt assets were secured by worthless business assets.

Knickerbocker needed a bailout, and approached the New York Clearing House for a loan and was denied.

This bailout denial created a big financial problem for the owners of Knickerbocker because, under free banking, shareholders of the bank faced double liability.

If a bank failed, the shareholders could be forced to pay an additional assessment in order to compensate depositors and other creditors.

In other words, the owners lost both the value of their investment in the bank, and also faced double liability to compensate depositors, who lost their savings when the bank went bust.

The intent of the banking reform, beginning with the Aldrich-Vreeland Act, aimed at eliminating this double liability of bank shareholders, but the creation of the FDIC required another economic collapse, in 1929, to be implemented.

Like the delegation of Congressional authority to the Federal Reserve Bank to coin money, the Federal Reserve subsequently re-delegated the double liability of bank collapse back to an independent government agency, in 1933, called The Federal Deposit Insurance Corporation,

The two banking reform acts, the Fed, in 1913, in conjunction with the FDIC, in 1933, created a new type of "free banking," where banks gained freedom of liability from wrongful acts committed against the depositors.

As we noted above, after the creation of the Fed, increased government spending on the military-industrial complex, at the beginning of a war, tended to bring the economy out of collapse, but generally, not for very long.

The increased government spending on guns versus private sector capital investment, does not create lasting economic growth, unless of course, there happens to be the coincidence of a series of new wars to continue to spend more government money on wars.

Members of Congress had noticed this pattern of routine, periodic, economic collapse, and beginning in 1907, Congress passed a law, titled The Aldrich-Vreeland Act, to study the pattern of collapse and to prepare a report to Congress on solutions to the economic instability.

The Act had several components, in addition to creation of the National Monetary Commission.

One of the provisions of the Act was to provide an emergency injection of currency into the economy [bailout] in order to permit national banks to issue additional security on bonds of states, cities, towns, and counties, as well as private commercial paper, secured by the corporate promise that their investments would yield "real" economic growth.[real bills doctrine].

Michael Bordo and William Roberds, in A Return to Jekyll Island. The Origins, History, and Future of the Federal Reserve. (Cambridge University Press, 2013.), describe the motive to form the Aldrich-Vreeland Commission.

They write,

"Following the Panic of 1907, Congress passed the Aldrich-Vreeland Act of 1908…Senator Nelson W. Aldrich (R-RI) was largely responsible for the Aldrich-Vreeland Currency Law and became the Chairman of the National Monetary commission. The co-sponsor of the legislation was Representative Edward Vreeland, a Republican from New York…By 1910, the 18-member commission could not agree on a plan [to create a more stable national economy]."

Bordo and Roberds note that Aldrich was frustrated by the Commission's lack of progress, and decided to pursue an independent, personal, secret initiative, directly with four of the biggest banks to create a central bank.

As they note, the Aldrich initiative required utmost secrecy to avoid alerting foes of their plan to create a national bank.

They write,

"Aldrich was well aware that his meeting with bankers outside of the commission proceedings [beyond consent] would generate controversy, for that reason the group met in [secret] in a private remote location."

Part of the secrecy of the group was an early agreement to call the new bank the "Federal Reserve," and not a "National Central Bank."

Another part of their secrecy was to only call themselves by their first names in meetings and in public.

To this end, members of the Jekyll Island group traveled to Jekyll Island by first name only.

Aldrich was not an ordinary, middle-class citizen. He was a powerful member of the Northeastern ruling class. He was referred to by the press and public alike as the "general manager of the Nation."

As we noted above, we rely on the description of the Ruling Class by Angelo Codevilla, who wrote,

"The American ruling class is the set of citizens in the Northeast who live in the same neighborhoods, go to the same universities, join the same social business networks and marry each other, [in order to inbreed.] (The Ruling Class: How They Corrupted America and What We Can Do About It. Angelo M. Codevilla, Beaufort Books, 2010.)

For example, Aldrich's daughter, Abigail married American banker John Davison Rockefeller Jr., who was the son of Standard Oil co-founder John D. Rockefeller.

Aldrich owned his own rail car, and was also a member of an exclusive social club, located on Jekyll Island. The other attendees of the meeting rode down to Jekyll Island on Aldrich's train car.

Attending the Jekyll Island meeting with Aldrich were:

• Prominent European banker and Kuhn, Loeb, & Co. partner Paul Warburg, who would later serve on the Federal Reserve's first Board of Governors, and whose knowledge of European central banking was crucial to the meeting's success. [because the model of the U. S. central bank looked just like the Bank of England.]

• J.P. Morgan & Co. senior partner Henry Davison.

• National City Bank of New York president Frank Vanderlip.

• Banker's Trust of New York vice president Benjamin Strong, who would later head the Federal Reserve Bank of New York.

• A. Piatt Andrew, Assistant Secretary of the Treasury.

Attendee Frank Vanderlip later wrote in his autobiography,

"None of us who participated [in the secret meeting] felt we were conspirators; on the contrary we felt we were engaged in patriotic work... Yet, who was there in Congress [elected representatives] who might have drafted a sound piece of legislation dealing with the purely banking [Ruling Class] problem with which we were concerned?"

We agree with Vanderlip. Their patriotic work was based upon their understanding of Madison's version of the American Dream of a plutocratic society.

Plus, as he noted, no one in Congress was competent to draft the legislation that met the needs of the Ruling Class.

At the meeting on Jekyll Island, Paul Warburg introduced a plan that was modeled on European central banks. The European banks were privately owned, and operated independent [beyond the consent of citizens] of the national governments of Europe.

The primary function of the European banks was to act as a "reserve" bank to provide regional banks with reserves to meet economic emergencies, and to rapidly increase the money supply to provide liquidity to avoid a run on the bank's deposits.

Thus, the origin of the term "Federal Reserve."

In 1914, when Benjamin Strong left Bankers Trust Company to preside as the first Governor of the Federal Reserve Bank of New York, Strong stated that he,

"Wanted to endow the New York Fed with the dignity and prestige of the Bank of England."

According to James Livingston, in Origins of the Federal Reserve System, Money, Class, and Corporate Capitalism, 1890-1913, (Cornell University Press, 1986.) Warburg intended to eliminate small business as a source of competition for capital, with Big Business.

As we noted above, the general consensus of the Ruling Class, during the collapse of 1893, was that loans to small, entrepreneurial companies, were "unproductive," and tended to create the economic condition of "over production," which was the primary Ruling Class explanation for the periodic economic collapses.

Warburg's proposal aimed at granting power to the Federal Reserve to deny credit to small businesses, based upon the Fed's rules of the credit worthiness of small business loans.

According to Livingston,

"Warburg proposed to separate the money and capital markets by using the central bank to redefine acceptable bank assets, making it virtually impossible for small entrepreneurs to obtain capital to make investments in "unproductive" enterprises."

In other words, under the "Real Bills Doctrine," only loans to Big Business created real economic growth. Loans to small businesses created over production.

Livingston notes the prevailing Ruling Class animosity to small business entrepreneurs by citing an editorial in the leading Business Magazine, in 1907:

"From the standpoint of the corporate-industrial business community, the magazine defined as a benefit [of a central bank] was precisely the problem with assets currency [providing small business with capital]... it would apparently benefit mainly small or marginal producers. Asset currency would not meet the requirements of an investment system dominated by large industrial corporations." [global imperial corporations].

Warburg explained that his reason for creating the central bank was to control loans of regional banks to small business, by noting that,

"If individual banks were granted the power of note issuance on their general assets, small or regional entrepreneurs would be able to convert currency [small business profits] into capital. [to make investments]. A central bank that had a monopoly on the right of note issuance was critical to the restriction of unproductive capital investment." [by small entrepreneurial businesses].

Aldrich had previously toured central banks in Europe, and he agreed with Warburg that the European central banking model was worthy of emulation.

Aldrich was particularly fond of the feature of the private European central banks that their deliberations were secret, and not publically transparent. He intended to replicate this feature of secrecy of the Fed, in his ensuing Congressional legislation, called the "Aldrich Plan."

In other words, not only was the meeting on Jekyll Island to create the Fed a secret, but the future deliberations of the Fed's Board of Governors would also be secret, when they met to manipulate interest rates and the money supply. [coin money].

The participants in the meeting discussed how to evade the Constitutional provision in Article I, Section 8, whose first clause states,

"The Congress shall have Power To lay and collect Taxes, Duties, Imposts and Excises, to pay the Debts and provide for the common Defence and general Welfare of the United States; but all Duties, Imposts and Excises shall be uniform throughout the United States;"

The fifth clause of Article I, states,

"[The Congress shall have the Power] To coin Money, regulate the Value thereof, and of foreign Coin, and fix the Standard of Weights and Measures;"

According to the internet website, Constitution Annotated,

"The power "to coin money" and "regulate the value thereof" has been broadly construed to authorize regulation of every phase of the subject of currency. Congress may charter banks and endow them with the right to issue circulating notes, and it may restrain the circulation of notes not issued under its own authority."

The reason for the delicacy of public disclosure and secrecy of the Jekyll Island group related to their intent to replicate the European central bank model, which could easily be construed, by their foes, as the intent to subvert the authority of Congress, and the Constitution.

Upon their return to Washington, the Jekyll Island group began a public relations campaign headed by Warburg, and funded by Big Banks, to promote the "Aldrich Plan."

At the time, Senator Carter Glass, a Democrat of Virginia, opposed the Aldrich Plan.

Glass stated:

"We object to the Aldrich Bill on the following points:

Its entire lack of adequate government or public control of the banking mechanism it sets up.

Its tendency to throw voting control into the hands of the large banks of the system.

The extreme danger of inflation of currency inherent in the system.

The insincerity of the bond-funding plan provided for by the measure, there being a barefaced pretense that this system was to cost the government nothing.

The dangerous monopolistic aspects of the bill."

At the same time that Senator Glass was making his case against the Aldrich Plan, another committee, in the House, released its findings on the existence of a "Money Trust," in the American economy.

The Pujo Committee, a subcommittee of the House Banking Committee, found that:

"If by a 'money trust' is meant an established and well-defined identity and community of interest between a few leaders of finance ... which has resulted in a vast and growing concentration of control of money and credit in the hands of a comparatively few men ... the condition thus described exists in this country today ... To us the peril is manifest ... When we find ... the same man a director in a half dozen or more banks and trust companies all located in the same section of the same city, doing the same class of business and with a like set of associates similarly situated all belonging to the same group and representing the same class of interests, all further pretense of competition is useless."

The language that we use in our historical economic continuity thesis to describe an "established and well-defined identity and community of interest between a few leaders of finance," is the "Ruling Class."

The established and well-defined identity of the Banking Trust had a community of interest that we call social class consciousness.

Our thesis of the social class consciousness of the Ruling Class explains the reason for the on-going history of economic collapse in the United States. Rather than virtue, their decisions reflect their social class ideology to protect their financial interests.

In 1914, the U. S. economy collapsed again, about 7 years after the collapse of 1907.

According to Marycela Diaz-Unzalu, of the Atlanta Regional Federal Reserve Bank, in her power point presentation for teachers and educators to use to educate young people about the secret meeting on Jekyll Island, [no date provided].

"In 1914 when the first great financial panic of the 20th century befell the world, necessitating the closure of the New York Stock Exchange. Secretary of the Treasury William Gibbs McAdoo appeared in New York City and assured the public that ample stocks of emergency banknotes had been prepared in accordance with the Aldrich–Vreeland Act and were available for issue to the banks. [bailout]. The crisis abated only when three events took place:

• the U.S. Treasury intervened [to add reserves to the banking system].

• John D. Rockefeller contributed $10 million of his own fortune [to the reserves].

• J.P. Morgan, acting as self-appointed head of the financial system, prevailed on solvent New York City financial institutions, including his own, to extend a total of $25 million in emergency funds.

• Secretary of the Treasury George Cortelyou's $25 million pledge of government funds shored up deposits in New York City banks, and the efforts of J.P. Morgan prevented a complete shutdown of the city's stock exchanges.

• Morgan's leadership also included the creation of a public relations campaign to help calm the public's fears about the economy and the financial system. John D. Rockefeller's personal contributions served to bolster the reserves of the National City Bank of New York, ensuring the solvency of the institution which is known as Citibank today."

We note, in passing, that the set of Ruling Class elites and banks who attended the Jekyll Island meeting to come up with the Aldrich Plan also participated in the banking rescue mission, during the collapse of 1914.

We also note, in passing, the odd treatment of the Jekyll Island meeting by Marycela Diaz-Unzalu, in her educational power point, where she emphasizes the instruction of the natural beauty and history of Jekyll Island.

She concludes her power point with the following advice to teachers:

"Handout 1: Explore Jekyll Island.

Island history:

1. Where is Jekyll Island located?

2. Who were the first visitors to the island? Why did the Spanish call Jekyll Island "Isla de Ballenas"?

3. What important events happened on the island in 1733 and 1734?

4. What was the Wanderer? What happened to those involved in bringing it to Jekyll Island?

Club history:

1. How did Munsey's Magazine describe the Jekyll Island Club? What members' names are recognizable to you?

2. What was the result of the meeting held on the island following the Panic of 1907?

3. What important milestone occurred at Jekyll in 1915?

4. Why is it ironic to call the homes built on the island "cottages"? In what styles were some of the most prominent homes built?"

In his book, Inflated: How Money and Debt Built the American Dream, R. Christopher Whalen, (John Wiley & Sons 2010.), cites the economic research of Nouriel Roubini on the cause of American business cycles.

Whalen writes,

"In Roubini's opinion, much of the current recession's cause [after the 2008 collapse] is due to "boom-and-bust cycles," and he feels the US economy needs to find a different growth path in the future. "We've been growing through a period of time of repeated big bubbles," he said. "We've had a model of 'growth' based on overconsumption and lack of savings. And now that model has broken down because we borrowed too much."

Roubini's analysis of the boom and bust economy is similar to our own analysis of plunder and collapse, but we tend to emphasize the social class political dynamics of the Ruling Class, as an explanation of the cause of economic collapse, more than he does.

According to Whalen,

"Roubini [explains] that repeated cycles of asset bubbles and credit bubbles, leading to financial crisis, is driven by excessive debt and leverage in the private sector leading to excessive public sector debt accumulation, via socialization of private losses, [crony capitalism] that leads to twin risks of outright default or the use of the inflation tax through monetization of fiscal deficits at the federal level."

Roubini uses the royal "We," similar in historical context to Madison's use of the term, "We, the people." We, the people did not borrow too much, and We, the people" did not create the inflation tax by monetizing the Federal debt.

The responsibility for too much debt and too much money rests with the Ruling Class elites who control the Federal Reserve Board of Governors and each of the 12 elites who serve as Presidents, on the regional banks.

There is no macro economic theoretical reason why the U. S. economy traces out a recurring pattern of economic collapse. A free, competitive entrepreneurial economy, would trace out an economic growth pattern to a point of Pareto Optimality.

Roubini can identify that too much money and too much loose credit leads to economic collapse, but fails to explain the cause of too much money and too much easy credit.

We rely on the theoretical work of James Buchanan, a past professor of George Mason University, who explained that Ruling Class elites are maximizing the social welfare of the social class to which they belong.

Buchanan addressed this issue of the Ruling Class social class self interest, in his book, The Theory of Public Choice, II, (University of Michigan Press, 1984.).

Buchanan explained that once a government bureaucracy is created, that is removed from the consent of the governed, the bureaucracy develops its own interpretation of the social welfare function it presumes to maximize.

If the bureaucracy was created to serve the needs of a special financial interest group, such as the banking industry, then that group's personal private preferences become the surrogate social welfare function of all citizens.

As Buchanan has pointed out, that surrogate social welfare function contains variables that promote the welfare of the politicians and bureaucrats who created it.

The welfare function that they maximize turns out to be their own. The Ruling Class social welfare function is not subjected to on-going citizen consent, sunset or recall.

The bureaucracy, in this case, The Fed, becomes a permanent feature of Madison's Ruling Class plutocracy.

We apply Buchanan's Public Choice theory to the operation and social class function of the Fed, in our article, "Does the Fed's Job Performance Justify Its Independence? (Laurie Thomas Vass, Social Science Research Network (SSRN), 2019.).

On its website, the Fed states that their decisions are independent and objective, and are, "based on the best interests of the nation, not the interests of a small group of politicians."

This argument by the Fed is intended to justify its independence to make decisions that improve the social welfare of all citizens.

We would modify their statement to read, "not the interests of a small group of politicians," to the interests of "a small group of bankers." [12 of them to be exact].

Our counter-argument against the Fed's independence is based upon our observation that the workings and functions of the free, competitive market would lead to better Pareto Optimal social welfare outcomes than the private, secret, decisions of 12 members of the Ruling Class.

There is nothing in Madison's framework of checks and balances that authorizes citizens to restore the Fed's mission back to Jefferson's original goal of improving economic growth rates of the domestic U. S. entrepreneurial capitalist economy.

Our argument concludes that the Fed's economic performance has resulted in a systematic series of boom-bust cycles, where the financial welfare of common citizens is devastated, while the privileged wealthy elite bankers escape unharmed.

We conclude that the Fed's arbitrary discretion to manipulate the economy by setting interest rates and manipulating the supply of money, must be taken away from them.

A better goal for national economic policy is to target increased rates of gross domestic private business investment, which leads to high rates of technological innovation, which create new future markets, which reduce wealth and income inequality.

We write, in our article,

"Since 1947, the Fed has manufactured a series of asset bubbles, caused by a sequence of easy money, followed by a policy of tight money, primarily by raising the rate of interest on overnight bank deposits, that are held at the 12 regional Fed banks…

The sequence of events is initiated by a Fed announcement that it is considering lowering interest rates to promote aggregate economic demand. The announcement, itself, not the Fed's actual interest rate adjustment, causes increased speculation among bankers and the Ruling Class investors, who bid up the price on fixed assets, primarily bonds and real estate, held in the accounts of the most wealthy citizens and banks. In other words, by announcing its intentions, the Fed initially acts to benefit the financial interests of the wealthy class, because the market price of fixed assets goes up when interest rates decline. The Fed repeatedly overshoots the interest rate target, resulting in rampant inflation, which the Fed is required by law, to control. As a result, the Fed tightens money supply, the economy contracts, and inflation is brought under control."

Our argument about the Fed's abysmal job performance can be observed with the benefit of statistical hindsight.

The Federal Reserve Bank of St. Louis publishes the GDP-Based Recession Indicator Index, which looks at past economic data and measures the probability that the U.S. economy was in a recession during the indicated quarter.

The statistical hindsight of the St. Louis Fed is better than the real-time NBER estimate of the beginning of a recession which is based upon contemporaneous subjective data, which are usually not released to the public for several years.

The Fed Index describes a perfectly symmetrical, recurring five year cycle of Fed induced economic chaos. The great benefit of this index is that its construction is entirely mechanical, and is based solely on real, not subjective, GDP data.

The Fed's data indicates that after 1970, the frequency of economic collapse increased, from the historical average of one every 10 years, to one economic collapse every five years.

Diagram 6. St. Louis Federal Reserve Bank GDP-Based Recession Indicator Index. 1967 – 2020.

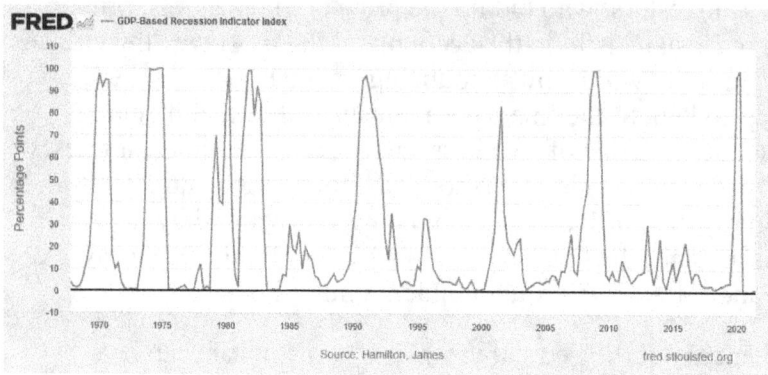

The economic performance of the Fed, described in the index, is not "based on the best interests of the nation," their performance is based upon stabilizing the global economy, and rewarding wealthy global banks, through a coordinated central bank global policy of asset-based speculation.

The welfare function being maximized by the Fed is not a Bergsonian national social welfare function, it is, instead, a James Buchanan selfish private welfare function of 5 private banks, who became co-equal partners with the Fed, after the 2008 Fed-induced chaos.

The financial focus of the Big 5 banks is global in operation, not the sovereign domestic financial interests of American citizens. Their financial focus is based upon a shared cultural world view of what is in the best financial interests of the global Ruling Class.

In his 2013 comments about the Fed's bailout of Big Banks, after the 2008 economic collapse, Richard Fisher, former President and CEO of the Federal Reserve Bank of Dallas, stated,

"I will argue that the big banks represent not only a threat to financial stability (of the U. S. economy), but to fair and open competition, that they are the practitioners of crony capitalism and not the agents of democratic capitalism that makes our country great."

Prior to the 2008 collapse, the biggest 5 banks owned about 41% of all domestic financial assets.

After 2008, the 5 banks owned 49% of all U. S. domestic assets. The increase in assets of the 5 banks is entirely due to the Fed's policy decisions to eliminate small banks, in order to consolidate power in the 5 big banks.

The chairmen of the Fed, and the Secretary of the Treasury, during the time of the 2008 crisis were former employees of the 5 big banks.

Fisher noted that there are about 6000 smaller, regional banks, and 10 big banks, primarily located in New York, who obtain special banking privileges at the Fed's New York Federal Open Market window.

As a result of their privileged status at the Fed's Open Market Window, the big banks obtain an insurance policy from the Fed that insulates them from credit risk, and the economic chaos inflicted on ordinary American citizens, by the Fed's boom-bust policies.

Fisher explained,

"A dozen megabanks today control almost 70 percent of the assets in the U.S. banking industry. The concentration of assets has been ongoing, but it intensified during the 2008-09 financial crisis, when several failing giants were absorbed by larger, presumably healthier ones. [crony capitalism]. Today, these megabanks—a mere 0.2 percent of banks, deemed candidates to be considered "too big to fail"—are treated differently from the other 99.8 percent and differently from other businesses... Without fear of failure, these banks and their counterparties can take excessive risks."

The Big Banks know that they can take excessive risks, during the plunder-bubble phase, because they know that the Fed will use tax dollars to bail them out when their loans and investments, during the bubble phase of the economy, go bust.

We disagree with Bordo and Roberds, in A Return to Jekyll Island, about the source of economic instability in U. S, economic history.

They believe that the culprit of the boom and bust economy is the Real Bills Doctrine.

They write,

"The Fed was established to bring stability to the US financial system through the creation of an elastic supply of liquidity…the policy tool [FOMC] created to reduce the probability of banking panics, like 1873, 1893 and 1907, became the policy source of the worst economic disaster and banking collapse in American history…The key source of the Fed's error was adherence to the real bills doctrine which failed to distinguish between supply and demand shocks in the loan market or between real and nominal interest rates…The Fed should have should have interpreted the increase in reserves as indicative of a decline in loan supply, [because the banks were holding reserves to earn risk-free interest from the Fed] but instead the Fed saw the increasing reserves as a decline in loan demand, and the Fed accommodated that decline in loan demand." [by jacking up the M-2 money supply].

Their analysis of the Fed's actions is perfect. But, the source of the economic instability is not the Real Bills Doctrine.

The source of economic instability lies in Madison's rules that created a plutocracy, which eventually became a Leviathan disconnected from the consent of the governed.

Our analysis of the pattern of economic collapse is similar to Carmen M. Reinhart and Kenneth S. Rogoff, in their article, "International Aspects of Financial-Market Imperfections: The Aftermath of Financial Crises." (American Economic Review, Vol. 99, No.2. (2009.).

They describe a pattern of money creation, speculation, and economic collapse like Roubini.

They state,

"Severe financial crises share three characteristics:

First, asset market collapses are deep and prolonged. Real housing prices decline an average of 35 percent over six years, while equity prices collapse an average of 55 percent over a downturn of about three and a half years.

Second, the aftermath of banking crises is associated with profound declines in output and employment. The unemployment rate rises an average of 7 percentage points over the down phase of the cycle, which lasts, on average, over four years. In addition, output falls, from peak to trough, an average of over 9 percent, although the duration of the downturn, averaging roughly two years, is considerably shorter than for unemployment.

Third, the real value of government debt tends to explode, rising an average of 86 percent in the major post–World War II episodes…the main cause of debt explosions is not the costs of bailing out and recapitalizing the banking system. The main cause of debt increases are the inevitable collapse in tax revenues that governments incur as a result of deep and prolonged output contractions, and the countercyclical fiscal policies in advanced economies aimed at counteracting the downturn."

Unlike Roubini, who cites the culprit as the real bills doctrine, Reinhart and Rogoff cite the relationship between the economic collapse and the downturn in government tax revenues, as the culprit.

In their telling, the government cannot obtain enough tax revenues, after the collapse, in order to engage in more Fed manipulation of the money supply aimed at "countercyclical fiscal policies aimed at counteracting the downturn."

We argue that the cause of the economic instability is caused by the Fed, Board of Governors who consistently get the monetary policy wrong, primarily because the Fed staff cannot tell the difference between supply and demand.

We agree with George Selgin, William D. Lastrapes, and Lawrence H. White, in their article, "Has the Fed Been a Failure?" (SSRN, 2012.).

They cite a consistent pattern of monetary policy mistakes made by the Fed, over a long period of time. They write,

"Our model also shows no clear improvement after World War II in the dynamic response of output to aggregate demand shocks. Whereas one might expect the Fed, in its role as output stabilizer, to tighten the money supply in the face of positive IS (investment-spending) shocks and to expand it in response to positive shocks to money demand, [LM, liquidity money], the response functions we estimate indicate instead that the Fed has tended to expand the money stock in response to IS shocks, causing larger and more persistent deviations of output from its natural level than would have occurred in response to similar shocks during the pre-Fed period. At the same time, the Fed was less effective than the classical gold standard had been in expanding the money supply in response to unpredictable reductions in money's velocity."

While we agree with their analysis of the Fed's poor performance, they shy away from answering the question that they raise about the Fed' policies after the 2008 collapse.

They ask:

"On what grounds did it [the Fed] determine that Bear Stearns andAIG were too big to fail, while Lehman Brothers was not? Bear Stearns, like Lehman Brothers, was an investment bank, and AIG was an insurance company and CDS issuer…, the Fed has never explained the precise nature of the systemic risk justifying its intervention in these instances. Nor has it ever made public its criteria for determining which failures posed a systemic threat [too big to fail] that could not be handled in classical fashion."

The answer to their question about the bailouts, and why they rescued Bear Stearns and not Lehman, provides the evidence for our argument about the Ruling Class preferences of the Fed lies with the actions of the New York Federal Reserve Bank's Open Market Window.

Bear Stearns was a protected, favored bank of the Ruling Class, while Lehman was not. We argue that the Fed will never reveal this truthful criteria for their bailouts.

We argue that 12 Ruling Class bankers, meeting in secret, to manipulate money and credit do not achieve better welfare outcomes than the free market.

Our argument is similar to John Taylor, in his article, "Systemic Risk and the Role of Government." Speech given at the Conference on Financial Innovation and Crises, Federal Reserve Bank of Atlanta, Jekyll Island, Georgia, May 12th, (2009.).

Taylor writes,

"In short, the Federal Reserve System, as presently constituted, is no more worthy of being regarded as the last word in monetary management than the National Currency System it replaced almost a century ago...More generally, government should set clear rules of the game, stop changing them during the game, and enforce them. The rules do not have to be perfect, but the rule of law is essential."

George Selgin, et. al., also cite the rule of law in their analysis of the Fed's persistent failure. They write,

"At the most philosophical or jurisprudential level, the case for a constitutional constraint on monetary policy-makers derives from the general case for —the rule of law rather than rule by authorities. The rule of law means constraints against arbitrary governance so that citizens can know what to expect from their government."

We slightly disagree. It is not "so that citizens can know what to expect from their government," It is the government of the Ruling Class, that Madison's constitutional rules empowered.

George G. Kaufman, a professor of economics, and consultant to the Chicago Regional Federal Reserve Bank, explained in his 2000 article, "Banking and currency crises and systemic risk: Lessons from recent events (Federal Reserve Bank of Chicago, (first published, 2000.),

"It is a common misconception to think that imposing losses on [bank] management and shareholders, while shielding counterparties and creditors, is enough to contain moral hazard. [plunder]. So long as bank creditors can expect high returns on the upside, with implicit government guarantees against losses on the downside, they will lend too cheaply to risky poorly diversified banks, making overly high leverage (thin capital) [worthless investments] an attractive strategy. Normal market discipline against risk-taking is thus significantly undermined." [because the remaining 5 Big Banks are too-big-to-fail and will be bailed out by the Fed].

The New York FOMC operates without Congressional oversight, entirely disconnected from the consent of the governed, and makes decisions based upon their Ruling Class social backgrounds, not on behalf of the interests of common citizens.

In Lewis v. United States, 680 F.2d 1239 (1982), the U. S. Supreme Court ruled that the regional Federal Reserve Banks are,

"Independent, privately owned and locally controlled corporations", and there is not sufficient "federal government control over 'detailed physical performance' and 'day to day operation'" of the Federal Reserve Bank for it to be considered a federal agency."

As a private, for-profit business, the business model of the regional banks is a fool-proof, guaranteed-profit enterprise, whose operations are guaranteed to make a profit, each year.

First, all banks that desire to affiliate with the Federal Reserve system must join, and buy stock in the corporation.

According to the 2011 GAO Audit of the Fed,

"Member banks must subscribe to stock in their Reserve Bank in an amount that is related to the size of the member bank. Holding of the stock does not confer any rights of ownership and the member bank may not sell or trade the Federal Reserve district bank stock. Member banks receive a statutory fixed annual dividend of 6 percent on their stock and may vote for six of the nine members of the board of directors of the Reserve Bank."

In other words, commercial banks transfer capital to the regional Federal Reserve Banks, based upon the size of the assets of the bank. In exchange for the transfer of capital, the member banks are "guaranteed" a dividend of 6% on their stock.

The regional directors of each bank charge fees for conducting services for the commercial bank members, such as clearing checks and performing consulting services.

The Federal Reserve Bank loans money to the banks, in overnight loans, to help the banks meet the daily reserve requirements, set by the Board of Governors.

The Federal Reserve makes money on its loans to banks called the "discount rate of interest." Whenever the Fed wants to make more money on its loans, it simply raises the discount rate of interest.

The Federal Reserve System also makes a guaranteed profit from the interest paid from owning U.S. Treasury notes it acquired as part of open market operations.

The New York Regional Federal Bank acts as a broker to buy and sell U. S. Treasury notes through its Open Market Window. The New York Regional Bank makes commissions and fees from acting as the broker for the U. S. Treasury.

A great portion of the U. S. Treasury bonds are bought and held by the Federal Reserve Bank.

Currently, of the entire $31 trillion in U. S. debt, the Federal Reserve Banks owns about 20%, on which it receives a guaranteed rate of interest, paid by the U. S. Treasury.

The left hand of the government, the Treasury issues bonds, and the right hand of the Fed buys the bonds, and makes a guaranteed profit. In the language of the Fed, this transaction is called "quantitative easing."

The Fed also receives interest and profits on its foreign currency investments, when the New York Regional Bank engages in foreign currency exchange markets.

Because the U. S. dollar serves as the global reserve currency, the New York FRB is in a perfect position to forecast the movement of the U. S. dollar against other currencies, because the Fed controls the rate of money expansion and money contraction.

In other words, the Fed has a very beneficial insider insight to profit on the currency exchange market because other currency reserves are denominated in U. S. dollars.

The Fed uses its guaranteed profits to pay all of its fixed operational costs, including the lavish salaries of the Directors, professional staff, and Presidents of the Fed and regional banks.

After the Fed pays all of its fixed operational costs, it returns the leftover profits to the U. S. Treasury.

This business model is called "Win-Win," for the Fed and U. S. Treasury.

In 2020, the Fed earned $90.5 billion in profits. Of this, $1.6 billion was paid out in dividends on stock owned by the member commercial banks of the regional Fed banks.

After the payment of corporate operating costs of managing and administering the Fed and the regional banks, the Fed sends the rest of the profits back to the U. S. Treasury.

The right hand of the Fed makes guaranteed profits, and the left hand of the U. S. Treasury obtains the profits from the Fed at the end of each year.

The annual remittance of profits from the Fed back to the U. S. Treasury provides the ideological justification for the Fed's statement that its mission is to serve the public.

In the 2011 GAO Audit of the Fed, the GAO asked each FRB Director in whose financial interests that they served.

The results of the GAO survey are provided below:

Section II: Your Roles and Responsibilities as a FRB Director

We are interested in learning about your duties as a Federal Reserve Bank director.

6. As a FRB Director, which of the following do you primarily represent? (check only one box)

	Frequency	Percent
The public	56	61.54
Your business/company	3	3.3
Banks in your district	23	25.27
Other businesses/companies in your district	3	3.3
Other (please specify below):	6	6.59

Over 61% of the directors said they served the public interest, which is odd, considering that the public does not own stock in the private corporation, and the directors have a legal fiduciary obligation to serve the member bank stockholders.

Over 25% of the directors provided a more transparent and honest answer that they served the member banks who own the stock of the Fed.

We argue that the ideological bias of the Ruling Class Directors of the Fed is easily seen in the beneficiaries of their bailouts, after the collapse of 2008.

The grand total of bailouts of the Fed, according to the sparse data released by the GAO audit, appears to be around $16 trillion. This estimate is hard to verify because much of the bailouts were kept secret, with no outside oversight or accounting.

The GAO audit released a data chart describing the 10 biggest banks in the United States, shown below.

Diagram 7. GAO Audit: Appendix IV: Ten Largest Domestic Bank Holding Companies by Total Asset Size as of December 31, 2010.

Domestic bank holding companies	Total Assets as of 12/31/10 (Dollars in thousands)
1. Bank of America Corporation	$2,268,347,377
2. JPMorgan Chase & Co.	$2,117,605,000
3. Citigroup Inc.	$1,913,902,000
4. Wells Fargo & Company	$1,258,128,000
5. The Goldman Sachs Group, Inc.	$911,330,000
6. Morgan Stanley	$807,698,000
7. Metlife, Inc.	$730,905,863
8. U.S. Bancorp	$307,786,000
9. The PNC Financial Services Group, Inc.	$264,414,112
10. The Bank of New York Mellon Corporation	$247,222,000

Source: GAO analysis of data from the National Information Center

In several different locations in the GAO report, they also provided data on the domestic U. S. banks who obtained the bailouts. We provide that data below in Diagram 8.

Diagram 8. Data from GAO Audit on the Five Banks Who Obtained The Biggest Federal Reserve Board Bailouts During the 2008 Economic Collapse.

Bank of America: $1.344 trillion ($1,344,000,000,000)
JP Morgan Chase: $391 billion ($391,000,000,000)
Citigroup: $2.5 trillion ($2,500,000,000,000)
Goldman Sachs: $814 billion ($814,000,000,000)
Morgan Stanley: $2.04 trillion ($2,040,000,000,000)

The GAO audit also revealed the identity of foreign banks who obtained the largest bail outs. We show that data, below, in Diagram 9.

Diagram 9. Data from GAO Audit of Five Foreign Banks Who Obtained The Biggest Federal Reserve Board Bailouts During the 2008 Economic Collapse.

Barclays PLC (United Kingdom): $868 billion ($868,000,000,000)
Royal Bank of Scotland (UK): $541 billion ($541,000,000,000)
Deutsche Bank (Germany): $354 billion ($354,000,000,000)
UBS (Switzerland): $287 billion ($287,000,000,000)
Credit Suisse (Switzerland): $262 billion ($262,000,000,000)

Our argument about the Fed's Ruling Class ideological bias for protecting the Ruling Class, and not the public interest, is based upon Buchanan's thesis of the social welfare function being maximized by the Fed.

The social welfare function that the Fed is maximizing contains variables of the preferences of foreign banks, not the general public of the citizens of the United States.

In their logic of claiming to represent the interests of the public, they would be forced to explain how the preferences of foreign banks fit into the Bergsonian national social welfare function of the domestic U. S. economy.

The Fed does not have a social welfare function of common citizens, as described above in the GAO survey responses, for whom the directors represent, because the Fed has never defined the social welfare of common citizens as a part of their deliberations on interest rate manipulations and increased money supply.

The so-called "public interest," of common citizens has never been defined, because the only interests that count, in the Fed's world view, are the interests of the Ruling Class.

But, we argue, in our historical economic continuity thesis, that whatever the public interest of common citizens may be, it most assuredly is not served by the series of boom-bust economic collapses engineered by the Fed.

We argue that putting a token farmer, or mechanic, or factory worker on the Fed Board would not solve the problem of the anti-democratic operation of the Fed's decisions because working class and middle class citizens do not see themselves as a collectivist group.

Middle class and working class do not have a unified, coherent social class awareness, like the Ruling Class.

In the absence of social class consciousness, a token farmer, or working class citizen, would not possess a social class awareness that would inform their decisions as members of the Fed, and common citizens do not have comparable research staffs, or lobbyist groups, like the National Chamber of Commerce, to prepare research to support their collective social class interests.

In any event, the issue of middle class representation on the Fed Board is moot. The GAO Audit released data on the social and professional class backgrounds of the directors of the Fed, as described below, and there are no middle class/working class citizens on the Board.

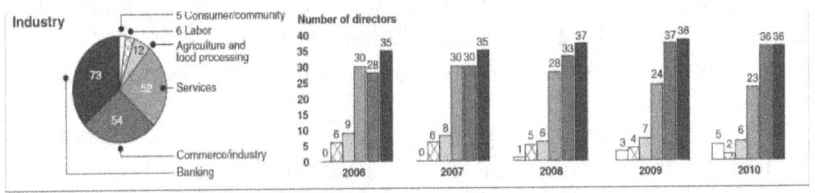

Of the 202 Director members of the Fed, during the 2008 crash, 73 were bankers, 54 were financial services members from brokerage houses and transfer agents, and 52 were from professional services, mostly lawyers, whose firms represent the banking industry.

Nearly 90% of the 202 directors were linked to the Ruling Class financial interests, and all of them possess a Ruling Class social class perspective of what is good for America.

For most of the time of the survey, during the crash, the so-called "labor" interests were union reps and executives who represent 11% of the U. S. workforce, which is not the same thing as working or middle class interests.

The social class composition of the directors in the U. S. Fed is different than the comparable central banks, in the world.

The GAO 2011 Audit presented data on how the membership of the Fed compares to other nations, as shown below:

Table 4: Size and Composition of Boards of Directors of Federal Reserve Banks Compared with Those of Selected Entities, as of August 2011

Characteristics	Reserve Bank of Australia	Bank of Canada	Bank of England	European Central Bank	Financial Industry Regulatory Authority	Federal Home Loan Banks	Federal Reserve Bank
Size of board	9	15	12	23	22[a]	13-18[b]	9
Number of board members who are independent[c]	5-6[d]	12	9	0[e]	11	At least 2/5 of board	6[f]
Number of board members representing member institutions	Not applicable	Not applicable	Not applicable	17	10[g]	No more than 3/5	3[h]
Number of board members employed by the institution or government	3-4	3[i]	3	6	1	0	0

The GAO categorization of 6 independent members on the U. S. Fed is laughable. The so-called "independent" members are bankers, selected by other bankers, to serve on the Board.

While those independent directors may be defined as independent, all of them possess the Ruling Class social class consciousness that informs their decisions about what is good for the American Ruling Class.

The absence of outside over sight, and absence of a social class consciousness of working and middle class citizens, on the Fed, allows the members of the Fed to engage in self-dealing and corruption, much like the Ruling Class during the Gilded Age.

We argue that if this Fed corruption and self-dealing had occurred under the rules of the Financial Industry Regulatory Authority [FINRA], shown in the above GAO diagram, that the acts would be deemed illegal.

The GAO Audit provided data on the self-dealing and corruption.

The GAO audit reports:

"For example, FRBNY officials said that General Electric Company (General Electric), whose chief executive officer was serving as a Class B director at the time, was one of the largest issuers of commercial paper [under the real bills doctrine] and General Electric was one of the companies FRBNY consulted when creating the emergency program to assist with the commercial paper market. FRBNY officials said they contacted institutions for this purpose irrespective of whether one of FRBNY's directors was affiliated with the institution... The GAO found that William Dudley was issued a waiver in 2008 to keep his shares in companies including those that received federal assistance, such as American International Group Inc. (AIG), while he was still the executive vice president of the New York Fed Markets Group...

In another case, General Electric CEO Jeffrey Immelt was a New York Fed board member at the same time GE helped create a Commercial Paper Funding Facility during the financial crisis. The Fed later provided $16 billion in financing to GE under this emergency lending program."

The waivers and exemptions for self-dealing of the Fed directors are granted to each other, under the rules of the Fed. For example, William Dudley's self-dealing in stocks that were part of the bailout was granted to him by other members of the Fed.

The GAO Audit described that the members of the Fed have obtained Congressional authorization for their secret self-dealing.

The GAO stated,

"According to FRBNY officials, a director providing information to FRBNY management and staff in his or her role as chief executive officer of an institution does not equate to "participating personally and substantially"—as defined by 18 U.S.C. § 208, discussed below

because the director is not playing a direct role with respect to approving a program or providing a recommendation."

In other words, the members possess a type of dual personality, much like the testimony before the Supreme Court of William Conkling, noted above.

"Conkling both represented the railroad in the case before the Supreme Court, and also provided direct testimony, and introduced evidence, based upon his work in drafting the 14th Amendment."

Applied to the Fed's self-dealing, when the member appears before the Board seeking a waiver, in her capacity as an executive of a private bank, that would be considered self-dealing because that bank executive and the bank would possibly benefit from obtaining the waiver.

However, if the director appears before the Board to seek a waiver, in her capacity as a member of the Board, that act would not constitute self-dealing, because the Board member was representing the broad public purpose, and not her own personal, private financial interests.

In any event, in the absence of the 2011 GAO Audit, this information on the Fed's self-dealing and corruption, during the 2008 crash, would never had been made public, because the deliberations of the members are secret, just as Senator Aldrich wished, in his Aldrich Plan, formulated in secret at Jekyll Island.

Our argument about American economic history begins with our observation that there are two competing versions of the American Dream.

In Jefferson's version of the American Dream, common citizens share social cultural values of equal opportunity for economic prosperity, which tends to bind citizens to voluntarily obey the rule of law.

In Madison's Dream, the cultural values of shared plunder and corruption by the natural aristocracy, under Madison's plutocracy, lead to rule evasion by the elite, and rule enforcement of common citizens, by the Leviathan, and a national social welfare function heavily skewed to the benefit of the Ruling Class.

As we noted above, in citing Buchanan, once the agency of government is created, that escapes the consent of the governed, that agency, like the Fed, becomes a permanent part of the Leviathan that Madison's constitution created.

We describe the overall macro economic risk to common citizens of the future continuation of the Fed's poor decision making in a series of diagrams below:

First, the strength of the U. S. dollar, as the global reserve currency, is based upon a relationship between U. S. economic growth, and the ability of the U. S. Treasury to repay national debt.

Other nations who maintain a reserve of U. S. dollars in their own central banks, to pay for international trade, assume [deeply believe] that the U. S. economy will continue to be the strongest economy in the world.

Sometime, around 2010, the national debt exceeded the national GDP. Currently, the national federal debt is about $31 trillion, and the GDP is around $20 trillion, which means that there is about $11 trillion of debt that is not backed by U. S. GDP.

Diagram 10. U. S. National Debt to GDP.

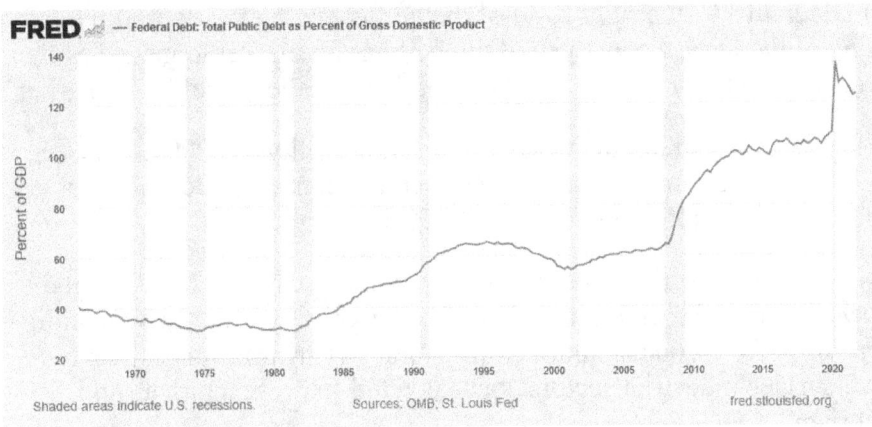

Of the $31 trillion dollar federal debt, the Fed owns about $5 trillion, as a result of quantitative easing, after the 2008 collapse, and more significantly, after Biden assumed office in 2020.

Diagram 11. Total Assets of Federal Debt Owned by Fed.

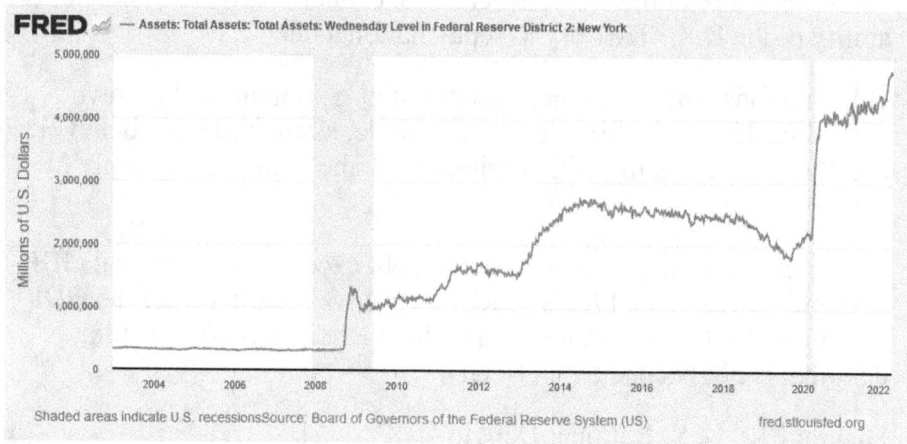

In Diagram 11., the right hand of the Fed is buying the debt of the left hand of the U. S. Treasury, and the Fed has no market to get rid of the worthless debt by selling it to other nations, in the global bond market.

After China entered the World Trade Organization, in 2001, the U. S. economy transitioned to a "service sector" economy, because most manufacturing jobs were shipped to China.

Diagram 12. describes the current components of U. S. GDP. Of the $19 trillion dollar GDP, in the fourth quarter of 2021, only $4 trillion was in durable goods manufacturing, and $11 trillion was concentrated in 7 service industrial sectors, such as retail trade, restaurants and tourism.

Increased government spending, and increased government debt, do not generate real economic growth, and the service sector does not possess the income and employment multipliers for distributing economic growth to the broader society.

As a result of the transition to a service sector economy, the U. S. economy does not possess the capacity to generate future economic growth because private consumption now constitutes about 80% of all GDP, and service sector jobs constitute about 70% of all jobs.

Diagram 12. Components of U. S. GDP:

Table 1.2.6. Real Gross Domestic Product by Major Type of Product, Chained Dollars: Quarterly

Line	Name	Q4 2021	Q3 2021	Q4 2020
1	▼ Gross domestic product	19,810.572	19,478.893	18,767.778
2	Final sales of domestic product	19,549.007	19,453.436	18,664.756
3	Change in private inventories	171.249	-66.771	88.799
4	Residual	90.316	92.228	14.224
5	▼ Goods	7,294.650	6,997.840	6,661.750
6	Final sales	7,005.295	6,978.252	6,553.749
7	Change in private inventories	171.249	-66.771	88.799
	▼ Goods by type of product			
8	▼ Durable goods	4,064.397	3,882.431	3,705.492
9	Final sales	3,952.480	3,959.906	3,683.839
10	Change in private inventories	75.293	-85.085	20.522
11	▼ Nondurable goods	3,228.499	3,113.239	2,955.584
12	Final sales	3,053.120	3,019.662	2,870.657
13	Change in private inventories	95.866	23.742	68.735
14	Services	11,275.279	11,189.478	10,742.906
15	Structures	1,413.028	1,427.421	1,469.722
16	Residual	-54.493	-56.231	-86.603

The key factor in future real economic growth is private domestic investment, which is currently not great enough to bring the U. S. economy out of the Nash equilibrium of the 2008 economic collapse.

The increased government spending, and increased debt, in conjunction with the structural economic change to a serve sector economy, squeezes private capital out of the market, in favor of government spending.

Diagram 13. Gross Private Domestic Investment.

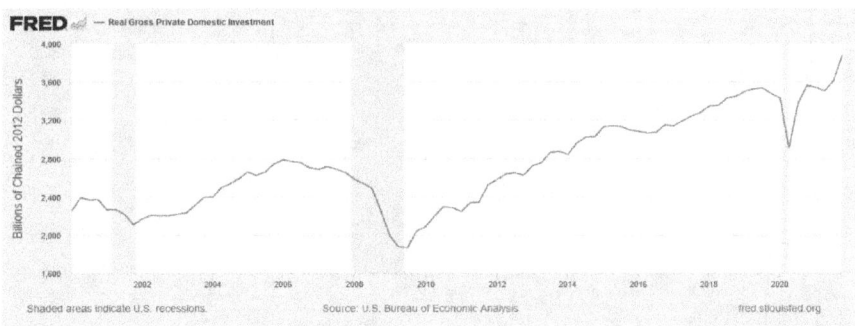

Our argument is that the Fed is focused on maintaining the privileges of plunder of the Ruling Class, and not focused on increasing the rate of private domestic investment in manufacturing.

As we argued above, Ruling Class plunder and worthless speculative investments, do not create real economic growth.

Ruling Class plunder, based upon speculative investments for too-big-to fail banks, creates economic collapse, while maintaining the social class privileges of the Ruling Class.

From the perspective of the Ruling Class, the Fed has not failed. The Fed has been a success for Madison's American Dream.

From the perspective of Jefferson's American Dream, the Fed's performance in generating economic collapse, every five or ten years, for common citizens is a failure.

Our conclusion that the Fed has failed middle class and working class citizens does not, by itself, indicate that it would be practical to entirely dispense with some sort of public monetary authority.

It does, however, mean that that new monetary authority would be created under a new constitutional set of rules that aims at reconstructing Jefferson's Dream of an entrepreneurial capitalist society, whose Preamble targets the preservation of liberty and equal rights for all, with special privileges for none.

Chapter 9. Re-constructing A Fair Constitution Under Jefferson's American Dream of an Entrepreneurial Capitalist Society.

To summarize our arguments, Madison's constitution was immoral because it perpetuated slavery, because it disenfranchised the consent of the governed of common citizens, and was implemented in a fraudulent ratification process.

Common citizens never provided prior consent to be ruled by the natural aristocracy, and did not provide legitimate consent to ratify Madison's constitution.

The only shred of legitimacy of consent of the governed in Madison's rules was the ability of the common citizens to vote, periodically, on the elites who would rule them.

And, that last shred of legitimacy was violated on November 3, 2020, when the Democrat Marxists overthrew the representative republic to install their version of a more perfect Marxist union.

We disagree both with the historical analysis of Democrat Marxists that America was founded upon the sin of slavery, in 1619, and we also disagree with their solution that the remedy for "the founding" is a collectivist communist tyranny.

America was founded in 1775, under Jefferson's promise of liberty, [The Causes and Necessity of Taking Up Arms], and codified under the Articles of Confederation, of 1781.

Jefferson's promise of liberty is one version of the American Dream for common citizens.

In contrast, the United States Government was founded in 1787, under Madison's constitution that empowered the elite over the common citizens. Madison's Ruling Class plutocracy is the second version of the American Dream, for the Ruling Class.

The Democrat Marxists are correct that Madison's constitution protected slavery, not because slavery was the essential value that held national elites together, but because in order to implement Madison's constitution, protecting slavery in the South was essential to maintaining elite rule in the North.

Madison said that the Senate needed to be a "check on the democracy. It can not be made too strong."

That "check on democracy" is now in the hands of Marxist Democrats, who staged America's second coup, in November 2020, overthrowing Madison's representative republic.

It was the flaws in Madison's rules for creating the British social class system in America that allowed the Marxists to gain their illegitimate power. In their ascendancy to illegitimate power, they gained unchecked control over Madison's Leviathan.

There is no force in Madison's constitutional framework to compel the elected representatives, of either political party, to represent the common good, or the public purpose.

Once the elected representatives arrive in DC, they collaborate with the special financial interests to enrich themselves. The Democrat Marxists collaborate with global corporate elites to maintain the power of the Leviathan.

We argue that, during the Gilded Age, there was no logical or moral justification, for common citizens to have been mistreated by the Plutocrats. Under a different constitutional configuration, that promoted Jefferson's concept of the American Dream, they would not have suffered.

We argue that there is no macro-economic marginal price theoretical reason for the economy to collapse every ten years. The economic instability is caused by Madison's constitutional rules, in collaboration with Hamilton's financial system, not by a failure in the price system of the competitive free market.

We revise Sumner's phrase "the forgotten man" to mean, today, that the financial and economic interests of working and middle class citizens are not represented in the centralized, corporate, deep-state, Marxist tyranny.

We argue that the Ruling Class, from 1787, onwards, had a coherent, unified social class consciousness that allowed them to politically pursue their social class preferences, under Madison's constitution.

The middle class and working class citizens never developed a social class awareness of their financial interests, and have never politically pursued their social class preferences, except for the brief moment in history of the Agrarian Revolt.

Our argument concludes that natural rights conservatives and patriots, today, who are trying to resurrect, or reconstruct Madison's constitution, in order to defeat the Marxist Democrats, are on a fool's errand.

In the current time period, there are no common cultural values holding the citizens of this nation together in a common mission.

The current unfair constitution finally evolved into a centralized, elite globalist crony capitalism that is impossible to eradicate because the Marxists do not share the same cultural values as conservatives.

Attempting to replace the crony capitalist system with European socialism, but keeping the existing constitution in place, would not solve the dysfunction in the American economy, or society.

Restoring Madison's centralized government would not eradicate the grip that the Democrat Marxists have on the deep state Leviathan.

Madison and Hamilton created a ruling class plutocracy, and going back to their "founding" would not resolve the conflict in the two versions of the American dream.

Madison's two social class constitution was an unfair social class conflict constitution, based upon rules that elevated the financial interests of the natural aristocracy over common citizens.

Madison's two party political system cannot be reformed. It is a permanent feature of Madison's political framework, built upon Madison's conception of the British two-class society.

The Fed is a permanent feature of Hamilton's banking system. The Fed cannot be abolished or reformed, as long as Madison's constitutional rules remain in effect.

The legal framework of Madison's rules worked in tandem with the unfair power of Hamilton's banking system.

The two conceptions of the American Dream are incompatible and irreconcilable. The appearance of the Democrat Marxist in the American political party apparatus changes the strategy for how to transition from Madison's Dream to Jefferson's Dream.

Our argument about the fallacy of going back to Madison's constitution to eradicate Marxism echoes Lincoln's argument about the Slaveocracy going back to Madison's constitution, instead of seceding.

As noted by Feldman, Lincoln stated,

"The only solution Lincoln offered to the crisis was to "go back to [the] old policy. If you would have the peace of the old times, readopt the precepts and policy of the old times."

That advice to the Southern states was as false then for dealing with the issue of slavery, as the strategy of resurrecting Madison's constitution is today for dealing with the issue of Marxist Democrats.

We agree with the Marxist Democrats that the Civil War did not solve the issue of slavery, or the issue of racism, because racism, as a political tool in the hands of the plutocracy is too vital a weapon to keep the Ruling Class in power.

A better idea to solve the issue of slavery, in both 1787, and 1860, would have been to let the slaveocracy "go in peace."

A better idea, today, is to let the two incompatible versions of the American Dream to "go in peace."

We offer a better strategy for common citizens to eradicate both the Marxist threat to liberty, and to eradicate the power of the global corporate state that undermines national sovereignty.

A better idea is to start over at the point of history of Jefferson's Declaration, and reconstruct Jefferson's American Dream of an entrepreneurial capitalist society.

In other words, we propose to follow Madison and Hamilton in their strategy of over throwing the Articles of Confederation by offering citizens in each state the pathway out of the Leviathan, and into a democratic representative republic, based upon fair constitutional rules.

We cite Kenneth Arrow on the elements of an individualist constitution and the imperative of stating the end goals in the Preamble of the constitution. (Social Choice and Individual Values, 1951.).

The logical consequence of constitutional rules that fail to establish a shared sense of civic mission, in the Preamble, is that no set of constitutional rules can be ranked and ordered in priority against each other to determine which constitutional arrangement contributes most to the Preamble's public purpose.

Individual choice in attempting to rank and order different constitutions, all which of have different or implicit end goals, will not lead to rational social choice or rational political outcomes.

As a result of this failure, the constitutional public purpose, in Madison's Preamble, means whatever the special interests in control say it means, at the time in history that they happen to be in control.

In Arrow's conception of social welfare, national social welfare is a function of individual welfare, not social class group welfare.

Arrow cites four primary conditions for obtaining maximum social welfare, under an individualist configuration of constitutional rules:

Social welfare is a function of individual welfare, and individual welfare can be mathematically aggregated into a national social welfare function.

Individual well-being is known best by the individual, not by a panel of political elites or state bureaucrats.

Individuals are rational and act to make themselves better off to improve their welfare both in political and economic decision-making.

Voting in fair elections reflects the expected welfare improvement of the citizenry, under a specific configuration of constitutional rules.

The rules of the individualist constitution must be fair and aim at achieving a specific set of goals:

- Allowing individuals to obtain fair reward for work.
- Providing incentives to work.
- Providing an equal path to individual prosperity.

In Logical Foundations of Constitutional Liberty, (1999), Buchanan relies on a philosophy of logic to explain how the end goals of a constitution, clearly stated in the preamble, create the binding allegiance of citizens to follow the rule of law.

The constitutional public purpose in an individualist society is served by promotion and adherence to common external values of trust, fair dealing, truthful representations, and promise keeping.

Citizens are morally obligated to follow the laws that they give to themselves, following Jefferson's principle that all legitimate authority is derived from the consent of the governed.

In contrast to Madison's social class collectivism, the social authority patterns of individualism assume that each individual is capable of making rational decisions about the individual's self-interest.

No political elite is assumed to have a greater ability or authority to make decisions on behalf of the welfare of either the individual or aggregations of individuals.

The individual's identity is not first and foremost defined by the group or tribe, but through the rational mental process of imagining the individual's own identity and taking the further mental step of imagining the identity and welfare of another individual.

Obligation to serve the public purpose, as offered by Jefferson, is derived from the recognition of reciprocal advantage in achieving individual independence that is obtained from social cooperation in civil rule making and rule enforcement.

Each individual citizen is assumed to have the rational capacity to see the self-evident truth of the reciprocal advantage to be gained through cooperation.

Jefferson's faith in the rationality of citizens results in reciprocity in political authority, and is based upon an exchange of trust that citizens will honor the claims and rights of others.

As Michael Zuckert noted in his writings about Jefferson, (The Natural Rights Republic: Studies In The Foundation of The American Political Tradition, Michael Zuckert, University of Notre Dame Press, (1996.),

"We come to respect those rights in others which we value in ourselves. Rights in the proper sense arise when human beings come to recognize a need for reciprocity in rights...that to claim a right for oneself requires accepting the same right in others...claims of rights become rights with duties reciprocal to them."

The constitutional contract involves the concepts of reciprocity, mutuality, and obligation, primary in defense of each other's freedoms.

The medium of exchange in the individualist constitutional is trust.

The rules of political cooperation developed through the process of reciprocal exchange of trust continually bind the individual to the system of authority because the individual can imagine that political rules and rights could easily be reversed, or worse yet, be dictated by a self-interested political elite.

As Buchanan points out, voluntary allegiance to the rule of law results from the realization that it is in one's rational best interest for his or her life's mission to be consistent with the public purpose of the constitutional rule of law.

Voluntary cooperation between individuals occurs when the individuals assume, prior to entering into any political or financial exchange process, that other citizens share common cultural and political values.

Common cultural values depend further upon a set of social and political institutions that act as the medium through which the future obligations are discharged.

Cultural values, in other words, provide an essential set of conditions for pro-social rule adherence in political exchanges involving trust.

Yet, common cultural values that emphasize the discharge of future obligations are not sufficient, by themselves, to insure that the obligations are discharged.

The function of the political institutions is not to balance political power, as they would under Madison's conception, or to facilitate exchanges of private property, as they would under Locke's conception of the social contract.

In The Theory of Public Choice, (1972) Buchanan states that,

"Uncertainty about just where one's own interest will lie in a sequence of plays or rounds will lead a rational person, from his own interest, to prefer rules and arrangements, or constitutions that will seem fair, no matter what final positions he might occupy we can simply define a person in terms of his set of preferences, his utility function. This function defines or describes a set of possible trade-offs among alternatives for potential choice."

With the uncertainty of rule adherence, individuals tend to abandon cultural values of trust, truth and honesty in favor of self-oriented values.

The issue of the uncertainty of rule adherence highlights the importance in a democratic republic of allegiance to the "rule of law" as applied to all individuals once the constitution has been created.

The equal application of the rule of law however requires an institutional framework through which the application can be applied. If the institutions are designed to adjudicate rights, then the rule of law can be applied uniformly.

If, on the other hand, institutions were conceived in the initial constitution as the mechanism to separate and balance political powers, then rights adjudication becomes more uncertain, contributing to the social uncertainty about rule adherence.

The institutions act as the equivalent of the price-based market mechanism that coordinates voluntary behavior in free market transactions.

In the political exchange, the voluntary hypothetical exchange of values takes place in a social setting where the common currency is common cultural values.

Once the constitutional contract has been established, the on-going mediums of exchange that coordinate voluntary joint behavior, without the application of power, are a unique set of commonly-held shared cultural values.

In order to perform the function of coordinating mutually beneficial joint behavior that has as its consequence pro-social rules adherence, the institutions must reflect the underlying cultural values of trust and truth, which must be universally held by all individuals who are parties to the contract.

Individuals continue to obey social rules when they have mutual dependency on sharing benefits with other individuals.

The issue of trust involves the reliance of a citizen that another party to a financial exchange will reciprocate in the future on keeping promises that involve a future payment.

The main point of Buchanan's constitutional model is that the level of rule obedience depends on how the rules are interpreted by an individual citizen in affecting that citizen's life plans.

Voluntary allegiance to the rule of law, in the natural rights republic, results from the fact that all citizens have an equal opportunity for upward mobility and individual prosperity.

Buchanan suggested that different constitutional rules produced different social welfare outcomes and different patterns of income distribution.

Change the constitutional rules, suggests Buchanan, and you change the distribution of income in the society.

We agree with Buchanan that there is only one configuration of constitutional rules, and only one method of citizen participation, in the making of fair constitutional rules, which creates both maximum individual liberty and maximum rates of economic growth.

We argue that the single constitutional configuration is Jefferson's entrepreneurial capitalist society, which citizens in America created in 1776, when they left the state of nature to form their first constitutional contract, called the Articles of Confederation.

That single constitutional configuration creates the maximum level of trust among citizens, so that citizens can trust each other to obey the rule of law.

Coincidentally, that same constitutional configuration also creates the maximum rates of knowledge creation and knowledge diffusion among citizens.

Maximum rates of knowledge creation create the social conditions for maximum rates of technology innovation, which creates maximum rates of economic growth.

In The Reason of Rules, (2000), Buchanan and Brennan explain the importance of how citizens create fair constitutional rules, when they provide prior consent to follow the rules that they give to themselves.

"Just conduct," writes Buchanan, "consists of behavior that does not violate rules to which one has given prior consent."

We argue that one of Madison's moral flaws is that common citizens never provided prior consent to be ruled by the natural aristocracy.

Buchanan suggested that different constitutional rules produced different social welfare outcomes and different patterns of income distribution.

The issue of fair distribution of income and wealth can be resolved, according to Buchanan, when citizens are involved in the deliberations about creating the constitutional contract.

The differences in the level of citizen rule obedience between societies was explained by Buchanan in terms of the perceived "fairness" of the rules related to income distribution.

Buchanan applies this concept of the limited power of institutions to his suggestions about the relationship between free markets and governmental power.

He states that,

"...for most persons, the independence offered by the presence of market alternatives offers the maximal liberty possible. But we have not yet designed institutions that will satisfy the individual's search for community in the impersonal setting of the market order without, at the same time, undermining the very independence that this order affords."

The point he makes is that certain types of institutional arrangements in government damage individual freedom gained in free market economic exchange.

Buchanan's rules link individual choice, in the free market system, to individual choice in the political system, because economic individualism is linked to equal political natural rights.

No other constitutional configuration starts out with this set of equal natural rights, aiming at the social goal to create "maximum" individual happiness.

Equal natural rights create maximum economic growth, which, in turn, creates maximum social welfare.

We explain in Chapter 10, that the relationship between constitutional individual freedom and national economic growth is through the ability of individuals to create new technology ventures that commercialize new technology products.

In the individualist society, the role of government institutions is to reduce the chance situations that other individuals, or the police power of the state, will be used to override the individual's freedoms of choice in pursuing their sovereign life mission.

The government serves this function by administering a framework of collective decision making whose goal is to secure just outcomes to the laws that individuals give to themselves.

The constitutional public purpose of government is not to increase the wealth of the nation, or to increase the welfare of one group over another group, or to obtain the equal distribution of incomes that conform to a collectivist vision of fairness.

The public purpose of government is to enforce the equal application of the rule of law.

Jefferson provided some elaboration on his concept of decentralized self-government, which leads to the second principle of constitutional rules.

Jefferson's rules, as defined in the Articles of Confederation, would establish a priority of local and state governments based on the principle that those bound most tightly by collective rules must be given the greatest say in the making and enforcing of the rules.

This priority of local government over national government has a very subtle point about equality before the law.

If all individuals are equal in the making and enforcing of the law, and the law is applied most stringently at the most local level of the community, then no individual is greater than the law.

In order to promote the greatest level of individual freedom, all individuals must be bound, in equal capacity, by the same law that they have given to themselves.

The priority of local government is related to how local laws most directly affect the individual in his or her every day pursuit of sovereignty.

Chapter 10. Re-constructing Jefferson's Entrepreneurial Capitalist Society.

We have argued that there is no macro-economic theoretical reason for the U. S. economy to collapse every ten years.

The economic instability is caused by Madison's constitutional rules, in collaboration with Hamilton's financial system, not by a failure in the price system of the competitive free market.

We have argued that the legal framework of Madison's rules worked in tandem with the unfair financial power of Hamilton's banking system to benefit Madison's natural aristocracy, to the detriment of common citizens.

The historical weakness in the U. S. economy is caused by money manipulation, which causes investment speculation, which does not result in real economic growth.

Re-constructing Jefferson's free, fair, competitive national entrepreneurial economy, would trace out an economic growth pattern to a point of Pareto Optimality, where no person's welfare could be improved, without damaging the welfare of another person.

Madison's version of the American Dream changed permanently, beginning around 1992, when the national corporate plutocracy shifted from a commitment of improving sovereign economic welfare to a global borderless market orientation.

Globalism is based upon an ideological premise that a centralized group of corporate elites are better at making social and economic decisions than individual choice in free market transactions.

This ideological orientation of corporate globalism is compatible with the ideology of Democrat Marxism, which is based upon a perspective that a small group of political elites would make better decisions for social welfare than the outcomes generated by the democratic free choice of voters.

Madison's constitutional flaw of elevating the power of the natural aristocracy over common citizens is compatible with both the corporate and the Marxist version of elite rule.

We assert that globalism is an economic failure for the vast majority of American citizens. There is nothing in Madison's constitution that defines a "more perfect union," in terms of the protecting the sovereignty of American citizens.

As a result of globalism, the national economy and regional economies, like the Detroit metro region, have lost the internal economic dynamic that caused regional economic growth.

The internal domestic structure of the U. S. economy has been hollowed out by global trade, leaving only a skeleton of consumer and government spending in place of economic growth caused by domestic private capital investment.

In the absence of domestic capital investment, the national and regional economies have ratcheted down through an economic ratchet because the regional economies do not possess the ability to generate real economic growth.

The political cause of the economic decline in American metro regions is that regional elected representatives willingly became the agents of the global corporations, who needed legislation to operate more easily across national boundaries.

We described that the American national economic structure changed, after China entered the World Trade Organization, in 2001.

After China entered the WTO, the U. S. economy transitioned to a "service sector" economy, because most manufacturing jobs, and industrial supply chains, were shipped to China.

Capital investments in manufacturing industries are the most critical factor in causing domestic economic growth, and the industrial supply chains are the most critical factor in distributing the benefits of economic growth to the middle and working class citizens.

The economic term to describe the wide distribution of benefits to society is income multipliers, which means that income generated in manufacturing production is widely shared among all social classes as the economy grows.

As a result of the transition to a service sector economy, the U. S. economy does not possess the internal economic structure required to generate future economic growth because the former strength of the manufacturing sector has been replaced by the economic weakness of consumer and government spending.

Private consumption now constitutes about 80% of all GDP, and service sector jobs constitute about 70% of all jobs, while manufacturing employment is down from around 17,000 to 11,000, in the period after China was admitted to the WTO.

Increased government spending, and increased government debt, does not generate real economic growth, it generates corruption and investment speculation.

The increased government spending, and increased debt, in conjunction with the structural economic change to a service sector economy, squeezes private capital out of the market, in favor of more government spending.

Prior to the implementation of the global trade policies, technology businesses hired 40 percent of high technology workers, such as scientists, engineers, and computer workers, right out of U. S. colleges.

After the entrance of China to the WTO, those U. S. college graduates cannot find high wage, technology jobs in America because the corporations have shifted to hiring foreign workers, located in foreign nations, right out of foreign colleges.

The transition to the service sector economy makes the U. S. economy more vulnerable to the Fed's boom-bust-bubble economy, which is why the historical frequency of economic collapse has increased, after China's entrance to the WTO, from a historical average of around 1 collapse every 10 years, to the more recent experience of 1 collapse every 5 years.

Since the passage of globalist laws in 1992, regional economic development in the United States has stagnated.

There is limited metro regional economic growth and little high wage private sector job creation because globalism destroyed the ability of metro regions to innovate, to create new technical knowledge, and to make capital investments in new technology ventures.

In place of self-sustaining, self-renewing regional economic growth, elected officials and large corporations engage in a corrupt rent-seeking competition to see which region can hand out the biggest tax incentives to recruit low wage global branch manufacturing plants.

The recent International Monetary Fund (IMF) report, World Economic Outlook, examined the economic effect of 88 banking crises, in selected national economies, over the past four decades.

They found that, on average, seven years after a bust, an economy's level of output was almost 10% below where it would have been without the crisis.

The national economies, in the IMF study, are not recovering to the economic levels of output attained prior to the transition to corporate globalism.

A level of GDP that is repeatedly 10% lower, after each economic collapse, does not look like a return to a prior equilibrium, it looks like an economy stuck in a Nash equilibrium.

Using Japan's economy as an example of the downward ratchet, beginning with the economic crisis in 1988, Japan's economy stagnated. By 2002 Japan's output was almost 23% below its 1988 GDP.

The U. S. rate of private domestic capital investment in small technology ventures is currently not great enough to bring the U. S. economy out of the Nash equilibrium, resulting from the 2008 economic collapse.

As the research by Decker, Ryan & Haltiwanger, et al., (2017), shows, the rate of new venture creation, eight years after the 2008 collapse, is too low to sustain macro economic growth. (Declining Dynamism, Allocative Efficiency, and the Productivity Slowdown, AER, 2017.).

Their research indicates that 70% of all new ventures fail within the first five years. The other 30% of new ventures that survive are responsible for most of the economic growth in the economy.

Economic growth requires a huge birth rate of new ventures every year, because the death rate of new ventures is so high, and yet, it is the new venture survivors that generate most of the economic growth.

The service sectors do not possess the income and employment multipliers for distributing the benefits of economic growth to middle class and working class citizens, which explains why the plutocracy is getting richer under globalism.

While globalism is an economic failure for 70% of the American population who are stuck in dead end, low-wage service sector jobs, from the perspective of global corporations, the Fed's management of the new global economy has been a success, measured by corporate profits and retained earnings.

Since 1992, corporate rates of profits have never been higher, or increased faster.

We have argued that the Fed's economic performance has resulted in a systematic series of boom-bust cycles, where the financial welfare of common citizens is devastated, while the welfare of the privileged wealthy, domestic and foreign, elite bankers escape unharmed, because the Fed bails them out.

We concluded, in Chapter 9, that there is a global macro economic risk of world-wide economic collapse for common citizens, if the Fed is allowed to continue its poor decision making, in the new global borderless economy.

The stability of the world's economy rests upon the mirage of economic strength of the U. S. economy which serves as the logic of the Bretton Woods agreement making the U. S. dollar the reserve currency of the world.

Beginning around 1998, with the Fed's bailout of the Russian long term debt, the Fed has increasingly become "banker-for-the-world," and not constrained to focus on stabilizing the U. S. domestic economy.

We assert that the Fed's arbitrary discretion to manipulate the economy by setting interest rates, manipulating the supply of money, and bailing out foreign banks after each collapse, must be taken away from them because they no longer act to preserve and promote national economic sovereignty.

Our conclusion that the Fed has failed American middle class and working class citizens does not, by itself, indicate that it would be practical to entirely dispense with some sort of public monetary authority.

It does, however, mean that that new monetary authority would be created under a new constitutional set of rules that aims at re-constructing Jefferson's Dream of an entrepreneurial capitalist society, whose Preamble targets the national sovereign preservation of liberty for citizens and equal rights for all, with special privileges for none.

Jefferson's Dream is based upon prosperity for small entrepreneurial firms who create future economic growth.

The key factor for stimulating national future real economic growth is increased rates of private domestic investment in small entrepreneurial firms, primarily in 9 high technology industrial sectors, primarily in each of the 300 metro regional economies.

We explained, in Chapter 9, that the relationship between constitutional individual freedom and national economic growth is through the ability of individuals to create new technology ventures that commercialize new technology products.

We argued that there is a single constitutional configuration that creates the maximum level of trust among citizens, so that citizens can trust each other to obey the rule of law.

Coincidentally, that same constitutional configuration also creates the maximum rates of knowledge creation and knowledge diffusion among citizens.

Maximum rates of knowledge creation create the social conditions for maximum rates of technology innovation, which creates maximum rates of economic growth.

A better goal for national economic policy, than the Fed's manipulating interest rates and money supply, is to target increased rates of gross domestic private business investment, which leads to high rates of technological innovation, which create new future markets, which create new flows of income, which reduce wealth and income inequality.

We argue that the new U. S. economic strategy, under a new Jefferson version of a decentralized constitution, would have the following policy goals:

Increased rates of private sector capital investment in the 300 metro regions with a population over 150,000, the minimum size for self-renewing, self-generating entrepreneurial economic growth.

Targeting private sector capital investment to new product technology commercialization and new venture creation, within those 300 regions.

Integration of metro economic opportunity zones policy into an advanced technology cluster strategy in each metro region, so that technology firms that like to be located close to each other can trade with each other and share tacit knowledge.

Integration of advanced high skill training apprenticeship programs into the 9 advanced technology cluster strategy so that future new ventures, in each metro region, have a consistent supply of highly trained middle class and working class technology workers.

Providing each region's private commercial real estate consulting firms with new econometric models, developed by a new type of Bureau of Economic Analysis, in order to target the geographical location of capital investments, in each metro region, to the development of regional industrial value chains and inter-industry supply chains that service the new technology clusters.

Modifying the existing SEC crowdfunding rules, in a new type of SEC, for raising private capital by broadening the scope of the existing Reg D Rule 506, and creating new forms of metro regional closed end funds that pool and target capital to the region's new and existing firms in the emerging technology clusters.

Implementing an explicit system of metro regional tacit technology knowledge creation and diffusion, using blockchain technology, to share regional technological knowledge among investors and entrepreneurs.

Technology innovation as regional tacit knowledge networks.

Brink Lindsey, of the Niskanen Center, (2017), aptly summarizes what has become a widespread consensus among scholars from many different fields within the economics profession:

"The long-term future of economic growth hinges ultimately on innovation. Indeed, as Sachs and McArthur have stated, "The more we think about it, the more we realize that technological innovation is almost certainly the key driver of long-term economic growth." (The Captured Economy: How the Powerful Enrich Themselves, Slow Down Growth, and Increase Inequality, 2017.).

We agree that future long term economic growth is dependent on the creation and diffusion of technological knowledge, but would add that "tacit" technical knowledge is geographically specific to each metro region.

The first step in re-constructing Jefferson's economic version of the American Dream is creating regional knowledge business-social networks in each metro region.

Technology is the application of scientific and engineering knowledge to economic production, and internet communication technology (ICT) is the technical computer hardware network that connects information flows to knowledge creation.

In their recent research on regional economies and innovation, Frédéric Miribel, Christian Le Bas, William Latham, and Simon Condliffe (hereinafter MBLC), examine the relationship between regional knowledge creation and economic growth by breaking the innovation effects of ICT into two parts. (Agglomeration Economies within IT-Producing and IT-Consuming Industries in U.S. Regions Center for Applied Demography and Survey Research, University of Delaware, July 21, 2008.).

In the case of MBLC, they emphasize the benefits of the local regional IT firms being located close to each other and they cite three regional economic benefits that result from IT localization economies:

The benefits of labor pooling among small firms that are located in close proximity to each other.

The cost reductions for purchased inputs when economies of scale are realized in the industries that produce the purchased inputs, and,

The better communication and more rapid spreading of knowledge or intra-industry knowledge spillovers.

MBLC cite market demand as the single greatest factor in stimulating economic growth. In other words, the direction of causality for future economic growth is from market demand to innovation to economic growth.

Their work emphasizes "local" economies and the benefits of "localization." They conclude that economic growth is based on technological innovation that occurs in "localization" economies.

Audretsch and Feldman (1995) have suggested that a tendency exists for high-technology industries to be geographically clustered, because proximity to sources of knowledge spillovers was crucial for the firms to succeed in producing new knowledge through their Research and Development (R&D) activities. (Innovative Clusters and the Industry Life Cycle, David B. Audretsch and Maryann P. Feldman, SSRN, 2001.).

Jörg Thomäa and Volker Zimmermann (2019), argue that the focus on small technology firms is the best strategy for creating regional economic growth. (Non-R&D, Interactive Learning and Economic Performance: Revisiting Innovation in Small and Medium Enterprises, ilf Working Paper No. 17/2019.).

They write,

"The innovation strategies of smaller firms are often characterized by attributes that extend beyond R&D (see e.g. Baldwin and Gellatly 2003; de Jong and Marsili 2006). when SMEs closely interact with their customers and exploit certain advantages associated with a smaller firm size. According to classical theoretical literature on small firm innovation (see Rothwell and Zegveld 1982; Rothwell 1989; Noote-boom 1994), such advantages of non-R&D-performing SMEs are largely behavioural and closely related to informal interaction within and outside the firm."

Their research on the economic benefits of small new venture creation suggests that small businesses contribute tacit knowledge to the technological innovation process in a distinct metro region, while at the same time, strengthening the income multipliers in that region.

MBLC cite Marc Porat (1977), for his research on technology knowledge spillovers. (The Information Economy: Definition and Measurement, Marc Uri Porat, U. S. Department of Commerce, O. T. Special Publication 77-12(1). 1977.).

The value of Porat's intellectual framework is that it allows for an easy to understand way to see how information as knowledge can easily flow between industrial sectors, at both the regional economic level and at the national level.

Porat's analysis raises the issue of uncertainty and instability of ICT for global corporate managers because as the information as knowledge flows across global industrial sectors, everyone sees the same information as everyone else, at the very same moment in time.

Everyone is connected. Everyone has access to a global macro structure of communication and production technology. The outcome of global ICT is a form of global macrotechnology that favors the existing status quo distribution of economic benefits to the largest global corporations.

However, as Porat's analytical framework points out, being connected to ICT is not the same thing as automatically deriving knowledge from the connection.

Deriving tacit knowledge, in contrast to codified knowledge, requires personal relations, mostly face-to-face, communication, among technology workers in a defined geographical location.

In the re-construction of Jefferson's entrepreneurial capitalist economy, economic growth is caused by the creation and diffusion of new tacit knowledge about how things work.

Capital investments in new regional technology ventures causes new income flows to be created where none had existed before.

Part of the new income is a result of increased manufacturing productivity, meaning that ICT causes production output to increase with reduced inputs in the production unit.

Part of the new income is in the form of profits related to new goods produced by new production units, which are then sold in new future markets.

Another part of the income is in the form of wages and salaries paid to people who work in the new venture firms.

In Jefferson's version of the American Dream, technological progress is related to the attainment of individual freedom because new technological knowledge opens up new pathways for individuals to achieve their own sovereignty through owning their own small business.

Jefferson's entrepreneurial capitalist economy is decentralized, democratic, and based upon private capital investments in an economy of continuous technological innovation.

Jefferson's innovative economy, in other words does not aim at maintaining the global status quo of social class divisions and political power, as does Madison's version of the American Dream, under the management of the economy by the Fed.

Blockchain model of regional knowledge creation and new venture creation.

The decentralized decision making in regional knowledge creation can be modeled as a blockchain information network that aims at replicating the entire private capital market investment process, from idea generation to profit reinvestments, after a venture exit.

Blockchain is a form of internet communication technology (ICT) that acts as a tool for converting computer information to technical knowledge.

A blockchain is a computer programming algorithm of time-stamped records that describe the source of new knowledge, or new ideas, contributed by the people involved in regional innovation economic development.

Each new idea, or piece of new knowledge, in each block of data (i.e. block) is secured and bound to each other block using computer algorithms, (i.e. chain).

The blockchain computer programs work in conjunction with the human social-business networks of people involved in the knowledge creation/deal creation process in each metro region.

The economic development value of the blockchain tool is the guidance it provides to the social-business networks to help people target the capital investments to regional technology firms in each regional technology cluster.

Those initial capital investments in technology firms, if they survive, will create new intermediate demand supply chains that distribute income to middle class and working class citizens in the regional economy.

Any region may have many different blockchains operating at the same time, reflecting the different technological clusters of knowledge in a region.

Clayton Christensen cited the new blockchain technology as a tool to help promote economic growth, and we extend and modify his idea to include regional blockchains that go from idea creation to private securities exchanges for capital market transactions for private regional technology stocks.

Christensen writes,

"Blockchain is a public, decentralized, distributed digital ledger that is used to record electronic transactions. Each "block" in a blockchain contains specific information that cannot be altered, due to the distributed nature of the technology. In a blockchain-based economy, the market-creating innovation [new venture investment] and the institution governing it [social-business networks] are fundamentally intertwined." (The Third Answer: How Market-Creating Innovations Drives Economic Growth and Development, Clayton M. Christensen, et al., Innovations, Volume 12, Number ¾, 2018.).

Christensen sees innovation as a dynamic way of life that continually modifies market institutions by opening up new markets and new occupational opportunities.

He states,

"Innovation is the process by which institutions that are critical to development emerge. It is through innovations that create or connect to new markets that societies can create jobs, pay taxes, and, ultimately, build strong and lasting institutions... From an economic development standpoint, innovations can be market-creating or sustaining, that improve [production] efficiency."

We envision each regional new venture blockchain as an imaginary deal creation pipeline, consisting of five major blocks of knowledge:

- Deal Ideas.
- Deal Creation.
- Deal Funding.
- Deal Exits.
- Deal profit reinvestment.

The new venture creation process envisioned by the block chain model can be described as a series of "if-then" contingent statements, where any citizen in the region with an interest in promoting economic growth could participate by contributing ideas on new ventures.

The series of "if-then" statements can be placed into a type of Bayesian prediction model that suggests that the prior industrial technology clusters in the region act as the foundation for future new venture creation:

• If deal exit events, in the past, create a pool of entrepreneurial profits, then if,

• The entrepreneurial profit is available to be used to fund new ventures that create new products, then if,

• Consumers and markets select new products, then if,

• Complementary intermediate markets are created, then if,

• New patterns of income distribution are created, then if,

• New technological knowledge is created, then if,

• New technological knowledge is diffused, then if,

- New production assets are "called forth" from the expanding production possibilities frontier, the assets have a greater probability of being "inherited" by subsequent generations of products to strengthen the regional technology clusters.

The entire process of regional new venture creation is envisioned to take place in a black chain network of computers, geographically located within 50 miles of the metro region.

The regional new venture creation blockchain is maintained by a social-business peer-to-peer network. The network is a collection of nodes that are interconnected to one another.

The "peer-to-peer network" partitions the entire regional economy into technology clusters to allow access by participants, called "peers," who are all equally privileged to contribute ideas to the blockchain.

Nodes are individual computers that take in data, and perform functions that provide an output of modified data that is converted to knowledge by the people in the regional social-business networks.

Each "block" in a blockchain contains specific proprietary information that cannot be altered, due to the distributed nature of the computer algorithm technology.

Each person with a peer computer on the node can add or modify data, with the ability to claim ownership of the new data, if the new data ends up creating a new business venture.

As a result, the blockchain technology has the potential to reduce uncertainty around ownership of new venture ideas and intellectual property rights, and other property claims, by providing transparent verified records, and thereby strengthening allegiance to the rule of law.

At the stage of raising private placement capital for a new venture, the likelihood of corruption, misunderstanding, and administrative errors is significantly reduced when a transparent, distributed, and immutable system is used to manage the transfer of knowledge assets from one party to another.

In the first block of regional new venture idea creation, any computer node peer member can add ideas and comment on other ideas for new ventures. This block is envisioned as an open forum to generate ideas for ventures that may work in that regional economy.

The first block in the regional block chain is the social-business organizing tool to bring a set of potential entrepreneurs, and knowledge workers, together to collaborate on new venture ideas.

The value of the first block in the block chain is that it facilitates communication among potential entrepreneurs who may not have previously known each other, and did not have the social contacts to meet other people in the social-business networks.

The communication in the first block supports and supplements the in-person, face-to-face networking events that currently occur in the entrepreneurial and angel capital forums.

Potential entrepreneurs come from the personnel ranks of existing production units. Entrepreneurs have been involved in the existing production units in a number of collaborative relationships with their peers about how things work, and how to make things work better.

Ideas that gain community traction among participants in the first block are gated through to the second block for further processing into more definitive new venture ideas.

The communication in the second block brings in the set of professional advisors and other interested parties to view the progress of a potential new venture transaction.

In a process similar to current chamber of commerce networking events, potential angel and venture capital investors also have unlimited access to the shared data about a venture in the second block.

This process in the second block is commonly called "deal creation," where various legal and financial professionals collaborate with nascent entrepreneurs to refine the venture idea.

Any computer on the node can freely contribute ideas in the second block.

The open nature of information flows changes in block 3 changes to be more like a private member pass word access node of computers. The members of the node would be professional advisors or self-certified qualified private capital investors under the SEC rules for private investing.

If the new venture idea gains traction, the new venture team would prepare a private placement memo to place online in the third block, and conduct online forums for all interested investors, in order to present the venture concept and answer questions.

After the funding has taken place, only members who contributed private capital to the venture would be allowed access to on-going financial performance reporting on the progress of the ventures, in block four.

This periodic performance reporting would be somewhat like the 10-Q of listed public companies, but with less stringent auditing standards.

In the fifth, and final block, private investors could place bid and ask prices for the venture and transact private secondary market exchanges of the venture's securities.

If, and when, there was some type of exit event, the existing investors would be eligible to participate in the subsequent investment event, and obtain capital gain tax relief for capital reinvested into subsequent new ventures.

The capital profits from the exit events are envisioned to be re-deployed in new venture creation, creating a self-renewing, self-sustaining rate of economic growth.

In the case where there is no exit event, the investors can continue to monitor the performance of the venture, and continue to trade their ownership interests, in the closed, private, regional blockchain stock exchange, much like they currently do in the NASDAQ pink sheets.

The initial partitioning of the regional technology clusters is facilitated by an econometric tool, created by Professor Ed Feser. (Using Feser's Input-Output Model of Technological Affinities To Target Innovation Investments To Regional Industrial Value Chains, Laurie Thomas Vass, SSRN, 2008.).

Feser, (1997), pioneered a modification in the conventional regional input-output analysis of regional economic structure. ("Industrial Complexes Revisited: A Test of For Coincident Economic and Spatial Clustering, Feser, E. J., and Sweeney, S. H. Working Paper, Department of City and Regional Planning, University of North Carolina, 1997.).

Feser's modification added the step of factor analysis to the national input output tables in the technical coefficients matrix, commonly called the A matrix.

The additional step of factor analysis allowed for the discovery of underlying technological affinities in manufacturing and production technology that exist between different industrial sectors.

Feser's factor analysis method results in the discovery of technological affinities that do not, on first glance, appear to be in obviously related regional industrial sectors.

Most cases of radical innovation involve the market commercialization of technology in products and services that are "new-to-the-world," and are not obvious.

This same idea of "shared specific knowledge" between what first appear to be unrelated industrial sectors was described by Bryce and Winter, (2006), as the "general inter-industry relatedness index." (A General Inter-Industry Relatedness Index, David, J., Bryce, and Sidney, G. Winter, CES Working Paper 06-31,2006.).

Bryce and Winter provide the example of the shared knowledge relatedness between the Metal and Partitions Sector, (SIC 2542), and the Automatic Vending Machines Sector, (SIC 3581), otherwise known as razor blades and drink machines.

The analytical results of the Feser and Bryce/Winters methods would suggest to entrepreneurs and private investors which industrial sectors in the region would be potential investment targets because they were "members" of the regional industrial clusters whose interindustrial multiplier relationships were not obvious.

Based upon the existing structure of technology in the region, the econometric models, in conjunction with regional blackchain networks, could generate predictions about possible future economic scenarios of economic growth based upon the existing firms in the industrial structure of the region.

The blockchain technology reduces the confusion and uncertainty that entrepreneurs face in the early part of new venture creation, during the period of time that product development professionals call the "fuzzy front end."

Metro regional entrepreneurship.

Self-sustaining regional growth is contingent upon human business-social networks which have the potential to create and diffuse new technological knowledge.

Regional economic growth occurs as a result of an entrepreneur taking old knowledge, gained from using the old technology, in the old unit, with her when she leaves with her new technological knowledge, to create the new venture.

The new ventures are more productive, and achieve higher overall production output per unit of input than the old production units.

To the extent that a region has a high rate, or pace of technical learning, and has accumulated technical knowledge, it will have a high rate of technical change in production processes, and consequently, a high rate of economic growth, as a result of entrepreneurs creating new ventures.

However, innovating firms, and the presence of social-business networks, and the accumulation of technological knowledge, are not distributed uniformly across regions.

Piero Saviotti notes that innovative firms,

"...tend to cluster in those (areas) that were already innovating countries...this specificity cannot be explained by factor endowments, but is more likely to be caused by specific institutional configurations, and by the cumulative, local and specific character of the knowledge that the institutions possess." (Technological Evolution, Variety and the Economy, Piero Saviotti, Edward-Elgar, 1996.).

This tendency of firms to concentrate in a geographic region contributes to the development of a regional economic "macrotechnology."

According to Saviotti, the reason one metro region economy develops a macrotechnology, as opposed to any other region is related to the,

"...specific institutional configurations and by the cumulative, local, and specific character of the knowledge that the institutions possess."

The geographically-specific technological knowledge in a metro region facilitates the ability of all the firms to absorb new technological knowledge, which we argue is enhanced by the blockchain technology described above.

All of the 300 metro U. S. regions share a certain type of macrotechnological entrepreneurial culture, characterized by many periodic chamber of commerce business social networking events, and angel capital conferences, where entrepreneurs make pitches to raise capital.

Each unique regional social-business network promotes tacit knowledge creation and is characterized by unique cultural values associated with individual risk taking and creating new ventures.

Richard Florida, in "The Distinct Personality of Entrepreneurial Cities," (2015), explains the connection between the entrepreneurial culture and tacit knowledge creation.

Florida states,

"The entrepreneurial culture (an environment that fosters entrepreneurship) creates an economy where entrepreneurs have the drive and resilience to overcome obstacles, are more open to new ideas, and are able to connect with people, build and lead teams, and get things done... The entrepreneurial culture interacts with and connects to local (tacit) knowledge and talent. As Renfrow puts it, "new knowledge will have a greater propensity to generate entrepreneurship in regions with a pronounced entrepreneurial culture where the predominant attitudes and norms reinforce an individual's decisions to act upon entrepreneurial opportunities." (Bloomberg, 2015.).

In other words, an existing regional metro social-business network of skilled individuals, working in a similar technology production units, share some specialized technical knowledge about a production process or a production technology.

Within this social-business network, potential entrepreneurs meet with each other and discuss the feasibility of starting a new venture, based upon their shared technical knowledge and their understanding of the potential market for the products produced.

All of the engineers, scientists, mid-level managers in the region communicate with each other about how the new process would work, and when they leave to create their own new venture, it is that new production process that forms the basis on their own equipment and machinery purchases.

We cite the historical example of the difference between corporate textile production in Lowell, Massachusetts, and the entrepreneurial textile production in Philadelphia, to describe how different types of economic growth results from different types of entrepreneurial cultures.

The example of the two regions is relevant to the issue of corporate globalism, today, versus regional metro economic development.

In Proprietary Capitalism: The Textile Manufacture at Philadelphia, 1800 – 1885, Philip Scranton (Cambridge UniversityPress,1983.), notes that.

"By the 1880s Philadelphia had erected a manufacturing system that stood as a fully realized alternative to the corporate industrial model of Lowell…the difference between a mature small business alternative to industrial gigantism."

Scranton describes how,

"High levels of flexibility and specialization in Philadelphia gave its hundreds of small mills a special character that stemmed from a network of material and sociological factors…

they constructed an alternative pathway to [capital] accumulation… the high level of productive flexibility [in small firms]…allowed them to alter production according to the wants of the season…using workers whose skills and experience was qualitatively richer than that of machine tenders [in Lowell]."

We argue that each of the 300 metro regions in the U. S. has the same entrepreneurial potential to create regional economic growth as Philadelphia did in the 1880s.

Given a set of blockchain computer nodes and econometric new tools, business social networks could embark on an entrepreneurial development pathway, consistent with Jefferson's version of the American Dream.

Regional Capital markets.

We cite an economic relationship between technological knowledge diffusion and a close geographical proximity to a supply of local private capital that invests capital in the new ventures. (Creating the Private Capital Market Infrastructure for Sustainable Innovation Economics, Laurie Thomas Vass, SSRN, 2008.).

Part of the barrier to regional innovation is the absence of a capital market institutional infrastructure. The existing venture capital networks, and angel funding forums, are not adequate for the level of new venture creation required to stimulate regional economic growth.

Part of the issue is that the investment capital required by small manufacturing firms and startups to support innovation is so small that it is not attractive to the VCs.

And, part of the issue is that the preferred quick VC exit strategy does not contribute to long-term economic growth at the regional level.

In other words, there is a financial conflict of interest between the short-term financial interests of the venture capitalist community and the long-term goals of regional self-sustaining economic growth.

More venture capital, as it is currently deployed, will not solve the capital equity gap for regional innovation. (Will More Venture Capital Spur Regional Innovation? Laurie Thomas Vass, SSRN, 2008.).

A new regional capital market infrastructure must be built in each region that targets investments into the region's industrial value chains.

The new capital market infrastructure must address the small amounts of capital required at the front end of the innovation pipeline and the best exit strategy that promotes economic growth at the back end of the pipeline.

The regional capital market infrastructure, that funds regional new technology ventures, functions in the same way that roads, bridges, and sewer lines functioned in the older industrial recruitment economic strategy.

Bruno and Tyebjee (1982), identified the supply of venture capital as one of the top three factors that seemed to explain where entrepreneurs came from before they became entrepreneurs. (The Environment For Entrepreneurship, A. Bruno, and T. Tyebjee, in C. Kent, D. Sexton, and K. Vesper, The Encyclopedia of Entrepreneurship, Prentice-Hall, Inc. 1982.).

The supply or absence of capital in a region seems to be a matter of historical contingency in the ability of the Ruling Class to control the process of economic development. (W. J. Cash, 1941.).

Unlike the existing set of natural resource factor endowments in a region, the creation of a pool of new venture capital is determined by human history.

No region is initially born with new venture capital, but some regions, as a result of history, are lucky enough to resist the return to the plantation, in order to create a supply of it.

The fifth block, in the above blockchain model of deal creation, is aimed at creating a mechanism for the reinvestment of capital gains from venture exits, back into the regional innovation process.

The new monetary authority.

We argued above that a new type of monetary authority, under the authority of a new constitution, should replace the independent Fed.

The intent of the new constitution is to bring monetary policy under some version of citizen democratic control by placing the monetary authority under the jurisdiction of national elected representatives.

One of Madison's flaws was the weak link in his grant of Congressional authority to coin money with the absence of rules for the administrative authority to manage the money supply.

In the Jefferson version of the entrepreneurial capitalist economy, a stable money supply allows entrepreneurs the ability to predict future prices when they are planning a new venture.

It is as result of the relationship between money supply in financial markets and commodity production markets, at the aggregate national level, that the supply of money is related to regional economic growth.

When an entrepreneur leaves the old unit to create a new venture, she goes through a process of guessing at prices in the future, and also guesses at the rate of profit to use in the spreadsheets for the new venture business plan.

Old production units provide some base line for these guesses, as far as they relate to cost of production to produce a new product.

The experience gained in the old units are not a very helpful guide for guessing at future prices, new markets, new production relationships or how consumer preferences may change.

Stable national monetary policy reduces an entrepreneur's uncertainty, and provides some context of stability for the entrepreneur as she makes her guesses about the future.

Money supply is linked to technical change at the regional level through its effect on the entrepreneur's expectations on the future.

This is similar to the Keynesian conclusion that the rate of investment reflects the entrepreneur's present view in period one to her view of possible future outcomes, in period two.

If the supply of money flowing into the region is stable or rising, the economic conditions are favorable for continued technical change. As long as the entrepreneur can predict the direction of technical change, she has the confidence to make guesses about future prices in planning her new venture.

In other words, stable national monetary policy can create the conditions for regional economic growth because it provides a base line of stability for the guesses that the entrepreneur is making about future demand and future prices.

Simon Kuznets described part of the effect of national monetary policy on economic growth with an analysis that relied upon business cycles for an explanation.

He also identified the main conceptual relationships between technical change and economic growth in his 1930 book, Secular Movements In Production and Prices. (Houghton, Mifflin, 1930.).

Using the framework of a three period cycle of time, Kuznets described how, in the first period, technological innovation created entirely new industries.

In the second time period, the newly created industries grow rapidly, compared to older industries because the older industries had lower demand elasticities, and as prices dropped, there was little increase in demand for older industry products.

In Kuznet's third time period, future economic growth depends on the continued development of new products, and the changing mix of industrial sectors brought about by technical change.

While Kuznet's objective was to place national economic growth into the analytical framework of business cycles, much of what he described could be translated into the analytical framework of Jefferson's entrepreneurial capitalist economy, because Kuznets explains the role of a stable money supply for creating the conditions of future economic growth.

The growth rate of money supply is tied to the rate of increase in population, in a "rule-based" monetary authority, overseen by national elected representatives.

The rule-based monetary authority establishes transparent, durable interest rates, with the current 6% interest, paid by the Fed to member banks on stock ownership in the Fed, as the benchmark for intermediate term interest rates.

As an alternative to the New York Regional Bank's discretionary authority to set overnight discount rates, a market-based futures commodity market would allow short-term bank borrowing rates to be set by market participants to meet daily reserve requirements.

The new monetary authority would act as the "lender-of-last-resort" to provide emergency reserve bank liquidity during a national crisis.

The current ability of the Fed to bail out its friends around the world would be abolished. In the future Jefferson version of the American Dream, no one, and no bank, is too big to fail.

An institutional authority, similar in concept to the existing regional federal reserve banks, would be tasked by national elected representatives, to collect the economic data, and organize the data into regional econometric models that can be used by citizens in the regional business-social networks.

The model for this new role of the regional Fed banks is the current function of the St. Louis Federal Reserve Bank's economic data gathering and economic modeling.

The regional banks, in the new model, would continue their function of monitoring and auditing private commercial bank reserves and lending practices, and issuing periodic reports to the national monetary authority.

Chapter 11. The Constitutional Economics of Jefferson's Entrepreneurial Capitalist Society.

The late James Buchanan, a professor of constitutional economics, at George Mason University, explained the relationship between a nation's rate of economic growth and the constitutional institutional rules of government that govern financial transactions in a free market competitive economy.

Under one configuration of constitutional rules, Buchanan predicted certain types of economic outcomes. Under a different configuration of rules, Buchanan predicted other types of economic outcomes.

Buchanan argued that there is only one, unique, configuration of constitutional rules that leads the nation to optimum rates of national economic growth.

These rules aim at maximum individual freedom to allow individuals to seek their own happiness, and that future economic outcome is called Pareto Optimality.

Buchanan explained that every set of constitutional rules has an internal end-goal to which the rules are directed.

We argued in Chapter 9 that Madison's constitution was defective because he did not state an unambiguous goal in his Preamble.

In the absence of a clearly stated end-goal, we explained that Madison's rules lead to Arrow's infinite regress of economic collapse, where the economy cycles over and over, through a series of speculative bubbles, followed by economic collapse.

In The Logical Foundations of Constitutional Liberty, (1999), Buchanan relies on a philosophy of logic to explain how the end goal of liberty in a constitution, creates the binding allegiance of citizens to follow the rule of law. (Liberty Fund; Volume 1, 1999.).

Buchanan relies upon the rationality of individual self-interest as a force that binds individuals to obey the rule of law, through a mental process of rationally minimizing risk in uncertain decision making environments.

In leaving the state of nature, and forming a constitution, Buchanan explains, individuals are placed in a position of uncertainty in the outcome of their life's mission.

No individual knows in advance where the individual may end up, given the choice between one set of constitutional rules or another.

His logic of individual rationality is that any individual, with a rational self-interest, would choose fair rules for all, aimed at the greatest freedom for all.

Buchanan argues that this unique constellation of rules is the most just and fair constitution, based upon an individual social welfare definition of justice, not on a social class definition of social welfare, as in Madison's rules.

In The Reason of Rules: Constitutional Political Economy, (2000), Buchanan explains that justice is obtained through process of how citizens provide prior consent to follow the rules that they give to themselves.

"Just conduct," writes Buchanan, "consists of behavior that does not violate rules to which one has given *prior* consent."

The end goal, or public purpose of the constitution, in this case of rational self-interest, is maximum individual liberty.

The public purpose in an individualist society is served by promotion and adherence to common external values of trust, fair dealing, truthful representations, protection of private property rights, and promise keeping.

Voluntary cooperation to obey the rule of law between individuals occurs when the individuals assume, prior to entering into any political or financial exchange process, that other citizens share these common cultural and political values.

In The Reason of Rules, Buchanan and Brennan write,

"Our specific claim is that justice takes its meaning from the rules for the social order within which notions of justice are to be applied…

To appeal to considerations of justice is to appeal to relevant rules. These rules provide the framework within which patterns of distributional end states emerge from the interaction of persons who play various complex functional roles."

In other words, fair distribution of income and wealth, under Buchanan, is obtained through just rules of financial and economic exchange.

Buchanan applies his concept of justice to his suggestions about the relationship between free markets and governmental power.

He states that,

"...for most persons, the independence offered by the presence of market alternatives offers the maximal liberty possible. But we have not yet designed institutions [Madison's rules] that will satisfy the individual's search for community in the impersonal setting of the market order without, at the same time, undermining the very independence that this order afford."

Rather than relying on the government's institutional separation of powers to deal with the problem of corruption, as Madison did, Buchanan relies upon the rationality of self-interest because the citizens provide prior consent to follow fair rules.

After the citizens give their prior consent to the initial creation of the rules, fair rules would allow them to give ongoing consent, after the government had been established.

Buchanan addressed this question of fairness in his book, The Theory of Public Choice, (1984), in terms of on-going citizen consent, after citizens give the initial grant of consent.

In the context of the application of fair constitutional rules, Buchanan makes a distinction between justice in political rules and justice in economic exchanges.

He described the difference between "economic man," in the context of economic exchanges, and "moral man," in the context of political rights. (University of Michigan Press, 1984.).

Economic man, according to Buchanan, is defined by his utility function, whose variables are weighted according to their contribution to monetary wealth.

"Economic man's behavior, in the economic relationship, is not influenced by ethical or moral considerations that serve to constrain his pursuit of his objectively defined interest."

Under a different constitutional arrangement, economic man's pursuit of unfair advantage would be tempered by the presence of moral man's principles of justice in the distribution of economic benefits.

As Buchanan notes, the welfare outcomes that the elites seek to maximize under Madison's rules, are the rules for economic man, because Madison never defined the role of morality in his constitution that sanctioned slavery.

In other words, as Buchanan explained, under Madison's rules, the social welfare that elites maximize is their own welfare, using the agencies of government to obtain unfair advantage over common citizens.

In Buchanan's political realm of moral man, appeals to justice take place within the political system of democratic representative government, and Jefferson wrote that citizens have a God-given right to alter or abolish those rules when the application of the constitutional rules become destructive of the ends for which it was created.

Private property is relevant to the creation of the new natural rights constitution because of property's relationship to an owner's ability to appropriate the fruits of his labor and returns on his investments.

The legitimacy of a claim of private property is related to an economicsystem of rewards based upon merit and individual achievement.

Following Jefferson, all legitimate authority is derived from the consent of the governed, and claims of private property made by agents of government that are not so derived from the sovereignty of consent, are illegitimate.

As we have argued, in the current period of history, citizens in the United States do not share common cultural values about the public purpose or national mission.

With the entrance of the Democrat Marxist ideology into the American political framework, there is no rational justification to keep the current set of rules in place.

A better idea is to start over, with a new constitution, at the point in history of Jefferson's ideology of liberty, and let the citizens of each state vote on the form of government that best serves their liberty and happiness.

The basic philosophical difference in the proposed referendum is between individualism and collectivism.

In other words, the conflicts, today, revolve around the differences between a natural rights constitution based upon individual rights and Madison's British social class mixed government constitution that aims at amelioration of conflicts between two social classes.

We cite four irreconcilable, permanent economic conflicts between Marxists and natural rights conservatives that warrant national civil dissolution.

- Open flows of technological information to create a wide range of new ventures.
- Open flows of private capital investment to create maximum rates of new venture creation.
- Maximum rates of technical change to create maximum knowledge diffusion.
- Maximum individual freedom, reward based upon individual merit to create an "entrepreneurial capitalist society" that promotes maximum rates of economic growth.

Jefferson's natural rights constitution has 11 constitutional provisions which establish the national framework of individual economic freedom:

The National Congress shall have the power to issue government bonds, and to borrow money on the credit of the Democratic Republic of America. All proposals to borrow money or issue debt shall occur once in the two year budget cycle, and all proposals to issue debt must be approved by 50% of the State legislatures of the Democratic Republic of America, no later than January 21 of the year of issuance.

The term of debt and interest on any issuance of debt shall not exceed 10 years, and must be paid in full by the end of the 10th year.

The National Congress shall have the power to regulate commerce and approve trade agreements with foreign nations, which are negotiated by the President.

The National Congress shall have the power to establish a uniform rule of citizen naturalization, and provide revenues for national border security to prohibit illegal entrance into the sovereign nation or any sovereign state.

The National Congress shall have the power to coin money, regulate the value thereof, regulate the circulation and creation of money and money instruments, regulate the national banking system and establish the currency value of foreign coin, and fix the Standard of Weights and Measures.

The National Congress shall have the power to provide for the punishment for the national criminal felony of counterfeiting the securities and money of the Democratic Republic of America.

The National Congress shall have the power to establish a national Post Office and a national system of roads and transportation routes, and national regulation of any form of internet communication that limits free speech.

The National Congress shall have the power to authorize regional capital securities markets, and to establish regulatory guidelines for the operation of regional private and public security exchanges designed to promote maximum national and regional economic growth rates.

The National Congress shall have the power to establish and maintain a national patent office to promote the progress of science and useful arts, by securing for limited times to authors and inventors the exclusive right to their respective writings and discoveries.

The National Congress shall have the power to protect the patents of citizens from foreign and domestic criminal usurpation of the right of citizens to enjoy the benefits of their invention.

The National Congress shall have the power to define and punish intellectual property piracies and criminal patent felonies committed against citizens of the Democratic Republic of America by foreign and domestic criminals.

We argued in Chapter 9 that Madison's constitution was defective because he did not state an unambiguous goal in his Preamble. We offer a superior Preamble for the new constitution:

The Preamble states:

We, the citizens of the Democratic Republic of America, establish this constitutional contract between our respective states and the National Government of the Democratic Republic of America.

"We solemnly swear and affirm that we establish this contract to preserve and protect the natural and civil rights of citizens in each state, and to protect and defend the sovereignty of each state and the nation, from foreign and domestic threats."

It is from this Preamble that the Guiding Principles of the National Government are created:

Guiding Principles of the Democratic Republic of America National Government.

By freely and voluntarily joining our state government into the union of the Democratic Republic of America, we affirm that the National Government will be guided by the following principles:

1. "...that all legitimate government authority is derived from the consent of the citizens governed..."

2. "...that as the consequence of the sovereign authority of citizens, citizens have an inalienable natural right to remove, within 30 days, an elected representative from office upon a referendum of 51% of registered voters in a state..."

3. "...that those governed by the laws and whose individual freedom is restricted by the laws should have the greatest say and consent in making of the laws..."

4. "...that those who make the laws and give consent to the laws, acting as representatives of the citizens, bind themselves and their constituents to following the laws..."

5. "...that the National Government is instituted to allow individual citizens to pursue individual happiness and to limit the arbitrary application of government power over the lives of individuals..."

6. "...that individual citizens who freely give their consent to form a government through constitutional conventions are bound by the original contract until the operation of the government becomes destructive to the original intent of obtaining individual freedom and the pursuit of happiness..."

7. "...that the citizens of each state have mechanisms in place in the constitutional contract to modify or abolish the governments that have been created that have become destructive to the ideals and goals under which the National Government is instituted, including the right to vote on remaining a member of the national government in a referendum to be held every 20 years from the date of admittance..."

8. "...that the parties to the constitutional contract are individual human citizens acting through their elected representatives at the state and national levels of government..."

9. "...that the National Government is created by this union of states and the National Government shall never usurp the sovereign power or authority of the individual states or the sovereignty of the citizens in each state and that states have an inalienable right to call a convention of the states, without Congressional approval, to modify, amend, or abolish this Constitutional Contract."

10. "...that an individual's private property obtained through legal contract and title transfer, their rights to appropriate income and profits from the use of their private property, and their

rights to dispose and transfer their private property are inviolate and derived from natural rights granted to them by God, and that no government or constitutional contract may ever abrogate or subordinate these natural individual rights, unless by free and voluntary consent of the citizen..."

11. "...that a citizens Grand Jury of 18 citizens is impaneled, for a term of 12 months, to protect and preserve the rights of citizens against the arbitrary application of government power against citizens..."

12. "...that a citizens Grand Jury of 18 citizens must inspect all national penal facilities within its district every 6 months, and report their findings to the Chief District Judge, who shall act to remedy the deficiencies found by the Grand Jury..."

13. "...that the 1776 Declaration of Independence established a representative democracy, ordained by God, to pursue individual human freedoms and liberty from oppression and is an exceptional model in human history to be preserved, protected, and cherished by the citizens and deployed by them and their elected representatives as the guiding principles in the Democratic Republic of America in its relationships with other nations and other people..."

Citizen Bill of Rights of the Democratic Republic of America.

We affirm and swear that all citizens in each of the respective States are guaranteed equal rights for all, and special privileges for none.

Among these rights are:

1. That all citizens have a natural right to worship and exercise their own religion and that the National Government is prohibited from making and enforcing any law respecting the establishment of an official national religion and compelling citizens to worship a national religion.

2. The National Government shall be prohibited from making or enforcing any law that restricts the natural right of a citizen's freedom of speech and freedom of conscience.

3. The National Government is prohibited from making or enforcing any law which restricts the right of citizens to peaceably assemble, and to petition the National Government for a redress of grievances.

4. That all citizens have a natural right to truthful and honest statements from government agents and from elected representatives, and that it is the duty of the free press to report the truth.

5. That all citizens in the respective states have a natural right to own and use weapons, and that the National Government, nor any state, shall make no laws which abridge the right of law-abiding citizens from owning, keeping and bearing weapons.

6. The National Government is prohibited from using agents of government or national resources to conduct searches and seizures of private citizen documents, or property, and that the possessions and documents obtained from illegal searches and seizures are inadmissible in any national court.

7. No citizen in any state shall be seized or imprisoned, or stripped of his rights or of his property or possessions, or outlawed or exiled, or deprived of his standing in any other way, nor shall agents of the government proceed with force against him, or send others to do so, except by the lawful judgment of a true bill of indictment by a majority vote of a grand jury of 18 citizens, or by the rules of judicial civil procedure of the National Government.

8. No warrants or judicial orders in any criminal investigation shall be issued by a national court, except upon probable cause, determined in a judicial hearing, supported by an oath or affirmation of the government agent describing the specific items or locations to be searched and a judicial description of the crime being investigated.

9. No person shall be held to answer for a capital, or otherwise infamous crime, unless on a presentment or indictment of a majority vote of a Grand Jury of 18 citizens who

conduct an inquiry into the legitimacy of the government's allegation of a national crime.

10. No citizen shall be subject for the same offence or to be twice put in jeopardy of life or limb; nor shall be compelled in any criminal case to be a witness against himself.

11. The National Government, and every State government, are prohibited from making or enforcing any law which shall abridge the privileges or immunities of citizens of the States; nor shall any State deprive any natural human person of life, liberty, or property, without due process of law; nor deny to any person within its jurisdiction the equal protection of the laws.

12. No citizen shall be deprived of life, liberty, or property, without due process of law; nor shall private property be taken for public use, without just compensation, determined by a majority vote of a Grand Jury of 18 citizens.

13. That all citizens are due the equal application of justice and that no citizen is entitled to special or unequal treatment of the application of the law.

14. That all citizens are judged innocent until proven guilty in a trial of due process, by a jury of 12 of their peers.

15. In all criminal prosecutions, the accused shall enjoy the right to a speedy and public trial, within 6 months of indictment, by an impartial jury of the State and district wherein the crime shall have been committed, which district shall have been previously ascertained by law, and to be informed of the nature and cause of the accusation; to be confronted with the witnesses against him; to have compulsory process for obtaining witnesses in his favor, and to have the assistance of counsel for his defense.

16. The right of trial by jury shall be preserved, and no fact tried by a jury, shall be otherwise re-examined in any Court of the States, than according to the rules of the common law then obtaining in the national judiciary.

17. Excessive bail shall not be required, nor excessive fines imposed, nor cruel and unusual punishments inflicted, nor imprisonment for longer than 5 days, in the absence of specific charges and allegation of crime.

18. That citizens have a civil right of action against elected representatives or agents of the National Government, for violation of these natural rights, upon a presentation of a motion of grievance to a Grand Jury of 18 citizens, who shall hear the case and determine the outcome and set the penalties for the violation by a majority vote.

19. The a citizens Grand Jury in any State retains the right of initiating a citizen initiative on legislative proposals by a petition to the House of Representatives, which must respond to the petition within 30 days of receipt.

20. The right of citizens of the States to vote, hold elected office, or deliberate in public debates, shall not be denied or abridged by the National Government or by any State on account of race, color of skin, sex, or religious beliefs.

21. The right of a citizen to vote in all elections is an inviolable inalienable natural right, and is constitutionally protected, in both the citizen's freedom to vote and in the legitimate count of the vote, in all local, state, and national elections and referendums, by Federal and State law enforcement agents.

Epilogue:

Jefferson's The Declaration of 1775, The Causes and Necessity of Taking Up Arms, states,

"We are reduced to the alternative of choosing an unconditional submission to the tyranny of irritated Ministers, or resistance by force. The latter is our choice. We have counted the cost of this contest, and find nothing so dreadful as voluntary slavery. Honor, justice, and humanity, forbid us, tamely to surrender that freedom which we received from our gallant ancestors, and which our innocent posterity have a right to receive from us."

The Patriots began their Declaration, of 1775, in the same place that we find ourselves today: on the fundamental purpose of government.

The Patriots wrote,

"Our forefathers, inhabitants of the Island of Great Britain, left their native land, to seek on these shores a residence for civil and religious freedom…Government was instituted to promote the welfare of mankind, and ought to be administered for the attainment of that end."

We believe that the differences in ideology between natural rights and Marxism are irreconcilable and unsolvable.

We believe that the only peaceful, non-violent solution to the differences is a civil disunion of the Former United States of America, where citizens in each state can vote to join the new nation, or to remain in a Marxist tyranny.

The strategy for adoption of the new constitution is similar to the process used by the Patriots, in 1776.

The Patriots relied upon the state legislatures to debate the proposed Articles of Confederation, and waited until 1781, for each of the 13 states to vote to ratify the Articles.

We propose a similar process, with the exception, that after each state legislature has debated the issue of leaving the former United State in order to join a new nation, that the legislature submit the proposal to the citizens for a vote.

States where a majority of citizens vote to approve the proposal can then meet, like the Continental Congress, and continue the work of drafting the final version of the constitution of the new nation.

Bibliography

A Constitutional History of the United States, Forrest McDonald and Ellen S. McDonald, Krieger Publishing Co., 1986.

A Government Out of Sight: The Mystery of National Authority in Nineteenth-Century America, Brian Balogh, Cambridge University Press, 2009.

A Nation Under Our Feet, Steven Hahn, Belknap Press, 2003.

A Politics of Tensions: The Articles of Confederation and American Political Ideas, Robert Hoffert, University Press of Colorado, 1992.

A Return to Jekyll Island. The Origins, History, and Future of the Federal Reserve. Edited by Michael Bordo and William Roberts, Cambridge University Press, 2013.

Against the Profit Motive: The Salary Revolution In American Government, 1780 – 1940, Nicholas Parrillo, Yale University Press, 2013.

American Populism: A Social History, 1877 – 1898, Robert C McMath, Hill and Wang, NY, 1993.

America's Revolutionary Mind: A Moral History of the American Revolution and the Declaration That Defined It, C. Bradley Thompson, Encounter Books, 2019.

An Economic Interpretation of the Constitution of the United States, Charles Beard, MacMillan Co, 1925.

"Banking and Currency Crises and Systemic Risk: Lessons From Recent Events," George G. Kaufman, Federal Reserve Bank of Chicago, 2000.

Beyond All Reason: The Radical Assault on Truth in American Law, Daniel Farber and Suzanna Sherry, Oxford University Press, 1997.

Born Losers: A History of Failure In America. Harvard University Press, 2005.

Capitalism and a New Social Order: The Republican Vision of the 1790s, Joyce Appleby, New York University Press, 1984.

Chinese President Xi's "Secret Philosopher" Analyzed America And His Findings Could Reverse Our Country's Decline, October 23, 2021.

Closing the Gate: Race, Politics, and the Chinese Exclusion Act, Andrew Gyory, UNC Press, 1998.

Collective Choice and Social Welfare, Amartya Sen, Harvard University Press, 1970.

Constitutional Economics, James M. Buchanan, Blackwell, 1991.

Corporations Are People' Is Built on an Incredible 19th-Century Lie: How a farcical series of events in the 1880s produced an enduring and controversial legal precedent, Adam Winkler, The Atlantic, 2018.

Creating the Private Capital Market Infrastructure for Sustainable Innovation Economics, Laurie Thomas Vass, SSRN, 2008.

Declaring Rights: A Brief History with Documents, Jack N. Rakove, Bedford Books, 1998.

Declining Dynamism, Allocative Efficiency, and the Productivity Slowdown, Ryan A. Decker, John Haltiwanger, Ron S. Jarmin, Javier Miranda, American Economic Review, vol. 107, no. 5, May 2017.

Democratic Promise: The Populist Moment in America, Lawrence Goodwyn, Oxford University Press, 1976.

Democracy in Desperation: The Depression of 1893. Douglas Steeples and David Whitten, Greenwood Press, 1998.

Does the Fed's Job Performance Justify Its Independence? Laurie Thomas Vass, Social Science Research Network (SSRN), 2019.

Does "We the People" Include Corporations? Ciara Torres-Spelliscy, ABA Groups, Volume 43, Number 2, 2021.

Echoes of War: Rethinking Post-Civil War Government and Politics, Gregory P. Downs and Kate Masur, in The World The Civil War Made, UNC Press, 2015.

Gilded Freedom: U. S. Government Exclusion of Chinese Migrants, 1848-1882, Robert Villanueva, University of Hawaii, 2016.

Government by Dissent, Robert Martin, NYU Press, 2013.

Has the Fed Been a Failure? George Selgin, William D. Lastrapes, and Lawrence H. White, SSRN, 2012.

Industrial Complexes Revisited: A Test of For Coincident Economic and Spatial Clustering, Ed Feser, and S. H Sweeney, Working Paper, Department of City and Regional Planning, University of North Carolina, 1997.

Inflated: How Money and Debt Built the American Dream. R. Christopher Whalen, John Wiley & Sons, 2010.

Inside the Fed Making Monetary Policy, William C. Melton, Dow Jones Irwin, 1985.

International Aspects of Financial-Market Imperfections: The Aftermath of Financial Crises. Carmen M. Reinhart and Kenneth S. Rogoff, American Economic Review, Vol. 99, No.2. 2009.

Jeffersonian Legacies Peter Onuf ed., University of Virginia Press, 1993.

Labor Market Institutions in the Gilded Age of American Economic History, Suresh Naidu and Noam Yuchtman, National Bureau of Economic Research, 2016.

Lawless, David Bernstein, Encounter Books, 2015.

Man Over Money: The Southern Populist Critique of American Capitalism, Bruce Palmer, UNC Press, 1980.

Many Excellent People: Power and Privilege in North Carolina,

1850 - 1900, Paul D. Escott, University of North Carolina Press, 1985.

Novus Ordo Seclorum: The Intellectual Origins of the Constitution, Forrest McDonald, University Press of Kansas, 1985.

Ordeal by Fire: The Civil War and Reconstruction. James M. McPherson. Alfred Knoph, 1982.

Origins of the Federal Reserve System, Money, Class, and Corporate Capitalism, 1890-1913. James Livingston, Cornell University Press, 1986.

Origins of The New South, 1877 1913, C. Vann, Woodward, Louisiana State University Press, 1951.

Plain Folk In The New South: Social Change and Cultural Persistence, 1880 1915, I. A. Newby, Louisiana State University Press, 1989.

Plain Folks Fight: The Civil War and Reconstruction in Piney Woods Georgia. Mark Wetherington, UNC Press, 2005.

Planters and the Making of a "New South": Class, Politics, and Development in North Carolina, 1865 1900, Dwight B. Billings, University of North Carolina Press, 1979.

Populist Vanguard: A History of the Southern Farmers' Alliance, Robert C. McMath, W. W. Norton, 1975.

Proprietary Capitalism: The Textile Manufacture at Philadelphia, 1800 – 1885. Philip Scranton Cambridge University Press, 1983.

Radical Protest and Social Structure: The Southern Farmers' Alliance and Cotton Tenancy, 1880 1890, Michael Schwartz, Academic Press, 1976.

Reason of Rules, James M., Buchanan, and Geoffrey Brennan, Cambridge University Press, 1985.

Rebels and Democrats: The Struggle For Equal Political Rights and Majority Rule During the American Revolution, Elisha, P. Douglas, UNC Press, 1955.

Reconstruction: America's Unfinished Revolution, 1863 – 1877, Eric Foner, Harper & Row, 1988.

Reconstruction and Redemtion in the South, Otto Olsen, Louisiana State University Press, 1980.

Second Treatise on Government, John Locke, Oxford University Press, 2016, first published 1689.

Secular Movements In Production and Prices, Simon Kuznets, Houghton, Mifflin, 1930.

Slavery in the State of North Carolina, John Spencer Bassett, Johns Hopkins Press, 1899.

Social Choice and Individual Values, Kenneth Arrow, Yale University Press, 1951.

Southern Capitalism: The Political Economy of North Carolina, 1880–1980, Phillip Wood, Duke University Press, 1986.

Southern Politics In State and Nation, Vladimer Orlando Key, with the assistance of Alexander Heard, A. A. Knopf, 1949.

Splendid Failure: Postwar Reconstruction in the American South. Michael Fitzgerald, Ivan R. Lee, 2007.

Supreme Court Rulings That Turned Corporations Into People, Alex Park, Mother Jones, 2014.

"Systemic Risk and the Role of Government," John Taylor, Speech given at the Conference on Financial Innovation and Crises, Federal Reserve Bank of Atlanta, Jekyll Island, Georgia, May 12th, 2009.

Technological Evolution, Variety and the Economy, Piero Saviotti, Edward-Elgar, 1996.

Theory of Public Choice: Political Applications of Economics, James M Buchanan, University of Michigan Press, 1972.

The American Revolution of 1800, Dan Sisson, Berret-Koehler, 2014.

The Antifederalists: Men of Great Faith and Forbearance, David J. Siemers, Rowman & Littlefield, NY 2003.

The Articles of Confederation, Merrill Jensen, University of Wisconsin Press, 1970.

The Broken Constitution: Lincoln, Slavery, and the Refounding of America. Noah Feldman, Farrar, Straus & Giroux. 2021.

The Burden of Southern History, C. Vann Woodward, LSU Press, 1968.

The Captured Economy: How the Powerful Enrich Themselves, Slow Down Growth, and Increase Inequality, Brink Lindsey and Steven Teles, Oxford University Press, 2017.

The Creation of the American Republic, 1776–1787, Gordon S. Wood, UNC Press, 1998.

The Death of Reconstruction: Race, Labor and Politics in the3 Post-Civil War North, 1865 – 1901. Heather Cox Richardson, Harvard University Press, 2001.

The Distinct Personality of Entrepreneurial Cities, Richard Florida, 2015),

The Doctrine of Sovereignty Under the United States Constitution, Hugh Evander Willis, Indiana University School of Law, 1929.

The Economic Origins of Jeffersonian Democracy, Charles Austin Beard, Macmillan Co., 1915.

The Environment For Entrepreneurship, A. Bruno, and T. Tyebjee, in C. Kent, D. Sexton, and K. Vesper, The Encyclopedia of Entrepreneurship, Prentice-Hall, Inc. 1982.

The Epic of America, James Truslow Adams, Simon Publications, 2001.

The Federalist: A Collection of Essays Written in Favor of the New Constitution as Agreed Upon by the Federal Convention, September 17, 1787, Alexander Hamilton, James Madison, and John Jay, Reprinted from the original text under the editorial supervision of Henry B. Dawson. Essays written by Alexander Hamilton, James Madison and John Jay under pseudonym of "Publius".

The Federalists, the Antifederalists, and the American Political Tradition, Wilson Carey et al editors, Greenwood Press, 1992.

The Forgotten Man, William Graham Sumner, 1883 lecture in Brooklyn, published posthumously in 1918.

The Framers Coup, Michael Klarman, Oxford University Press, 2016.

The Great Father: The United States Government and the United States Government and the American Indian, Francis Paul Prucha, University of Nebraska Press, 1984.

The Ideological Origins of the American Revolution, Bernard Bailyn, Belnap Press, 1967.

The Information Economy: Definition and Measurement, Marc Uri Porat, U. S. Department of Commerce, O. T. Special Publication 77-12(1), 1977.

The Jefferson Image In The American Mind, Merrill D. Peterson, Oxford University Press, 1960.

The Leviathan, Thomas Hobbes, T., & Gaskin, J. C. A., first published, 1651.

The Logical Foundations of Constitutional Liberty, James Buchanan, The Liberty Fund, 1999.

The Making of the American Constitution, Merrill Jensen, D. Van Nostrand Co. Inc., 1964.

The Mind of the Founder: Sources of the Political Thought of James Madison, Marvin Meyers, Brandeis University Press, 1973.

The Mind of the South: 1900 -1941, Wilbur Joseph Cash, Alfred A. Knopf, 1941.

The Moral Foundations of the American Republic, 3rd Ed. Robert Horwitz, University of Virginia Press, 1986.

The Natural Rights Republic: Studies In The Foundation of The American Political Tradition, Michael Zuckert, University of Notre Dame Press, 1996.

The Ordeal of the Reunion: A New History of Reconstruction, Mark Summers, UNC Press. 2014.

The Other Founders, Saul Cornell, UNC Press, 1999.

The Political Economy of American Industrialization, 1877 - 1900, Richard Franklin Bensel, Cambridge University Press, 2000.

The Political Theory of Possessive Individualism: From Hobbes to Locke, C. B. Macpherson, Oxford University Press, 1962.

The Populist Moment: A Short History of the Agrarian Revolt in America, Lawrence Goodwyn, Oxford University Press, 1978.

The Populist Persuasion: An American History, Michael Kazin, Basic Books, 1995.

The Promise of the New South: Life After Reconstruction, Edward Ayers, Oxford University Press, 1992.

The Quest For Progress: The Way We Lived in North Carolina, 1870-1920, Sydney Nathans, University of North Carolina Press, 2001.

The Radicalism of the American Revolution, Gordon S Wood, A.A. Knopf, 1992.

The Reason of Rules: Constitutional Political Economy, Geoffrey Brennan and James M. Buchanan, Liberty Fund, 2000.

The Republic for Which It Stands: The United States During Reconstruction and the Gilded Age, 1865 – 1896, Richard White, Oxford University Press, 2017.

The Restoration of the American Natural Rights Republic: Correcting the Consequences of the Republican Party Abdication of Natural Rights and Individual Freedom, Laurie Thomas Vass, GabbyPress, 2017.

The Rise of American Democracy: Jefferson to Lincoln. Sean Willenz, W. W. Norton, 2005.

The Road to Chinese Exclusion: The Denver Riot, 1880 Election, and Rise of the West, Liping Zhu, University Press of Kansas, 2013.

The Road to Redemption: Southern Politics, 1869 1879, Michael Perman, University of North Carolina Press, 1984.

The Roots of Southern Populism: Yeomen Farmers and the Transformation of the Georgia Upcountry, 1850 1890, Steven Hahn, Oxford University Press, 1983.

The Second Founding: How the Civil War and Reconstruction Remade the Constitution, Eric Foner. W. W. Norton, 2019.

The Slaveholders' Dilemma: Freedom and Progress in Southern Conservative Thought, 1820 1860, Eugene D Genovese, University of South Carolina Press, 1992.

The Theory of Public Choice – II, James M. Buchanan and Robert D. Tollison, Editors, University of Michigan Press, 1984.

The Third Answer: How Market-Creating Innovations Drives Economic Growth and Development, Clayton M. Christensen, et al., Innovations, volume 12, number ¾, 2018.

The Transformation of Southern Politics: Social Change and Political Consequence Since 1945, Jack Bass and Walter DeVries, University of Georgia Press, 1995.

The Unwritten Constitution of the United States: A Philosophical Inquiry Into the Fundamentals of American Constitutional Law, Christopher Tiedman, G. P. Putnam, 1890.

The World The Civil War Made. Edited by Gregory P. Downs and Kate Masur, UNC Press. 2015.

Slavery and Its Consequences: The Constitution, Equality, and Race, AEI Institute for Public Policy Research, Robert Goldwin, Art Kaufman, 1988.

Splendid Failure: Postwar Reconstruction in the American South. Michael Fitzgerald. Ivan R. Lee. 2007.

Social Choice and Individual Values, Kenneth Joseph Arrow, Wiley, 1951.

Unruly Americans and the Origins of the Constitution, Woody Holton, Hill and Wang, 2007.

Verily the Road was Built with Chinaman's Bones: An Archaeology of Chinese Line Camps in Montana, Christopher W. Merritt, Gary Weisz and Kelly J. Dixon, International Journal of Historical Archaeology, 2012.

We Have Taken A City: The Wilmington Racial Massacre and Coup of 1898, H. Leon Prather, Dram Tree Books, 2006.

Will More Venture Capital Spur Regional Innovation? Laurie Thomas Vass, SSRN, 2008.

About the Author.

GABBY Press is the publishing company of The Citizens Liberty Party News Network. The Gabby website is owned by Laurie Thomas Vass, the General Partner, and author of 11 books at Gabby Press.

She is a regional economist and a constitutional economist. Her political ideology is natural rights conservative.

She is a graduate of the University of North Carolina at Chapel Hill, with an undergraduate degree in Political Science and a Masters degree in Regional Economic Development Planning.

She was a solo practitioner registered investment advisor for 30 years. She was cited by Peter Tanous, in The Wealth Equation, as one of the top 100 private money managers in the nation.

She is the inventor and holder of a research method patent on selecting technology stocks for investment. (Method of Identifying A Universe of Stocks for Inclusion Into An Investment Portfolio. United States Patent 7,251,627).

The method explained in her patent is based upon her theory of how technology evolves. (Theory of Technology Evolution, Gabby Press, 2007.).

Prior to starting her investment advisory company, she was a regional economist and advisor to the Board of Directors of B.C. Hydro, and also served as an economic advisor to the N. C. Commissioner of Labor. She learned the retail stock trade as a broker, at E. F. Hutton.

www.ingramcontent.com/pod-product-compliance
Lightning Source LLC
Chambersburg PA
CBHW051421290426
44109CB00016B/1381